CW00661445

THE LETTERS OF THE FIRST VISCOUNT HARDINGE OF LAHORE TO LADY HARDINGE AND SIR WALTER AND LADY JAMES 1844–1847

THE LETTERS OF THE FIRST VISCOUNT HARDINGE OF LAHORE TO LADY HARDINGE AND SIR WALTER AND LADY JAMES 1844–1847

edited by

BAWA SATINDER SINGH

CAMDEN FOURTH SERIES
Volume 32

LONDON
OFFICE OF THE ROYAL HISTORICAL SOCIETY,
UNIVERSITY COLLEGE LONDON,
GOWER STREET, WC1
1986

British Library Cataloguing in Publication Data

Hardinge, Henry Hardinge, *Viscount*
   The letters of the first Viscount
   Hardinge of Lahore to Lady Hardinge
   and Sir Walter and Lady James,
   1844–1847.—(Camden Fourth
   series; V. 32)
   1. Hardinge, Henry Hardinge, *Viscount*
   2. Marshals—Great Britain.—Biography
   3. India.—Governors.—Biography
   4. India
   .—Politics and Government.—19th century
   I. Title   II. Singh, Bawa Satinder
   III. Series
   325′341′0954   DS477.1

ISBN 0–86193–110–6

Printed in Great Britain by Butler & Tanner Ltd
Frome and London

CONTENTS

PREFACE

An explanation of the origin, contents, and current location of the Hardinge letters is provided in the Introduction, the Editor's Note, and the Table of Correspondence.

I wish to acknowledge a deep debt of gratitude to the late Dowager Lady Hardinge of Penshurst for her help and interest in my work. I am also indebted to the Fourth Baron Northbourne of Betteshanger, the late Fourth Viscount Hardinge of Lahore and the Hon'ble Mr Julian Hardinge for their advice. I am most grateful to Professor Norman Gash of St Andrews University, the late Professor Eric Stokes of the University of Cambridge, Professor Robin W. Winks of Yale University, and Professor Parshotam Mehra of Panjab University at Chandigarh for their special interest in my research. I also wish to express my thanks to Professor John H. Moore, my colleague at Florida State University, and Professor Kenneth J. Perkins of the University of South Carolina for helping me solve problems in the letters which fell in their areas of expertise. I am especially obliged to Dr Joanne Tanenbaum for her assistance with the French sources. I am thankful also for numerous kindnesses extended to me by Mr Martin Moir and Dr R. J. Bingle of the India Office Library; Sir Robert Mackworth-Young of the Royal Archives at Windsor Castle; Mr Gerald French and Mr Gregory Buss of McGill University Libraries; and Miss Phyllis Holzenberg, Mrs Gay Dixon and Miss Marianne Donnell of the Florida State University Strozier Library. As always, my wife Karrie assisted me with every phase of this work, an assistance which I indeed value. I also wish to acknowledge my thanks for the gracious permission of Her Majesty the Queen to consult Queen Victoria's papers at the Royal Archives in Windsor Castle. I want to express my gratitude to the American Council of Learned Societies and the Florida State University for financial assistance which made research on the Hardinge letters possible. Finally, I am particularly indebted to Dr H. C. G. Matthew, the Literary Director of the Royal Historical Society, and to his predecessor, Dr Ian Roy, for their painstaking guidance in the preparation of this work.

May 1986   Bawa Satinder Singh

ABBREVIATIONS

Place of publication is London unless otherwise specified.

Aberdeen Papers	The papers of George Hamilton Gordon, 4th Earl of Aberdeen, in the British Library
Add. MSS	Additional Manuscripts in the British Library
Arthur Hardinge Letters, i	The letters of Arthur Edward in the Kent County Archives, Maidstone
Arthur Hardinge Letters, ii	The letters of Arthur Edward at South Park in Penshurst, Kent
B. G. L. D.	*Papers relating to the Articles of Agreement concluded between the British Government and the Lahore Durbar.* House of Commons, 1847
The Bombay Times	*The Bombay Times and Journal of Commerce,* Bombay
Briggs	*The History of Melbourne, in the County of Derby, including biographical notices of the Coke, Melbourne, and Hardinge families* by John Joseph Briggs. Derby, n.d.
Broughton Papers	The papers of John Cam Hobhouse, Baron Broughton, in the Home Miscellaneous Series, IOL
Charles Hardinge Letters, i	The letters of Charles Stewart, 2nd Viscount, in the Kent County Archives, Maidstone
Charles Hardinge Letters, ii	The letters of Charles Stewart, 2nd Viscount, in the McGill University Libraries, Montreal
Charles Hardinge Letters, iii	The letters of Charles Stewart, 2nd Viscount, at South Park in Penshurst, Kent
Clowes	*The Royal Navy, A History,* by Wm. Laird Clowes, 1900
Colchester	*History of the Indian Administration of Lord Ellenborough* ed. by Lord Colchester, 1874

Cunningham	*A History of the Sikhs* by J. D. Cunningham, 1849
Doble	'South Park, Penshurst: A House of History' by D. C. Doble, 1979 (unpub.)
Ellenborough Papers	The papers of Edward Law, 1st Earl of Ellenborough, in the PRO
E. S. L. I.	Enclosures to Secret Letters from India in the IOL
F. P. N. W. F.	*Further Papers respecting the late hostilities on the north-western frontier of India.* House of Commons, 1846
Gash	*Sir Robert Peel* by Norman Gash, 1972
Grey	*European Adventurers of Northern India* by C. Grey. Lahore, 1929
Hasted	*The History and Topographical Survey of the County of Kent* by Edward Hasted. 3 vols. Canterbury, 1797–1801
Hogg Correspondence	The correspondence of Sir James Weir Hogg, MSS. Eur. E. in the IOL
Hurkaru	*The Bengal Hurkaru and India Gazette,* Calcutta
IOL	India Office Library
Lawrence	*Essays, Military and Political* by H. M. Lawrence, 1859
Newman	*West Kent and the Weald* by John Newman. Harmondsworth, 1976
Parker	*Sir Robert Peel* ed. by C. S. Parker. 3 vols. 1891
Peel Papers	The papers of Sir Robert Peel in the British Library
Politics	*Politics in the Age of Peel* by Norman Gash. Hassocks, 1977
PRO	Public Record Office
Q. V. J.	The journal of Queen Victoria at the RA
RA	Royal Archives, Windsor
Recollections	*Recollections of India* by Charles S. Hardinge, 1847
Ripon Papers	The papers of Frederick John Robinson, 1st Earl of Ripon, in the British Library
Russell Correspondence	The correspondence of Lord John Russell in the PRO

S. C.	Secret Consultations in the Foreign Department Correspondence, National Archives of India, New Delhi
Singh	*A History of the Sikhs* by Khushwant Singh, vol. 2. Princeton, 1966
V. A. P.	The papers of Queen Victoria and Prince Albert, vol. 2, at the RA
Viscount Hardinge	*Viscount Hardinge* by Charles S. Hardinge. Oxford, 1891
Wellington Papers	The papers of Arthur Wellesley, 1st Duke of Wellington, at the National Register of Archives

INTRODUCTION

I T was in 1964 that I first had the opportunity to consult the private letters of Henry, Lord Hardinge, written from India during the years 1844–7. The bulk of the letters was then in the possession of the late Dowager Lady Hardinge of Penshurst, the widow of Henry Hardinge's great-grandson, the Second Baron Hardinge of Penshurst.[1] I had been so impressed by the overall significance of these letters that in 1975 I asked for and received Lady Helen Hardinge's permission to edit them.

A photocopy of the letters was supplied to me by the McGill University Libraries, which had received a microfilm of the Hardinge letters by special arrangement some years earlier. The collection of the original letters is now divided, part of it remaining at South Park in Penshurst, the rest preserved at the Kent County Archives in Maidstone and McGill University's Department of Rare Books and Special Collections in Montreal. A list of each of the letters included in this volume and its location is given in the Table of Correspondence.

The Indian letters of Hardinge were written to his wife, Emily Jane; to his stepson, Sir Walter Charles James; and to the latter's wife Sarah Caroline. There are indications that Hardinge's two daughters, Frances Elizabeth and Emily Caroline, also received some letters, but they were probably lost or destroyed since no trace of them has been found. These family members in turn wrote letters to Hardinge in India, but they too seem not to have been preserved. Out of a total of 137 Hardinge letters, written on paper of varying sizes and totalling over 900 pages, I have omitted twelve. The transcribing of the letters required not only familiarization with Hardinge's handwriting but also with that of Emily Jane who in 1850, for some unexplained reason, copied thirty-two of her husband's Indian letters (making occasional marginal comments of her own, some of which I have included in this work) before destroying the originals.

Hardinge seems to have spent a considerable amount of time writing during his tenure as governor general. In addition to his dispatches, Hardinge personally wrote almost all his official memoranda (nos. 22 and 115). It is possible that while in India he carried on more private correspondence than at any other time in his life. Although most of these letters were written to his family members in England, he also corresponded with others including Peel, Ellenborough, and Hogg.[2]

---

[1] Alexander Henry Louis Hardinge (1900–60).

[2] The Hardinge–Peel letters are at the British Library, and excerpts from them appeared in Parker, iii. Hardinge's correspondence with Ellenborough and Sir James Weir Hogg (1790–1876) is at the PRO and IOL, respectively.

Hardinge's letters to his family are a major source of research material for Anglo-Indian history of the 1840s. They dwell at length on the roles of such prominent figures as Gough, Tweeddale, and Charles Napier as well as Dwarkanath Tagore, Rani Jindan, and Gulab Singh. The letters record in detail not only the evolution of Hardinge's educational, social, and army reforms, but also the mechanics of his policies toward various states like Oudh, Panjab, Kashmir, and Nepal. Moreover, because of the personal nature of these letters, they give a rare insight into the life and thinking of a governor general. These letters contain a fascinating narrative, sometimes witty, sometimes poignant, of the work, travels, and experiences of Hardinge in India. They provide interesting details on the operation of the governor general's official household, the nature of the Englishman's social life in India, and the general attitudes of the British toward the Indians. Like a diary, they reveal very private opinions about the people and issues connected with the subcontinent, opinions which Hardinge often reminds his family are not to be shared with others.

There are also interesting observations on the volatile English political scene and its leading personalities such as Wellington, Peel, Russell, Disraeli, Palmerston, and Ellenborough. Hardinge's letters are far more informative and candid on the many controversies of the times, both in India and England, than his views contained in his official communications. Moreover, Hardinge was quite a talented letter writer who wrote particularly well when not under extreme pressure of official business. This gift is evident whether he is describing the Meriah practice of human sacrifice (no. 34), the Taj Mahal (no. 55), the marvels of nature in the Himalayas (no. 87), or the training of hunting hawks by a hill raja (no. 101). He is also at ease in narrating a nostalgic anecdote whether it deals with a Peel–O'Connell quarrel (no. 36) or the discomfiture of Alex Grant caused by a swarm of stinging bees (no. 111). The same minute attention to detail that Hardinge exhibited in official matters is illustrated in his letters dealing with personal affairs, such as the financial arrangements relating to his daughter's marriage or payment of his accounts in England, or the design of his heraldic insignia upon his receiving the viscountcy.

The selection of Sir Henry Hardinge as the eleventh governor general of India was in a way the direct result of the Afghan War. The calamitous rout of the British army in Afghanistan at the end of 1841 resulted in the replacement of Lord Auckland, the governor general, by Lord Ellenborough. Though the Court of Directors of the East India Company had sent Ellenborough to restore British prestige by punishing the Afghans, Ellenborough proved to be far more militant than it had wished. Not only did he avenge the British defeat by temporarily re-occupying Afghanistan in 1842, but he also brought about the controversial annexation of Sind in the following year. He then proceeded to concentrate troops in the Northwest with a view to invading and annexing the vast kingdom of Panjab. However, the Court of Directors was in no mood for new military adventures. Ellenborough's questionable policies in Sind only strengthened the Court's resolve not to allow him to become involved in Panjab. But the Governor General stubbornly persisted in his aggressive attitude[3] and further infuriated his masters by displaying in official correspondence his disdain for their views. Its patience exhausted, the Court, despite the opposition of Sir Robert Peel's Tory government, recalled Ellenborough in the spring of 1844.

The Court resolved its differences with the British government over Ellenborough's recall by offering the governor generalship to Hardinge, who had emerged as the most generally acceptable man for the position.[4] However, Hardinge, the secretary at war in Peel's Cabinet, had serious reservations about leaving England. In 1842 he had, despite Ellenborough's urging, turned down the position of commander in chief in India.[5] The reasons for his reluctance to accept a prolonged foreign assignment were personal. He was already 59, the oldest man who would serve as governor general of India. In addition, he believed his wife's health was such that she could not survive in the Indian climate. Hardinge was certain that he would have to leave her behind and thus endure a separation for an undetermined number of years. There were worries too about his four children who were all at a stage when he felt he ought to be near them. His elder son, Charles Stewart,[6] then 22, had been educated at Eton and Oxford but had lost a leg in a boating accident some years earlier. The younger son, Arthur (Ben) Edward,[7] 16, had chosen the

[3] Ellenborough informed Queen Victoria on 16 Feb. 1844, that, if necessary, he could cross the Sutlej by December. Encouraged by the chaotic conditions inside Panjab, he wrote to Wellington on May 9 that he would be militarily prepared to launch an invasion by the year's end and declared: 'Everything is going on there as we could desire, if we looked forward to the ultimate possession of the Punjab' (Colchester, pp. 115, 437).

[4] Even Ellenborough was pleased with Hardinge's selection. Ellenborough's first wife, Octavia Stewart, and Hardinge's wife, Emily Jane, were sisters. Ellenborough was convinced Hardinge would follow in his footsteps and told all important Indian princely courts 'that my successor, my relation and best friend, would act upon the same principles of policy and carry out all my views' (Ellenborough to Peel, 19 June, 1844, in Parker, iii, 258). The Queen confirmed Ellenborough's feelings by recording that he 'is delighted at the appointment of Sir Henry Hardinge which will show that the same policy is to be continued' (Q.V.J., 10 Sept. 1844, p. 56).

[5] Hardinge to Ellenborough, 6 May 1842, Ellenborough Papers, 30/12/21/7.

[6] The future 2nd Viscount Hardinge of Lahore (1822–94).

[7] Arthur Edward Hardinge (1828–92), afterwards K.C.B. and general.

army as his career and his education was far from complete. Hardinge's two daughters, Frances (Fanny) Elizabeth and Emily Caroline, were approaching marriageable age, and he believed that they would need his guidance now more than ever before. Finally, there was Hardinge's absorbing interest in South Park,[8] his country home situated at Penshurst in the rolling hills of Kent. Hardinge was planning to refurbish and expand South Park and live there permanently after his retirement, but all such plans would have to be delayed if he were to go to India. Because of his age he was unwilling to postpone the realization of a dream which he might not then live to enjoy.

Despite these concerns, Hardinge was finally persuaded to change his mind by at least three factors. First of all, there was the opportunity to crown his career with one of the most powerful and prestigious positions in the British Empire. Secondly, a governor general in India received a far more lucrative remuneration than a secretary at war in the British Cabinet, and hence there was the clear prospect of improving his family's fortunes. But probably the most important reason was the considerable pressure exerted on Hardinge by Peel to accept the offer. The two men were friends and allies of long standing, and there was no one whom Hardinge admired more, or was more loyal to, than Peel. Even at the expense of losing such a staunch supporter in the government, the Prime Minister wanted Hardinge to take the appointment. Peel considered him the most qualified man for the job and wrote to Lord Ripon, the President of the Board of Control: 'I think he is by far the best man that could be named.'[9] When Hardinge formally accepted, Ripon gratefully told him: 'You have made a noble sacrifice in accepting what has been offered to you. The country is deeply indebted to you.'[10]

Hardinge had impressive credentials to recommend him. Born at Wrotham, Kent, on March 30, 1785, he was the third son of Henry Hardinge, the Rector of Stanhope, Durham. Although he was to pursue a military and political career, his deeply religious upbringing had a lasting influence on him, as these letters often attest. He had his early schooling at Durham, joined the Queen's Rangers at 15 as an ensign, and was stationed in Canada until 1802. Hardinge became a lieutenant in 1802, a captain two years later, and entered the Royal Military College in 1806. In 1807 he was sent to the Continent and was engaged in almost the entire Peninsular War. He fought under

[8] He had purchased South Park in the 1820s. For more on Penshurst, see Richard Church, *Kent's Contribution* (Bath, 1972), pp. 100–2, 120–4; and Alan Bignell, *Kent Villages* (1975), p. 136.
[9] Peel to Ripon, 2 May 1844, Ripon Papers, Add. MS 40868.
[10] Ripon to Hardinge, 4 May 1844, Ripon Papers, Add. MS 40868.

Arthur Wellesley at Roliça and Vimeira, and was beside General Sir John Moore when he was mortally wounded. In 1809 General Beresford, then in the process of reorganizing the Portuguese army, appointed Hardinge to his staff where he remained until the spring of 1814. While serving as the deputy quartermaster general of the Portuguese army, he participated in the battles at Busaco, Albuera, Salamanca, Vittoria, and Bayonne. He was promoted to lieutenant colonel in the 40th Foot Guards during April 1814, and was awarded a K.C.B. early in 1815. On Napoleon's return to Paris in March 1815, Wellington placed Hardinge on the staff of Field Marshal Blücher to help coordinate military efforts with the Prussians. It was while fighting alongside Blücher at Ligny on June 16, 1815, that Hardinge's left hand was shattered by a French cannon shot. However, in spite of the severity of the wound, he remained on the battlefield. Several hours passed before he was examined by a Prussian surgeon, and the decision was made to remove his hand. Thirty-seven years later Hardinge recounted the circumstances of its loss to Queen Victoria, who recorded:

> [He] told me yesterday how he had lost his arm. It was at Ligny, 2 days before Waterloo, & he remained from 5 in the afternoon till eleven at night, when only it could be amputated. The next day he had a good deal of hoemorrhage [sic], & just as the surgeon had begun dressing the wound, they heard that the French had entered the village, and he. had to ride off to Lorraine, with his arm only just wrapped up!! That night another surgeon tied each vein separately to stop the hoemorrhage [sic].[11]

This misfortune kept him from action at Waterloo, but apparently he adjusted to the loss of his limb with courage and fortitude, for he continued to serve with the Prussians until the end of their occupation of France in 1818.

Returning home with a reputation for bravery, Hardinge in 1821, at the age of 36, married Emily Jane James, the widow of John James[12] and the daughter of the First Marquess of Londonderry.[13] Their marriage marked the beginning of a loving relationship, and Hardinge's attachment to his wife is quite evident all through these

---

[11] Q.V.J., 30 Sept. 1852, p. 1. That he did not receive the best medical attention is confirmed by his son: 'The operation was not skilfully performed as the ligatures subsequently gave way, and he suffered much from loss of blood' (*Viscount Hardinge,* p. 25).

[12] John James, son of Sir Walter James James, 1st Bart., married Emily Jane in 1814 and died in 1818. He served as minister to Holland.

[13] She was the sixth daughter of Londonderry by his second wife, Frances. The 2nd Viscount Castlereagh was thus her half-brother.

letters. In addition to their four children already mentioned, Hardinge welcomed into his home five-year-old Walter,[14] Emily's only child by her first husband, whom he treated throughout his life with much affection and consideration.

A year before his marriage, Hardinge entered politics as a Tory. He was elected to the Commons for Durham in 1820 and served as the clerk of the ordnance from 1823 to 1828. He was re-elected for Durham in 1826, and was the secretary at war in Wellington's Cabinet from 1828 to 1830. He received the rank of major general in 1830, and represented Launceston in the Parliament from 1832 to 1842. He served as chief secretary of Ireland in 1830 and again in 1834–5. In 1841 Hardinge became a lieutenant general, and when the Tories returned to power, he again became the secretary at war, occupying that position until he was sent to India. During the quarter of a century that he was on the English public scene he earned the reputation of a competent and indefatigable administrator although a somewhat partisan politician.

Hardinge was well aware of the desire in London for peace, and no sooner did he accept the governor generalship than he set about familiarizing himself with the current Indian situation. Victoria quoted him as saying that 'he had made himself master of the subject, and sees his way quite clearly'.[15] Ripon seemed quite satisfied with Hardinge's outlook and believed that he 'is not a man likely to overlook what is of real importance'.[16] Yet to make sure that he fully understood the sentiments against war, John Shepherd, the chairman of the Court of Directors, addressed him early in June at a farewell dinner: 'You, sir, know how great are the evils of war. And, we feel confident that, while ever ready to maintain unimpaired the honour of the country and the supremacy of our arms, your policy will be essentially pacific.'[17]

Accompanied only by Charles and Robert Wood, his nephew, Hardinge, on arriving in India, set up a strenuous schedule of work. Rising at five in the morning and going to bed by ten at night, he tended to official business from eleven to twelve hours a day. Although he thrived on all this labour, he confessed in one of the letters that 'no govr. genl. who accepts this office ought to complain, but I never knew what it was really to work until I came here' (no. 15). He held regular conferences with his council, but his closest confidants were Charles, who was his private secretary, and Robert, who served as his

[14] Walter Charles James (1816–1893), the future 1st Baron Northbourne of Betteshanger.
[15] Q.V.J., 19 May 1844, p. 160.
[16] Ripon to Shepherd, 28 May 1844, Ripon Papers, Add. MS 40868.
[17] *Viscount Hardinge*, pp. 49–50.

military A.D.C. Robert, then 30, was very close to the Hardinges, who treated him like a member of their own family.

Although he devoted some attention to the Kolapur insurrection during his first months in office, Hardinge also spent considerable time studying political conditions in Panjab. As desired by London, he hoped to prevent hostilities with the Sikhs. No one carried more weight with him on this point than his friend Peel, who in November wrote to him:

> If you can keep peace, reduce expense, extend commerce, and strengthen our hold on India by confidence in our justice and kindness and wisdom, you will be received on your return with acclamations a thousand times louder and a welcome infinitely more cordial than if you have a dozen victories to boast of, and annex the Punjaub to the overgrown Empire of India.[18]

However, his greatest contribution in 1844 lay in his encouragement and promotion of higher education. He was quite impressed by the intellectual prowess of the Indians attending government colleges and talked of the students 'spouting Shakespeare fluently—aye & explaining accurately all the most difficult passages' (no. 13). Charles too was similarly impressed and wrote: 'Many of them are really much better informed than our Cambridge & Oxford men.'[19]

Hardinge never quite adjusted to the summer heat and humidity of the Indian plains. He found the going particularly rough during his first months in Calcutta, which to him was a 'torrid zone', and he admitted: 'The damp far exceeds any idea I had formed of its penetrating effects' (no. 7). He took special precautions so that he and Charles would not fall prey to heat-related maladies. Charles was a gifted artist and spent much of his spare time sketching. His mentor was the landscape artist, J. D. Harding.

The Hardinge letters exhibit from the start the close relationship between Hardinge and his stepson Sir Walter, then M.P. for Hull.[20] They also reveal the admiration Hardinge held for his stepson's wife Sarah Caroline[21] and the trust he placed in her judgment. While he was in India Walter and Sarah lived at South Park and cared for Emily and her two daughters. The letters show in particular Hardinge's concern for Emily and the void caused in his life by their separation. Yet he hoped that she would not come to India, for he truly believed that her health was so fragile that she could withstand neither the strain of the voyage nor the sweltering climate of Calcutta.

---

[18] Peel to Hardinge, 6 Nov. 1844, Peel Papers, Add. MS 40871.
[19] Charles to Walter, 20 Oct. 1844, Charles Hardinge Letters, i.
[20] Educated at Oxford, he served in the Commons from 1837 to 1847.
[21] Sarah Caroline James (1812–90), married Walter in 1841. See note 50.

He did everything to dissuade her from making the journey. When
word reached him in October that she was in France determined to
attempt the journey in spite of his wishes, he manifested considerable
anxiety (nos. 6, 7, 8, 11, 13, and 14). Emily did indeed board a ship
for Alexandria in December, but she soon became ill and had to turn
back. She took her two daughters to Nice but allowed Arthur to
continue the voyage and join his father.

Not only domestic concerns turned Hardinge's attention to Europe
in 1845. As a split developed in the Tory party over the Maynooth
grant, his sympathy was clearly on the side of Peel, and in his letters
he bitterly denounced those Tories opposing the prime minister. In a
sentimental note during June, he told Peel: 'I must say that, however
inefficient in the House, I wish I were near you to express the devotion
& attachment so fully felt by yr. affec[*tiona*]te H. Hardinge.'[22] In a
similar vein, he wrote to Emily in July that Peel 'has been shamefully
treated & I wish I were by his side to say so' (no. 40).

In India Hardinge remained immersed in the responsibilities of his
office, wishing that he were '40 instead of 60 & could convert the 24
h[*ours*] into 48' (no. 32). He formulated policies on roads, canals, and
railways, and continued to work hard to improve Indian education.
While he believed that Indian climate 'breeds a love of idleness', he
remained convinced of the 'natural capacity' of the people. He felt an
obligation to improve the living conditions of the Company's subjects
and told Sarah that the English rulers 'are bound by every moral &
Christian obligation to educate & improve them' (no. 46). Remarkably enough, Hardinge, though a devout Christian, criticized those
who would convert Indians to Christianity by compulsion and
bribery. He held the simplistic belief that government-sponsored education and legislation, such as the Liberty of Conscience Bill,[23] would
ultimately lead to the rise of Christianity in India. 'The educated
classes are already deistic,' he wrote to Walter, '& this act will do
more eventually for Christianity than all the missionary societies'
(no. 34).

Hardinge divided his time between Calcutta and Barrackpore.
He found the cost of maintaining his official residences quite steep,
especially the one at Calcutta where all his aides lived with him. His
biggest expense, however, was the retention of a large contingent of
servants, each one of whom, thanks to social taboos, performed only
specific tasks. Charles recorded:

> I think they are about 500 in number, receiving for wages about
> £12 a month each man, who has his own separate duties to perform

[22] Hardinge to Peel, 12 June 1845, Peel Papers, Add. MS 40474.
[23] See note 167.

which [*are*] carried to an absurd extent. For instance, if you tell a man to wipe the dust off a book, he will immediately go off to the other end of the house & fetch a sweeper to do it. If you keep a dog you must get a man whose sole duty is to look after him.[24]

The incessant turmoil in Panjab soon provided the Hardinges with a chance to escape from the heat of Calcutta. The trip which had been discussed since late 1844 got underway on September 22. The journey up the Ganges River gave the Hardinges their first glimpse of the vast and often picturesque interior. Enjoying his first respite since coming to India, Hardinge exclaimed: 'I have no boxes chasing me for orders & suitors pestering me for interviews, but here I am without a breach of duty' (no. 54).

As Hardinge moved up to Ambala during November, there was a growing conviction in India of the inevitability of war with the Sikhs. The steady disintegration of the Lahore government, caused largely by its chaotic army, was gradually forcing London to alter its views towards the Panjab. Wellington, who had opposed the extension of the British frontier beyond the Sutlej, now merely hoped 'that by cutting up some of these marauding detachments of Seiks [*Hardinge*] may be able to keep matters in such a state on the frontier as to preserve peace for some time longer.'[25] Even Peel, who had so eloquently urged peace earlier, wrote to Hardinge: 'Whatever may be your ultimate decision with regard to our intervention in the affairs of the Punjaub ... I shall feel entire confidence that the decision has been taken after the calmest and most deliberate review of all the considerations which require to be maturely weighed.'[26] Yet Hardinge continued to believe even in early December that peace would prevail.[27]

This optimism was dashed by the sudden outbreak of hostilities which culminated in the bloody struggles at Mudki and Ferozeshah (nos. 62 and 63). On Christmas Day 1845, Hardinge wrote to Emily that, although he and their two sons were fortunate to have escaped injury, the English had paid a heavy price in the two battles (no. 64). In the final days of 1845, Hardinge and Charles made the rounds of the camp hospitals to comfort the wounded by 'showing them a governor general without a hand & his son without a foot' (no. 65). However, as word of the heavy English losses spread, Hardinge's conduct was fiercely condemned by segments of the press both in India and England. To make matters worse, the Sikhs were still

[24] Charles to Emily, 29 May 1845, Charles Hardinge Letters, iii.

[25] Wellington to Ellenborough, 9 Oct. 1845, Ellenborough Papers, PRO, 30/12/21/7.

[26] Peel to Hardinge, 26 Oct. 1845, Peel Papers, Add. MS 40475.

[27] Hardinge to Ripon, 3 Dec. 1845, Ripon Papers, Add. MS 40874; and Hardinge to Secret Committee of the Court of Directors, 2 Dec. (no. 15) and 4 (no. 16), *Secret Letters from Bengal and India*, clxxviii, MS. at IOL.

encamped across the Sutlej, and the war was not yet over. The British still had to fight at Aliwal and Sobraon before their victory was assured.

Even before the final battle in February 1846, Hardinge had, for a variety of reasons, decided against annexing the entire Sikh kingdom. One of those reasons was his reluctance to share a common frontier with any Muslim power to the north (nos. 69 and 71). He was well aware of the centuries of Muslim invasions through the Khyber Pass and thus he preferred the continuation of a non-Muslim power in Panjab to act as a buffer between Afghanistan and British India.[28] At the same time, he was not sympathetic to the idea of a subsidiary alliance with Panjab, saying: 'I am equally averse to the subsidiary system which by British bayonets enables a native govt. to grind the people to dust' (no. 71).

Once the Anglo-Sikh negotiators had drafted the treaty provisions, the governor general marched into Lahore late in February 1846 and was received by the Sikh government leaders more like the visiting head of a friendly state than the man who had just delivered a near fatal blow to their state.

Soon after the treaties were signed, Charles and Arthur, at the invitation of Gulab Singh, the newly appointed maharaja of Kashmir, left on a tour of his mountainous domains while Hardinge headed for Simla, arriving there early in April. He took up residence in the stately Auckland House and found he had difficulty adjusting, after the excitement of the previous four months, 'to red boxes & the humdrum business of the state' (no. 82). While keeping a close watch on how the new treaties were being implemented, he busied himself once again with irrigation and railroads. Later in May he heard that he had been created a viscount, and tributes for his victory and post-war arrangements began to reach him from England. He particularly prized the messages from the Queen and Peel (nos. 88 and 89). Victoria, in a personal note, 'expressed her extreme satisfaction at the brilliant & happy termination of our recent contest with the Sikhs . . . & knows how much she owed to Sir Henry Hardinge's exertions.'[29] Peel wrote with lavish praise:

> There is here universal approval and admiration of your conduct and policy from *first* to *last*. Above all things your moderation after victory is most applauded. It is thought and justly thought that it

---

[28] Upon the signing of the peace treaty which recognized this principle, Hardinge repeated his argument to Peel: 'I have done this on the principle that it is our policy to prefer Hindoo governments, or any race in preference to the Mahommedans on this great entrance into India' (19 March 1846, Peel Papers, Add. MS 40475).

[29] Queen to Hardinge, 6 April 1846, V.A.P.

adds a lustre to the skill and valour displayed in the military achievements. It is ten times more gratifying to the public mind than the annexation of the whole Punjab would have been. This is the common sentiment, the instinctive feeling of the whole mass of mankind.[30]

Throughout these months, Hardinge kept close watch on the political crisis in England, and the departure of Peel at the end of June, despite his success in repealing the Corn Laws, saddened him. 'You will see that we are *out*,' Peel wrote to Hardinge, 'defeated by a combination of Whigs and Protectionists.'[31] In an emotional letter, the governor general responded: 'Your retreat preceded by two most important victories has been a noble triumph. You fought until the battle was gained, & then fell with your face to the foe.'[32] With the appointment of Lord John Russell as prime minister, the prospect of working under a Whig government containing old political adversaries like Auckland, who was expected to join the Cabinet,[33] did not appeal to him. Hardinge offered to resign, but Russell, in a warm letter, asked him to remain, suggesting that in the aftermath of the Sikh war 'no other chief can so well consolidate the peace you have achieved as yourself.'[34] Peel, Wellington, Ripon, and Hobhouse, the new president of the Board of Control, also urged him not to leave his post (no. 97). This, combined with a concern that 'a precipitate retreat' so soon after receiving the viscountcy and a liberal pension might expose him 'to the imputation of acting on selfish considerations,'[35] persuaded the governor general to stay on for a while.

However, Hardinge was privately making plans for an early return to England as soon as circumstances would permit. He was busily purchasing land around South Park and steadily sending home meticulous instructions relating to its expansion, renovation, and landscaping (nos. 84, 89, and 95). He informed Walter: 'You see by these details that I am preparing to take up my abode for the remainder of my life at dear S. Park' (no. 99).

In spite of his desire to leave, Hardinge continued to work hard on

---

[30] Peel to Hardinge, 22 April 1846, Peel Papers, Add. MS 40475.

[31] Peel to Hardinge, 4 July 1846, Peel Papers, Add. MS 40475.

[32] Hardinge to Peel, 3 Sept. 1846, Peel Papers, Add. MS 40475.

[33] For a while, there was concern that Auckland might become the new president of the Board of Control, and Charles, obviously expressing his father's view, wrote disapprovingly: '[*He*] will be continually corresponding with his Indian friends here, which is very objectionable for many reasons' (Charles to Walter, 13 Aug. 1846, Charles Hardinge Letters, i).

[34] Russell to Hardinge, 8 July 1846, Russell Correspondence, 30/22/5B.

[35] Hardinge to Hogg, chairman of the Court of Directors, Hogg Correspondence, 21 Sept. 1846, 342/6.

governmental affairs, sometimes putting in as many as sixteen hours a day. 'I must omit nothing under Whig masters,' he wrote (no. 99). He had difficulty adjusting to the new government but admitted: 'I know Lord John is a man of honour & a fair man, & I sleep sound every night' (no. 104). In India, his main concern still was the Panjab. While his political aides worked out the details of a new Panjab agreement he had devised, Hardinge set out on an extended tour in late October to inspect the new territories acquired from the Sikhs. Accompanied by Charles and Arthur (the latter had rejoined his father after a long tour of Kashmir and Ladakh), the Hardinge entourage passed slowly through such mountainous towns as Mandi, Rajpur, and Kartargarh. Even while leading the 'gypsy life of a camp,'[36] he worked on the red boxes that pursued him and was badly jolted by the news of his wife's illness.[37] Reassured by family letters that she had made a quick recovery, the Hardinges continued their journey and Charles found more opportunities to use his brush. At Kangra he made a memorable sketch of its ancient fort, characterized by the Indians as 'the Key of the Himalayas.'[38] This drawing may be one of the best records of that fort now available since an earthquake at the turn of this century left it in ruins.

Descending into the plains in late November, Hardinge arrived at Bhairowal a month later. There he witnessed the signing of a new treaty with the Sikhs which put the British in virtual control of the Lahore government.[39] Charles perhaps best summed up the general British sentiment toward the Sikhs at that time: 'We had then only succeeded in drawing the reptile's fangs. We have now completely tamed & subdued him.'[40]

Early in January 1847 Hardinge paid a week-long visit to Lahore to chart the course for the changes provided for in the new treaty. Later in the month, when the Hardinges camped at Sobraon and Ferozeshah, they could barely recognize the sites where only a year before furious battles had been waged. At Ferozeshah, Charles observed that nothing 'remains to mark the different points of attack except the bleached skeletons of men and horses.'[41]

During February Hardinge visited the protected Cis-Sutlej states,

[36] Charles to Sarah, 3 Nov. 1846, Charles Hardinge Letters, i.

[37] Charles wrote to Sarah: 'You cannot imagine how severe the shock has been to him. Indeed, had the state of suspense in which he was for two days been prolonged, I am sure his health would have been affected.' The nature of Emily's illness was not specified. See letter of 19 Nov. 1846, Charles Hardinge Letters, ii.

[38] Hardinge to the Secret Committee of the Court of Directors, 4 Mar. 1846, F.P.N.W.F., p. 89. See also note 299.

[39] See note 306.

[40] Charles to Walter, 2 Jan. 1847, Charles Hardinge Letters, i.

[41] Charles to Walter, 20 Jan. 1847, Charles Hardinge Letters, i.

whose affairs had attracted his attention ever since his arrival in the Northwest. The governor general was annoyed by the protected rajas who 'confident of our support, ill-treat their people to an extent unknown in the Punjab,'[42] and had already removed two of them from their gaddis during the previous year. On this trip he persuaded the various rajas to agree to duty-free transit trade, but he recognized that much more needed to be done to improve conditions in these states (nos. 107 and 108).

Early in March the governor general visited the site of one of his favourite projects, the Ganges Canal. Thrilled by the potential of the canal and conscious of the government's paternal responsibilities, he hoped that this irrigation project would 'be some redemption of our character, for hitherto we have done very little for the people' (no. 110). In mid-March the Hardinges spent a few days hunting tigers in the Dun valley at the foot of the Himalayas. Seated on forty elephants which moved 'through the reeds as easily as we walk over a stubble field at home,' Hardinge was ecstatic when he brought down a tiger more than nine feet long. Calling him a 'noble monster,' he had it stuffed and made arrangements to send it to South Park (nos. 111 and 121).

During the last weeks of his tour, Hardinge carried on an angry correspondence with Gough over what he considered was an insinuation by the commander in chief that he, the governor general, had recommended, through two of his military aides, a retreat at Ferozeshah on the crucial evening of December 21, 1845 (no. 112). Hardinge and the two aides in question vehemently denied making such a suggestion. There was a suspicion in Hardinge's mind that Gough's wife had played a role in staging this controversy (no. 117). Charles was more categorical about it: 'My opinion is that Lady Gough is at the bottom of it all.'[43] After some initial hesitation, Gough attempted to patch up the quarrel upon the governor general's return to Simla later in March, calling on him and making 'many "salaams." ' Hardinge, however, was deeply offended, feeling that Gough had 'acted most shabbily towards him,'[44] and wrote to Walter: 'He has fallen greatly in my estimation' (no. 114).

On April 5 Hardinge wrote to Hobhouse that his task in India was nearly complete and that he definitely intended to leave India by the end of 1847. This decision he declined to change in spite of renewed requests from Russell and Hobhouse to remain.[45] His resolve was

[42] Hardinge to Ellenborough, 17 Jan. 1847, Ellenborough Papers, 30/12/21/7.

[43] Charles to Emily, 4 Mar. 1847, Charles Hardinge Letters, i.

[44] Charles to Walter, 3 April 1847, Charles Hardinge Letters, i.

[45] Hardinge to Hobhouse, 5 April 1847, Broughton Papers, dccliii; Hardinge to Hogg, 30 April 1847, Hogg Correspondence, 342/6.

strengthened by his perception that, although Russell and the cabinet as a whole wanted him to continue,[46] Hobhouse and Palmerston were not sympathetic to the recent arrangements in the Panjab. Hardinge felt that, while Hobhouse's private letters were cordial and supportive, his 'official letters are cold—almost to disapprobation,' and he complained to Ripon: 'The fact is, he [*Hobhouse*] & Palmerston are for direct annexation.'[47] Cognizant of Palmerston's fear of a Russian invasion of India, Hardinge wrote to Russell on April 20 that, because of military and geographical considerations, such a threat would not materialise.[48] Palmerston, however, rejected Hardinge's conclusion. Advocating that the British must push their frontier to the Khyber Pass, he told Russell: 'The advance of a Russian army is ... far from being as impossible as Hardinge seems to think it.'[49] Although the British frontier remained unchanged during the remainder of his governor generalship, Hardinge continued to denounce Palmerston's views in his private letters (nos. 115, 117, 121, and 125).

In his final months at Simla Hardinge again became a hostage to his gruelling work schedule and confessed 'the work is really too much for any man' (no. 120). A great deal of his time in 1847 was spent in balancing the budget by reducing the size of the army by 60,000 men (no. 125) amidst bitter criticism from the military-controlled Indian press. He also succeeded in cutting down the military expenditures while accelerating the construction of fortifications at Aden (no. 117). His political headaches had diminished considerably with the signing of the Bhairowal treaty, but he still had to deal with some minor problems in Panjab and more serious ones in Deccan and Oudh. In addition, Hardinge carried on an almost incessant correspondence on Indian affairs with his superiors in London and his council at Calcutta as well as with his governors and political agents. 'I am nearly worn out,' he told Emily early in July. 'Prepare the dusthole' (no. 119). He seemed determined to retire for good. When Emily wrote of a rumour that he might succeed Wellington at the Horse Guards, he dismissed it as mere gossip, adding, 'I am so surfeited by over-work that I loathe the very thought of losing my liberty regained' (no. 121).

Hardinge's main diversion from his labours continued to be his interest in the improvements being undertaken at South Park and in the activities of his two sons. While he fidgeted over Arthur's idleness and his need for a formal education, he was pleased with the growing

---

[46] Hardinge to Hogg, 23 June 1847, Hogg Correspondence, 342/6.

[47] Hardinge to Ripon, 20 April 1847, Ripon Papers, Add. MS 40877.

[48] Hardinge to Russell, 20 April 1847, Russell Correspondence, 30/22/6C. In a letter of the same date, he bemoaned to Hogg: 'They have again revived the bug-a-boo of Russian invasion' (Hogg Correspondence, 342/6).

[49] Palmerston to Russell, 9 June 1847, Russell Correspondence, 30/22/6D.

poise and maturity of Charles. He watched the progress of his artistry and felt that each 'successive sketch excels its predecessor' (no. 119). He was elated when many of Charles' sketches were accepted for publication in London even though Hardinge felt, after examining some advance lithographic prints, that 'they fall far short of the coloured originals' (no. 122). Later that year the large volume entitled *Recollections of India* appeared, containing twenty-six prints and accompanying text. Its fascinating subjects varied from pig-sticking hunts and Mughal monuments to the mountains of Kashmir.

Amidst tributes led by Gough (no. 123), Hardinge left Simla on October 26 for Calcutta to relinquish the reins of government to Lord Dalhousie. On the way he made stops at various cities and, despite the rush of farewell receptions, still found time to conduct government business and write official dispatches. Drifting down the Ganges early in December, he reminisced over his forty-two months in India. He felt he had fulfilled his mission by establishing peace on a firm footing and putting the government back on the road to economic recovery. Above all he believed he had introduced a new moral tone into the conduct of the government, which was already beginning to better the condition of the people. In his last letter to Walter from India, he wrote: 'Every part of the country is quiet—the harvest most abundant & the crops for the spring most promising, the river crowded with boats & trade increasing' (no. 125). With the firm conviction that he had done his job well, Hardinge, then nearly 63, left India in January 1848.

EDITOR'S NOTE

The Hardinge letters in this volume have been kept in their original form as far as possible. The abbreviations and the original spellings, including the variants of Eastern words, have been retained. Editorial insertions have been made at places for the sake of clarity, but they are always in square brackets and italicized. Only capitalization and punctuation have been modernized. The salutations and closings of the letters have been excluded to avoid repetition. Most of Hardinge's letters to his wife are addressed 'Dear' or 'Dearest Emily' and end with 'Ever yr. affec[*tiona*]tely devoted H.H.' Letters to Walter James and his wife usually begin with 'My dear Walter,' and 'My dear Sarah' and end with 'Ever yr. affec[*tiona*]te, H.H.'

TABLE OF CORRESPONDENCE*

* All of Hardinge's letters at South Park are copies in his wife's hand; the letters at Maidstone and McGill are in his own hand.

THE HARDINGE LETTERS

1. [*To Sarah.*] Marseilles. 14th June 1844

I cannot go into a new quarter of the globe without having a parting word with you to express how strongly I feel all the warmth of heart with which you identify yourself with our family distresses & successes, our sorrows & our joys. I have not been ashamed to show you my weaknesses & I shall always be proud of your love, for no daughter of mine could have shown me more affection than you have done at a moment of great tryal. On that subject our difficulties are great. I have written to Walter, but I have not been able to add a word to the long conversations we have had on this topic, & it is so painful that without any useful object I will not inflict it upon you. But I felt gratefully the goodness of yr. heart & the soundness of yr. judgements, & these deserve & ever will retain my devoted praises & thanks.

We are all well & sail this night at 10.

Last night at 12, a stage or two from Avignon, we were stopped by our postillions wishing to change horses. [*Robert*] Wood, who is the paymaster, declined. I had said, "Let them change," but he replied, "Sir, we shall never get on with these tired horses." When a voice from the other carriage said, "You are close to the post h[ou]se," I then said at once in French, "Change your horses. Why did you not say that you were close?" Wood had been rather rough. My French & voice, different from his, made the traveller call out, "Jim." "My Lord." "Ask if that is Sir H.H." The traveller proved to be Lord Vernon, returning from Greece & posting on to Milan. I immediately got out, shook him by the hand, gave him the last acct. of yr. father & mother when he very affecly. asked after you.[50] I gave him a very good acct. of you, but a better [*one*] of the baby.[51] He was courteous, or rather cordial, &, after giving him a very good report of Augustus,[52] we separated. In this case I may reverse the usual mode & say the father is very like the son. He was as brown as a sepoy & had a reading lamp, making the best of his time.

[50] George John Warren (1803–66), the son of Baron Vernon, was married to Isabella Caroline, the eldest sister of Sarah Caroline. They were the daughters of Cuthbert Ellison (1783–1860) and Isabella Grace of Hebburn, Durham. Cuthbert Ellison had served as the high sheriff of Hebburn. Sarah Caroline was his fifth daughter.

[51] Sarah (Sarina), daughter of Walter and Sarah James, was then apparently one or two years old. She grew up to marry the 1st Baron Kilbracken in 1871 and died in 1921.

[52] Augustus Henry Vernon (1829–83), eldest son of Lord Vernon, became the 6th Baron Vernon in 1866.

Pray learn as much as you can & tell Walter to do the same of dear Ben. Let Walter write to Sir Fredk.[53]

My captain[54] has called & I conclude.

2. [*To Walter.*] Alexandria. Sunday, 23rd June 1844

We arrived here last night just in time to get into the harbour for the night, the smell outside being very heavy & unpleasant. Thus in a fortnight from the day we left London we have gained this point, exceeding 2100 miles. Charles was sick the 2 first days & also for the last 2 days, the breeze having created a very heavy sea, & he could not leave his bed. The distance has been made in 8 days under very favourable circumstances; 9 or 10 days ought to be the probable period.

Our captain (Carpenter) is a very civil & obliging gentleman. I am going to take him with me to Cairo as he has not seen the Pyramids.

It is now 7 o'cl. & at 10 we are going to church. Thence in full dress I am to pay a visit of ceremony to Mahmut Ali,[55] but I shall be so pressed for time that I write whenever I can.

The subject uppermost in my thoughts is the power of yr. dear mother to stand such exertions as these. I shall write from Suez so that you will be in possession of any possible information. If this point could be settled with safety to her, my mind would be comparatively at ease.

I am remarkably well—my head clear & not oppressed by the heat, though it has generally averaged 82° in the cabin. I perceive by the Bombay papers of the 20th June that the recall was then not known. Tell yr. mother to send me any letters from Ld. Ellenborough. I shall conclude this note after I have seen the pacha & the other heirs & expect to be en route for Suez tomorrow even[in]g.

24th

After church at 4 o'cl. we visited the pacha in state, all in full dress. His carriage (very like Soult's at the coronation) with 4 horses was in constant requisition. A batt[*alio*]n of Egyptian troops [*gave*] us a g[*uar*]d of honor. Crowds of all chiefs & natives grouped together &, after passing up a marble staircase & through a marble hall, we were ushered by 30 or 40 well-dressed courtiers into the divan with a couch all round. The old pacha with great alacrity jumped off his couch & met me nearly halfway. He then resumed his seat, desiring all my people to be seated, consisting of almost a dozen. A pipe was brought

---

[53] Sir Frederick Smith was Arthur's tutor in England.

[54] Capt. Carpenter of H.M.S. *Geyser.*

[55] Also known as Pasha Mehmet Ali or Muhammad Ali.

for the pacha & for me, then coffee in little cups without bottoms, all
his people, ministers, etc. being kept standing.

I have written to your mother in detail & refer you to her.

We then returned to Cap. Lyons,[56] took off our finery, got into the
pacha's carriage & took boat for our ship, on which we found a very
good dinner & dessert at 6 o'cl. I then settled to write officially to
Artim Bey, minister for foreign affairs, & went to bed, having been
up before 6 & very tired.

This morning again up before 6. Went to the pacha before 9 o'cl.
& recd. by him in the same state as yesterday. I went through our
different points in detail, Artim Bey being the interpreter of my French
to the pacha. I then left the substance of the proposed agreement in
a letter addressed to him which he is in general terms to acknowledge
this day, thus gaining time & enabling me to steal away tomorrow
morning.

At 3 we are to drive with the pacha, & he is to drive me out in the
even[in]g.

                                                            9 o'cl.

The dinner was excellent—quite Parisian, the wines iced & well
prepared—& the old pacha beat us all in appetite.

He is not so tall as I am by 2 or 3 inches, rather corpulent, broad-
chested, a good countenance, white beard, & at once in his manner
you perceive that he is a distinguished character. I am tired to death
with making conversation which is so torn to tatters by the constant
interruption of a very bad French interpreter.

However, the fag is over. I have just finished my official letter to
Lord Aberdeen [*informing him that*] the viceroy [*Muhammad Ali, has
accepted*] most readily the proposed basis of an arrangement, & in 24
h[*ours*] I have done & accomplished as much as it was possible.

Charles & Robert have just come in from inspecting Cleopatra's
Needle[57] & Pompey's Pillar. I was too busy with my treaty to venture
to look at these works by moonlight & am so knocked up, having
been hard at work in one way or another from 6 o'cl., that I am
almost asleep whilst I am writing.

Give my love to dear Sarah. Charles has sent a sketch to his mother.
I found one on the table which I enclose for Sarah.

Let me know how Arthur is going on. I shall write from Cairo.

3. [*To Emily.*] Alexandria. 24th June 1844

I will not dwell on the disagreements of a week's passage on board

[56] Hardinge's escort at Alexandria.

[57] One of Cleopatra's two obelisks. Muhammad Ali presented one to England in
1819 which now stands on the Victoria Embankment. The other, apparently viewed
by Charles, was sent to New York and erected in Central Park in 1881.

the steamer. Suffice it that Charles, who was the sufferer, is now quite well & highly pleased with the picturesque Arabs, dromedaries & donkies [*sic*] one meets with at every turn. Having anchored late on Saturday night, I went to church on Sunday with our party & all the naval officers, which is a room with 4 bare walls, but in this wild Moslem country there was something affecting in the simplicity of the whole ceremony, & I fancied myself more attentive & devout than usual.

The person to whom I am consigned here is a naval captain of the name of Lyons, a brother of Sir Edmund's,[58] who with his wife, a nice little old woman, recollects Charles & all of us at Milford on the Hampshire coast ages ago.

After church I dressed in my uniform and went in the pacha's carriage to pay him a visit of ceremony. The whole thing was amusing—a sky-blue coach with glass windows like the Duke's [*Wellington*] lined with yellow silk, rich harness, grooms & guards & running footmen, the troops turned out on parade, etc. We then went up a marble staircase to the pacha's apartments, which are very handsome in the richest Parisian style of decoration, & were ushered by about 20 courtiers into the presence chamber in which an old man with a white beard, short & rather lame, scrambled off his ottoman, walking halfway down the room to receive me. A pipe for His Highness & his brother viceroy[59] were then introduced & all his courtiers kept standing, & then Artim Bey, whom you may recollect in England, interpreted my limping French into Turkish. The eye of this old man is very fine & inquisitive. I should say that he was naturally a good-natured man. He never took his eye off me, encouraged me to talk, but said little in reply & seemed to be rather anxious & nervous. I told him that I would not omit to pay my respects at the earliest period but that I must delay till tomorrow to make him a communication on the part of my government. He seemed more inclined to reconnoitre me than to originate any conversation, & in about half an hour I took my leave, going back in his state carriage with all solemnity as before. We then returned on b[*oar*]d the Geyser to dine & sleep, for I did not like to accept his offer to be accommodated in one of his palaces during the few hours I had to remain. I thought he might be offended if I went to an hotel & therefore got rid of the difficulty by remaining with Captain Carpenter, a very gentlemanlike man.

This morning at 9 o'cl. we went to the palace to communicate to

---

[58] Sir Edmund Lyons (1790–1858), later 1st Baron Lyons, a veteran of the Napoleonic wars.
[59] i.e. Hardinge.

the pacha the British govt.'s proposal. We were recd. as before. I went through all the points, & I could see by his eye & an occasional chuckle that he was highly delighted. I left a letter with his minister Artim Bey, stating the proposal. I shall receive his answer this evening & before I go to bed shall write to Lord Aberdeen & get rid of this affair altogether. Today at [?3] we dine with His Highness. Charles has made an excellent sketch of this extraordinary man.

9 o'cl.

From 3 to 8 I have been making conversation for the pacha. His interpreter speaks bad French, and every sentence is hung up & gibbetted & cut into quarters by the impatience of the interpreter to give your meaning to his master. In matters of dry business this is nothing but in familiar gossiping conversation this is fatal. However, we get on very well à force de compliments &, as this old fellow is a despot, nothing is too rank for his taste, altho' I believe him to be as practical a philosopher as any in the world & very much in advance of his age. He told me he could not *read* at 47 years of age; he then taught himself Arabic. He consoles himself for every misfortune either that it was so predestined or that the loss is a real gain. Thus he praises Lord Palmerston for combining agt. him to deprive him of Syria & part of Arabia.[60] These conquests required 50,000 men. The expense came from Egypt & was enormous. It threw his finances into disorder & into debt. By having Syria forced from him by England and the allied powers, there was no disgrace in his son Ibrahim abandoning Syria,[61] & he now boasts, 'I am richer than ever and better able to do my duty by Egypt.' He spends a gt. deal of his revenue in public works. There were only 2 good bridges.

We start at 6 tomorrow. I take the capt. & some of his offs. with me to see the Pyramids & I shall write by him from Cairo. I am afraid to say a word at present on the subject of your journey, & even when I arrive at Cairo I feel beforehand that it is a subject on which I shall fail to have the courage to speak.

Your duty & mine are to consider yr. safety. What would become of the children if anything happened to you?

[60] Palmerston, as the foreign secretary in Melbourne's government, helped to organize joint action with several European powers, including Russia and France, to stave off the dismemberment of the Ottoman Empire after Muhammad Ali's declaration of independence from Istanbul between 1839 and 1841. Although by the subsequent settlement the Ottomans recognized Muhammad Ali's hereditary position as viceroy in Egypt, he lost control over Syria and Arabia.

[61] Ibrahim Pasha, the eldest son of Muhammad Ali, fought in many military campaigns on behalf of the Ottoman Empire and his father. He served as the viceroy of Syria in the 1830s and was later assigned political and diplomatic responsibilities by Muhammad Ali, including a mission to France and England in 1845. Ibrahim took over the administration of Egypt in 1847, when Muhammad Ali was incapacitated by old age, but died in 1848, a year before his father.

4. [*To Emily.*] Ibrahim Pacha's palace, Cairo. 28th June 1844

On the morning of the 25th the viceroy's state carriages conveyed us to Mahmoudye's Canal,[62] 48 miles long, on which steamers go at the rate of 7 or 8 miles an hour, but at this season of the year the canal is low not only because the Nile is low which feeds it, but because the husbandmen of the surrounding country are allowed to fix water wheels worked by the mud buffalos which wallow in the mire of the canal &, being thus employed the greater part of the day, the canal was so low that the viceroy's steamer which he lent us was actually moving through liquid mud, & we were obliged to have a regt. of 600 to pull her through & keep her head straight. This was a curious sight. The officers had little whips in their hands, which were not required to be used, & by dint of their assistance we were actually dragged through the sand. These poor fellows every now & then fell out, went to the edge of the canal, washed their faces & hands & feet in the muddy water, then fell on their knees, turned towards Mecca, touched the ground with their foreheads, said a short prayer, & returned to their work.[63] The same devotions were constantly going on on board the steamer, & I never was so much struck with any exhibition of religious feeling which seemed to have such complete possession over its votaries as among these poor Musselmen. The villagers on the banks were in a state of the greatest misery, living in mud huts 3 or 4 feet high. We lost 4 or 5 hours by the state of the canal. When we got on the Nile, by means of large [*steamers*] we went at 6 miles an hour, but the viceroy's steamer is slow &, instead of arriving at 6 next day in the evening, we only reached Cairo at 11 in the evening of the 26th, taking 38 hours instead of 30.

[*Section missing.*[64] *Letter resumes with description of pasha's palace.*]

In the interior space there were a variety of lions & heads spouting out water in every direction, but it was Nile water, which is yellow turning to a red-brown, & the ceilings & ornaments were of wood badly painted. The floors were all of marble except the rooms which were inlaid with wood. I took this occasion in admiring this large fountain to observe that it reminded me of the famous Moorish palace of the Alhambra at Granada in Spain, which was considered very fine & of which we had in England very celebrated color'd prints. He had never heard of the Alhambra or the caliphs in Spain & seemed astonished at my admiration, & when I told him that we owed the invention of the watch to the Moors he was almost incredulous.

[62] The Al-Mahmudiyah Canal was built under Muhammad Ali in the late 1810s.

[63] Emily Hardinge's reaction was contained in a marginal note: 'How many Christians would do well to get over their anger in similar brief manner.'

[64] Emily's inserted comment explains: 'A sheet of this letter is lost which described the Pacha's garden & palace.'

He was, during the wars, a brave & good officer & is now chiefly occupied in planting & irrigating his lands, & by hydraulic machines made in England he is forcing the Nile water over its banks in every direction. Mahmut Ali & Ibrahim are Macedonians by birth[65] & Musselmen by religion. They are building very large expensive mosques, but they employ chiefly Greeks in their higher offices & are phylosophers [sic], drinking wine & setting Mahomet's [the Prophet's] precepts at defiance.

After visiting a large establishment for breeding horses & other places, we traversed the town on horseback, a party of about 40 horsemen mounted by the pacha whose people preceded us to clear the way. This is the most extraordinary town I ever saw. It is very large, full of mosques with beautiful minarets, the houses having very fine latticed windows worked in wood curiously carved, very like our oriel windows, projecting from the main walls of the buildings. I have no doubt many of our Gothic ornaments were introduced into England after the wars in the Holy Land. Charles & I were in admiration, which our friend the [Khunow] Bey[66] was scarcely able to comprehend. The streets are so narrow as almost to touch, & the top is generally covered during the great heats, as at present, which keeps the streets & houses comparatively cool.

We then went to the Citadel[67] which is undergoing a very substantial repair, the defences being raised more to keep the town in order than to resist an outward enemy. The population exceeds 300,000. Here in the Citadel Mahmut Ali invited the Mamelukes to dine with him. During dinner the Turkish janissaries by his orders surrounded the palaces & massacred their guests. One horseman made a tremendous leap with his horse of 35 feet into the ditch below. The horse was killed, & thus [he] was the only Mameluke out of the whole corps which escaped. Our old friend is not very scrupulous when he has a point to carry. In making his canal 20 years ago, he collected 300,000 villagers by force guarded by soldiers. In 3 years they formed the present canal excavated by their hands, having no spades. 10,000 died, according to Khunow Bey; according to others, 20,000 men. But this canal irrigates the whole country & has, as he says, multiplied the population & their comfort 100-fold.

The heat was excessive and we all stood it very well. At 4 we dined, at 8 I had an hour's talk with Ibrahim, & at 9 turned half undressed

[65] Muhammad Ali, though born at Kavala on the Macedonian coast, was probably of Albanian ancestry.

[66] An Egyptian official in attendance on Hardinge.

[67] The Citadel, located atop the Mokattam Hills, was built by Salah Al-Din Ayyub (Saladin) in 1183. Several significant monuments were later added to it, including the Soleiman Pasha Mosque, the Alabaster Mosque, and Joseph's Well.

into bed, having made our arrange[*men*]ts to ride 14 miles into the desert in order to view the Pyramids at sunrise & then to ride back before the great heat begins.

Charles came into me at 12 saying he had not closed his eyes. He had been so devoured by mosquitoes & red aunts [*sic*], but he had a net over his bed, & he & Robert Wood had amused themselves in chastizing the mosquitoes instead of going to sleep.

We went up the river 2 or 3 miles in the steamer, then landed & mounted our horses, the night being lovely—a full moon, a charming breeze, & the Pyramids generally seen indistinctly on the horizon. We had 6 or 7 men with long poles & a sort of iron-hooped grating on the top filled with dry wood. These men were distributed along the road, running at 4 or 5 miles an hour. The neighing & scampering of 40 horses & a few camels, the men on foot who are [*sic*] running, grooms belonging to the horses mixed with Arabs of the villages whom we picked up on the road, the partial obscurity & conflict between the light of the large torches & the beautiful moon, the singing of the camel drivers, the shouts of the men—all contributed to render it one of the most striking & extraordinary scenes I ever witnessed.

At 3 we got to the large Pyramid. The moon had gone down & it was quite dark. We went to the mouth of the great chamber. Charles insisted upon going into it, and he quite astonished the party by the manner in which he climbed up into the interior. I was rejoiced to see him come out of this stupendous tomb,[68] pleased at what he had seen & with himself. We then had a few minutes to wait before daylight enabled the younger portions of the party to ascend the gt. Pyramid. I kept Charles with me, making an interesting sketch by torchlight. One Bedouin Arab in 6 minutes with one of our large torches ran in the dark up to the top &, fixing his light like a red lurid star, shouted out to us below. Whilst the more active, assisted by Bedouins, went to the top of the Pyramid, we rode round the base & examined the next in size. The sun being up, we, all highly delighted with our excursion, rode back, reaching the palace by 7 o'cl. My poor bey, a man of 40, [*was*] quite knocked up. I am as fresh as when I started, having *rode 24 miles there & back*.

[*No closing*]

5. [*To Emily.*] Hindostan steamer, n[*ea*]r Aden. July 4, 1844

After I had closed my letter from Cairo we dined with Ibrahim Pacha, who treated us à la Turque. The cooking was Turkish & we

---

[68] The tomb of Khufu (Cheops).

eat [*sic*] with our fingers. He gave me a plate which I used as little as possible. The cookery was much approved, & at 5 in the broiling sun he took me in his carriage to see an estab[*lishmen*]t of Arabian horses on the road across the desert. He had previously offered me two horses which I declined. I saw one very remarkable horse; the others were scarcely worth notice.

I took my leave of this extraordinary man who has, during 30 years of his life, been a successful soldier & whose manner was frank & pleasant. We got into an English light britska, driven by an English man with a postillion on the leaders, horsed by 6 light native horses of the country. After a certain quantity of kicking & neighing, we got under weigh [*sic*] at full gallop, the whips cracking, & on each side a Nubian running by the side of the carriage at full speed who get up behind or even push themselves on the box, going at great speed & ready at any moment to get down to put the harness in order. Two other covered carriages on 2 high wheels followed with the servants & baggage, &, the moon getting up soon after our departure, we galloped over the wild tracks of the desert certainly at the rate of 12 miles an hour. We had been up the night before in visiting the Pyramids. Charles slept like a top, but I was so absorbed in the novelty of our position, the extraordinary skill of our English driver, & the sorts of breakneck adventure in which we were engaged that I talked to him & our conductor, an Italian & clever fellow, the whole of the way.

When we had galloped in this style abt. 50 miles, changing horses every 10 or 12, our poor postillion, who had determined to ride the whole way, 84 miles, was thrown by his horse, falling under the carriage. At first we feared he was killed, but on examination his foot was only bruised, so we put him into the baggage van with the doctor of the Hindostan, who had come with us from Cairo, & left him at the next bungalow, consoling him with an extra fee of £2 for his folly. We then went the remainder of the distance with 4 in hand, this Englishman driving with extraordinary skill & energy, & reached Suez an hour after sunrise, having completed the distance, including stoppages, on 12 horses.

I stopped to dress & wash in the same room that Napoleon occupied when at Suez, &, our boats being ready, I was on the Hindostan to breakfast by 9 o'cl. &, altho' we had fared well in the desert, we did justice to an English breakfast after a severe jolting during the night. We slept till dinner time.

Our cabin is comfortable, & every luxury was provided to make our passage agreeable. The thermometer was 89 but it gradually rose to 90, 92, & 93. Yesterday I was unwell. I took [*a*] blue pill & am better this morning. But the heat is very oppressive & I would not, d[*eare*]st, on any account [*?wish*] that you should have been exposed to the last 3 days' heat which we have experienced. I scarcely think you could have survived it.

We shall probably reach Aden at 9 this evening. It is a post not very honestly obtained from the Arabs, who have twice endeavored to take it from us, but a British batt[*alio*]n & a sepoy batt[*alio*]n of 1700 men continue to hold it, & I am to give a final opinion as to the mode of occupying & fortifying it. It is a halfway house between India & Egypt for our communications &, notwithstanding the expense (100,000 a year), must be held.[69]

Charles is quite well. He has the power of sleeping whenever he likes &, being very abstemious, he has suffered little. My indisposition is slight, caught by sleeping in a sharp current of air when hot. I am quite satisfied you could not have come out with me at this period of the year. The sea is 88, the engine room is 120, in the sun 106, & in this cabin 91 whilst I am writing. Fortunately we have few passengers, only 15 going out instead of 120, the usual complement, on account of the season. This practical proof must make you rejoice that you did not risk yourself & the children at this season. I thank God repeatedly to Charles that you are not with us. For the present, good-bye.

Aden. 5th July

We were up at 1/2 p[*as*]t 3 this morning, mounting on horses before daylight & getting to the ground as the sun rose. Now that I have seen this extraordinary mass of volcanic rocks, I can talk with the different depts. during the day & compare opinions, weighing objections & forming my opinion as to the system which ought to be adopted.

We found the 17th British & the 47th Madras Sepoys on the lines, on the alert to defend the Turkish lines, living under tents and mattings. The remainder of the guard was drawn out on parade to receive me, & I passed down the line at 6 o'cl. & have now been breakfasting with the political agent, having a sepoy to fan me whilst I am writing these hurried lines. I have to receive the officers & public dept. at 12 o'cl. & when the heat goes down I shall again mount my horse to see the town, which is wretched in appearance but is said to contain every Indian comfort.

A steamer from Bombay for Suez has come in. The steamer for Suez will sail in 3 or 4 hours. I may have letters from Ld. Ellenborough informing me of his intention of returning by this route, & I shall keep

---

[69] The strategically located Aden was occupied by a British force sent from Bombay in 1839, and it passed under the administrative control of the East India Company. The British strengthened Aden militarily because of local insurgency and the fear of French intrusion into the region.

this note open for an hour or two to communicate with you up to the last moment.

My head is quite free from any giddiness or headache. I take very little wine—2 or 3 glasses in the 24 hours, diluted with soda water. I am quite satisfied as to my stamina to endure heat. If I were quite happy about you, I should be happy, energetic, & ten years younger.

We sail tomorrow m[*ornin*]g at 10 o'cl. after having taken coal on b[*oar*]d for Ceylon, our next resting point. Then to Madras & lastly to Calcutta where we hope to land about the 24th. Now that we have got out of the Red Sea the sea breezes will keep me cooler, & you may calculate that we have got over the most oppressive part of our voyage.

I won't attempt a description of this curious chaotic mass of rock, which exceeds anything I ever saw in Europe or America. The Arabs of the neighbourhood are small active men, but our sturdy English-men, as I passed down the ranks, made me feel quite proud. In look & shape & make they have such a marked superiority over the sepoy, the Arab, & the Nubian that it was impossible not to discover in our race the real secret of our wonderful successes. This physical superiority, regulated & directed by Christianity & civilization (for in spite of much injustice, we have more respect for human life & divine precepts than any other conquering power), & this rule of conduct probably has secured for us more assistance than we should otherwise have had if we had imitated the infamous system of French *Ruzzias* in Algiers.[70]

God bless & preserve you and our dear children.

6. [*To Walter.*] Hindostan, off Madras. July 19th, [1844]

The only means of communicating with you by the present mail is to send my letter ashore at Madras. The Bentinck for Suez from Calcutta will be here in 3 or 4 days and, altho' I write in utter ignorance of any news from Calcutta, it is better to seize this oppor-tunity than to postpone our com[*municatio*]n for a whole month.

I have written to your dear mother by several opportunities which have occurred, & I have strenuously advised her to postpone her voyage, for the choice of evils is great. If at the present season we suffer from intense heat, at a later season this sea is much rougher & the vessel's motion worse to bear, altho' it is true that the climate of

---

[70] The word 'Razzias' is an English and French corruption of the Arabic term *ghazawat* (war). Here it refers to the large-scale and bloody French punitive military expeditions against the militant Arab tribesmen, who in the first half of the nineteenth century often raided French settlements in Algeria. See no. 89.

Calcutta in October is better than we shall find it to be on our arrival.

I therefore trust that your dear mother will, 'till she hears from me, give up her intention. Indeed, until I reach Calcutta I know not what may be my own movements. I confidently hope I shall find Ld. E[*llenborough*] at Calcutta. I hear he [*has*] taken a ho[*us*]e 1/2 mile from the Government Ho[*us*]e &, as the Auckland has been at his disposal for some time, I rejoice in the hope of having the advantage of much confidential conversation with him before he separates from me.

We expect to reach Calcutta the 24th, & I long to grapple with my difficulties. I have read a good deal on the voyage & with profit, &, altho' I do not conceal from myself the arduous nature of my duties, I am prepared to work with more [*rest lacking. Here Emily makes a reference, without explanation, to the loss of Hardinge's letters written from India between July 19 and August 17 relating to his arrival at Calcutta. Thus Hardinge's very first impressions of India have not been preserved.*]

7. [*To Walter.*] Calcutta. 17th Aug. 1844

I am anxiously expecting the arrival of the mail from England. Our mail must be made up this even[*in*]g, & every letter which is brought into the room ends in the disappointment of its not being from the dear friends we have.

I continue in excellent health. I ride every other morn[*in*]g at 5 for an hour & drive in the even[*in*]g. This, with sauntering in the large veranda, is exercise enough for an old gentleman who is never dry for one moment in this moist climate. The damp far exceeds any idea I had formed of its penetrating effects, & this house, exposed to the south on the main front, is quite green with vegetation. We have 2 months more of the bad season and are then to have 4 or 5 months of fine weather.

Charles has a cold & does not manage himself so well as I do. Sometimes he puts on a flannel waistcoat, then takes it off & over-exercises himself I think. But he is very temperate & gets through his business well.

The public business is already much simplified. Ld. E[*llenborough*] trusted no one & liked to do the inferior drudgery of every office from an insatiable necessity of being employed. He told me he could not live without excitement. I make the officers do their own business, oblige each secretary to state his opinion on a Minute covering each paper which he signs. We agree or disagree. I see everything as before but the written record of what is to be done is before us. The letters written accord with the Minute, whereas by the former system the letters were written with very few Minutes, & it [*was*] impossible to know what answers were sent, exclusive of the excessive toil of wading through a mass of papers which, after an hour's perusal, reqd. nothing to be done, etc. etc.

I have had to read lectures & admonish a king or two[71] since I last wrote, the style of which wd. amuse you, but the only quarters in which we have any business of real interest are the Punjab & Scinde.

We have no treaty with the Lahore govt. In the disturbed state of the Punjab, our relations are merely nominal. Our real position is that of an armed truce.

The army are the real rulers of the Punjab. The executive power is lodged in the hands of Heera Singh, a great favorite when a boy of Runjeet Singh's.[72] His uncle, Golab Singh, who raised himself from being a runner by the side of Runjeet's horse to be a raja or prince, has a large force & many forts in the hills.[73] His brother Suchet Singh, who was killed some months ago by Heera Singh, was the owner of some treasure, £150,000 in coin, at Ferozepoor. This money we seized on his death, informing the parties that we should hold it in custody for the rightful owners. We wrote 3 months ago to Golab S. & Heera S. & the widow. We have had no answer, &, as I am desirous of giving the strongest proof which barbarians can receive of our honesty, namely the surrender of money, I am now about to deliver it up to the Lahore govt. to be disposed of according to the laws & usages of the country, no answer having been sent to our letters for the last 3 m[onths] & no claimant appearing before us. This common honesty may dispel some of the alarm which they entertain of our hostile preparations.[74]

They have an army of 100,000 men of various sects, 500 guns, some

[71] This alludes to a letter from Hardinge to the nawab of Oudh, Amjad Ali Shah, on 10 Aug. 1844, reproaching him for widespread corruption and favoritism in his administration.

[72] Hira Singh, the minister since Sept. 1843, was one of the Jammu Rajas. Believed to be then in his mid-twenties, he was made the minister more out of sympathy for the bloody death of Dhian Singh, his father and predecessor, than for his own merits. An inexperienced and vacillating minister, Hira Singh found it impossible to cope with his office. He was murdered in Dec. 1844.

[73] Gulab Singh (1792–1857) was the eldest, and eventually the most successful, of the Jammu Rajas. He joined the Sikhs' service in 1809, and for his contributions in various military expeditions was made the raja of Jammu in 1822 by Ranjit Singh. After that Gulab Singh was seldom at Lahore, devoting himself to the acquisition of territories surrounding Jammu through a policy of intrigue and brutality. See Bawa Satinder Singh, *The Jammu Fox: A Biography of Maharaja Gulab Singh of Kashmir* (Carbondale and London, 1974).

[74] Raja Suchet Singh (ob. 1844), a dignitary at the Sikh court, was killed in a power struggle with his nephew. At first Hardinge seemed inclined to return the Raja's treasure at Ferozepur, the British cantonment on the Sutlej, but failed to do so because more than one claimant appeared.

with horses & manned, & probably 30,000 cav.[75] This army is in a
state of successful mutiny for pay on our frontier. The contagion is
unpleasant, for the real solution of the phenomenon of our Indian
army & its attachment to an alien govt. is pay. Our pay is the best.
We grant pensions & faithfully perform our stipulations, which no
native prince ever does.

But when a large army for several months together dictate what
pay they should receive, dismiss & appoint their officers (murdering
many), & before they perform any service making a bargain for pay,
the risk of a bad example to an army, which is a *foreign* army as it
regards its employers but a *national* army as it regards its own countrymen, is a state of things which must give uneasiness when
accompanied by symptoms of discontent & mutiny, such as those
instances in the 34th, 64[*th*], 10th Cav., & other corps on *that frontier*.
However, I have no doubt we shall get over our milty. difficulties
successfully, & in this vast empire, let your political economists say
what they will, our power rests exclusively on the fidelity of this native
army & must do so for several years to come, for the prejudices of
Muhommedans & Hindoos are very strong & hitherto we have made
very little impression.

To return to the Punjab. Golab Singh, the uncle of Heera Singh,
is the ablest man of the Jummoo family. They are Rajpoots & pure
Brahmins in religion.[76] The Sikhs are a fanatic sect of Hindoos, hating
all infidels, having by their courage & good fortune conquered the
Affghans who had settled in the Punjab.

This Goolab Singh was a foot orderly, as I have before said, to old
Runjeet S. Being a native of the hills, he was allowed by Runjeet to
make conquests, acknowledging R. as his lord paramount. In a few
years this man has conquered a small principality, subduing his
weaker neighbours & forcing them to pay tribute, & this territory is
nearly equal to the Punjab. His income is probably £600,000 a yr.
He is brave, skilful, & holds the Sikhs of the plain in contempt. He
has agreeable manners, full of information, provident, trusting only
to himself, but bloodthirsty & not hesitating to assassinate in his own
h[ou]se any guest whose property he covets or whose death may be
convenient. He played chess with Sooltan Khan of the hill state of
Bimber. He beat him (S.K.) at chess, then asked him to go upstairs
&, setting on him in front & rear with his armed men, murdered him.

---

[75] The numerical strength of the Sikh army rose from 65,835 in 1843 to 98,821 in
1845. These statistics include the infantry, artillery, and the cavalry but not the levies
supplied by the jagirdars. (S. R. Kohli, 'The Organization of the Khalsa Army' in Teja
Singh and Ganda Singh [eds.], *Maharaja Ranjit Singh* [Amritsar, 1939], pp. 70–87.)
[76] The Jammu Rajas were not Brahmans. They were Dogra Rajputs, all of whom
belong to the Kshatriya caste. Hardinge makes a similar error in no. 118.

This is the accomplished villain who is most anxious that the B. govt.
should acknowledge him as sovereign of the hill tribes. Being of a
different creed from the Sikhs, they hate him on religious prejudices,
& he is too crafty to place himself in the dangerous position in which
his nephew Heera Singh is placed at Lahore.

This Heera S. is about 25 years of age, very handsome, very
arrogant, & during the last year has displayed much courage & talent.
Runjeet S. always placed him in a seat next [to] himself. This privilege
he retained after Runjeet Singh's death, during the short reigns of
Khurrick Singh & Sheer Singh,[77] who have both met with violent
deaths. He displayed great spirit & promptitude in the attack on the
murderers of his father in the [Lahore] fort. He was equally successful
agt. his uncle Soochet Singh & agt. Utter Singh & Baee Beer Singh,
whom he destroyed.[78] He is a Hindoo by religion, & will only govern
the Sikh army as long as the treasure lasts. The most influential of the
Sikh sirdars have withdrawn from the Lahore court, keeping aloof &
waiting events.

Heera Singh is advised by Pundit Julla, a Brahmin who the Sikhs
detest on that score. His brother[79] is the spiritual adviser of the
Jummoo family, that is, Heera Singh's & Golab Singh's. He is obliged
to pay the army & is on every acct. very unpopular.

Heera Singh's power will probably not be destroyed by open violence. His chief danger is from some fanatic Sikh, of which class there
are bodies of fukeers banded together & who desire to revenge the
death of Baee Beer Singh, who was killed in a battle by Heera S. and
who was a holy man in great repute amongst the Sikhs. He will also
have all the desperate men who are seeking their fortune by enterprise
agt. him, & I expect [by] every post to hear that he has met with his
deserts & is no more.

The Maha-raja, the grandson of Ranjeet S., is Duleep Singh, a boy
of about 9 years of age, sickly & just recovering from the smallpox.[80]
He is probably safe for the present as his life is convenient to Heera
Singh.

[77] They ruled from June 1939 to Nov. 1840 and Jan. 1841 to Sept. 1843, respectively.
[78] Attar Singh was a leader of the anti-Dogra Sandhawalia faction which murdered
Sher Singh and Dhian Singh in mid-Sept. 1843. When Hira Singh avenged his father's
death by killing most of the prominent Sandhawalias, Attar Singh escaped to Ludhiana
in British India. In May 1844 he re-entered Panjab and, after an unsuccessful attempt
to oust Hira Singh, took refuge with Bhai Bir Singh, a venerated Sikh saint. Hira
Singh's troops, however, encircled the Bhai's camp. In the melee that followed, both
Bir Singh and Attar Singh were killed, and the 'head of Sirdar Attar Singh was cut off
and sent to Lahore' ('Abstract of Intelligence from the Punjab,' May 8, 1844, in H. R.
Gupta [ed.], Punjab on the Eve of First Sikh War [Hoshiarpur, 1956], p. 181).
[79] A Pandit Charan Das who lived at Jammu.
[80] Dalip Singh (1837–93) became the Maharaja in Sept. 1843.

Lehna S.[81] is a Sikh, govr. of Umritser, very well informed, a scholar, skilled in gunnery, very fond of pundits & learned men's society, & curious in Hindoo law & Persian poetry. He is too prudent to remain in the Punjab & has proceeded on a pilgrimage into our province. He is not a daring man but he is likely to be an important character hereafter, & I have therefore mentioned him. He is about 42 yrs. of age. I will not give you the characters of 1/2 a dozen other chiefs of some note who have survived the bloody intrigues of the last 2 years.

Well then, our position is this: we desire peace, but with such neighbours on our frontier, ready at any moment with a wild fanatic army to overrun our territory, we must make milty. preparations on a large & expensive scale. Whilst I hope we shall not be required to take any decisive act of interference, we must be prepared & be ready. This is annoying. If we do interfere, rely upon it, my case shall be a very strong one to justify the measures. In this state we are waiting events but, as the rivers are flooded, nothing can happen till October.

If I don't curb the speed at which I write, I shall send you a volume instead of a letter. But the fact is the climate has a most satisfactory effect upon my head. I am clearer & can work longer than in England. I think my memory is improved & I am so much more confident, now that I have admonished a king or two in diplomatic language, & can be much at home in the most important part of our business, that is the milty. branch, that I have no apprehensions. They were strong whilst I was in doubt &, as it is well-known that I do all the business myself, I am tranquil & confident & really have not time to be ill or to mind the climate.

Robert Wood is very attentive & laborious & does much good service. Charles will turn out very well, decidedly not so clever as Arthur but respected & beloved by those who know him.

I have been writing at least 30 sheets of paper since 5 this morn[in]g with many interruptions. I shall keep this letter unsealed till the last moment in the hope of hearing from you & Sarah. Every hour I am here I am grateful to Providence for our discretion in having prevented your mother & the 2 girls from coming here. How[eve]r, on all these points I reserve myself till I open my letters, having alas! only 4 h[ours] more before our mail closes. Give my love to all who care for me.

[PS.] I have just recd. Sarah's letter & a *very* short note from you, &, as I find your mother is not at any rush to embark before Decr., there will be ample time, I trust, to induce her to defer her journey.

---

[81] A member of the Majithia family, he had received the title of Hashm-ud-Daulah (Lord of the State).

Oh! what I [*would*] give if this torrid zone were but Canada or Kampschatka![82]

Charles' cold has been attended with some fever, very like ague. He is obliged to keep [*to*] his room & take calomel. In a day or two, I have no doubt, he will be quite right. He is better today than he was yesterday, & I write openly to you, being quite satisfied abt. him. But this slight attack only confirms me in my forewarnings not to trust my children who are younger to any unnecessary trial; & even if your mother, with all her noble energy & dauntless courage, could outlive the climate, I should be in alarm abt. the girls. I must entreat you to consult & advise with Ld. E[*llenborough*]. He knows the country & the climate better than I do. The conflict with me is a cruel one. I can bear the separation because it is my duty & I am incessantly occupied, but to deny anything to such a devoted wife is a cruelty & a task beyond my powers.

I must close this letter. I have many letters to sign & the hour is late.

[*PS.*] Always write under cover to Ld. Ripon.[83] The govr. genl.'s bag is recd. by dak 24 & 48 h[*ours*] sooner than the common post. Tell this to all my correspondents.

8. [*To Emily.*] Calcutta. August 17th, 1844

I have read with avidity & gratitude your invaluable letters from the day I left you to this moment. Thank God you are well & that our children prosper. Arthur will, I have no doubt, be everything which we can desire, & any arrangements which you make conducive to your comfort will, I know, never be detrimental to his interests. In various letters I have with perfect truth stated to you my fears at the risk you & the children will run by coming here. At the same time I never will prohibit you from doing what you consider to be your duty, but I cannot conceal from you that the weight of my responsibility, which I bear firmly whilst I know you & our children are in safety in a healthy climate, will be greatly increased.

At this moment, altho' I am not uneasy about Charles, I am unsettled & worried because he has a cold & a bilious attack. It makes me so anxious that I unconsciously get up to walk into his room at the other side of the house. With you & the two girls subject to these attacks, what would be my state as a public servant in a position requiring incessant labour? Even if I could get over my alarm about you, what must I not apprehend by the presence of two young creatures who could only sit under a punka all day, for the society here is really visionary. The climate is so hot & damp that every book is mildewed, every coat wet, the house very green, & this to last for 6 weeks longer. When I carefully weigh all these considerations, I know it is my duty to you & to my children to state them clearly & honestly, &, if I did not love you more deeply & respect you more strongly than I ever could any other woman, I should decidedly say, don't come. But with you who have such claims upon me I never will thwart your inclinations. I am ready to sacrifice my public life to you. But as far as your free-agency is concerned, I never will oppose you. You need not mind expense. If you come, take the best cabins. If you do not, pray recollect [*that*] the advantages which money can give the girls are a source of much consolation to me. I did not consent to come here for wealth, for I had refused the office of comd. in chief, which, in a pecuniary sense, is as good &, in a professional sense, was more to my taste. There was no difficulty in obtaining a successor & one who had a good claim by service to the preference. I relinquished it without a murmur, happy to remain with you. I could not relinquish this last honour so urgently pressed upon me, & it is a great gratification to me that the toil is to be accompanied by the means of making our children, when I die, comparatively independent. Therefore you will make me happy by denying them no advantage in matters which may improve & cultivate their minds. With yr. maternal devotion to your children I must leave the decision of yr. joining me to your own free choice. I am ready to support you, to love & cherish you, nay more, to approve of yr. decision & in every result, be it disastrous or happy, to attribute to you & your decision the only true notice by which you will be guided, the honour & success of yr. husband, the health & prosperity of yr. children. I have solemnly promised never to conceal from you that which as a mother & a wife you have so just a title to enjoy, the fullest & most complete confidence.

Charles four days ago complained of cold from checked perspiration & put on & took off his flannel waistcoat. He declined taking medicine &, I suspect, threw it away (as if medicine were not invented as a remedy for human infirmities).[84] We thought him well yesterday morning, but something like ague came on—quite well at one moment but heated at another. He is free from fever this m[*ornin*]g, but it will probably return in the middle of the day & in a day or two subside. I gave him some letters to read from Arthur & his sisters, which the

---

[84] Emily's maternal response to this was written in the margin: 'Just like Charles.'

doctor said had excited him. However, he liked his drive in the evening &, if we have no rain, he will go out again today. I wish this contretemps has [*sic*] happened earlier as I should have had the satisfaction of saying he was quite well.

With regard to Arthur I can say nothing positively, dearest, till I know what yr. decision will be. I should wish, if you postpone coming for a year, that he should remain till next Sepr. in England, then join me for the cool season. But a year is so large a space in the revolution of events here that I scarcely can say more than that I should wish to have him in the fine season when I shall be probably going up to the N.W. frontier. As the climate is good *there* & he would be under my eye, I think at 17 1/2 yrs. of age it would enable him to see more than in any other position & tend to form his character to become a useful & perhaps a distinguished servant of the public, for after all we best fulfill our brief vocation here if we are honest & good & useful to our country.

With regard to politics, I have written at full gallop to dear Walter on the most important point, namely the Punjab. He will show you my letter. I have only had a short note from him.

You must let me know your itineraire de voyage, in order that my letters may go from Marseilles to any other place if you decide on going abroad. But do not take a dislike to dear South Park. Love it for my sake &, rely upon it, Providence is merciful & kind. If we do what is right, we shall have the better chance of receiving our reward even in this world. Only conceive the delight after all our troubles & trials to be seated in our comfortable rooms hearing the girls play, the boys laugh, & receiving our friends & old neighbours with true English hospitality, substituting a good blazing fire for the punka, & sauntering on the terrace after my imprisonment here, for between 6 in the morning & 7 in the evening I am a state prisoner.

I went last Saturday evening to the country residence of the govr. genl. at Barrackpore, 15 miles from Calcutta. The park is not quite 200 acres, beautifully green & kept mown. Lord Ellenborough has made a very handsome terrace & greatly improved the place, but there, as here, that brilliant tyrant the sun keeps us in confinement, & night & day I live under a punka.

As regards myself, you will perceive by the quantity & the facility of my work that I am quite well. The climate, by great care & temperance & constant occupation, has not disagreed with me. I drink sherry & water, eat mutton for dinner, bread & butter & jam for breakfast, riding for upwards of an hour 3 times a week before 5 in the morning. If I could be assured about you, my dearest wife, I should be able to get through my drudgery, but, whilst I have *no nerves* on public matters, you have witnessed how *weak* I am on family affairs.

The mail closes in two hours but I shall keep this open an hour longer.

God preserve & bless you.

[*The first part of the following letter is missing. Its references to conditions in Panjab, Ellenborough's return to England, and the problems relating to Emily's desire to join Hardinge in India, seem to indicate that the letter was probably written sometime between August 17 and October 20.*]

9. [*To Walter James. n.d.*]

I have no doubt, how[*eve*]r, that a govr. genl. may easily lay bye half his income on £12,000 a yr.

These details will convince yr. mother that she need deprive herself of no comfort if she will consent to remain at home. I am, I can assure you, quite convinced that for 7 m[*onths*] in the year she could not exist at Calcutta, & from what I see of society, she & the girls would die of ennui. I am kept alive by constant employment. If this were to cease, I am sure I should give way.

In a few months, I shall be able to take a more safe & true survey of my position. I may be able to do good. I do not anticipate milty. operations in the Punjaub, altho' in India no man can say what a month may produce in a country of 120 millions of inhabitants governed by an army which is officered by aliens, whilst the mass of the force under these foreign offs. consents to co-erce [*sic*] their own countrymen, merely for the sake of pay & pension—*mesmerized* as it were by a handful of offs. exhibiting in the working of the system the greatest phenomenon that the world ever witnessed.

When you see Ld. E[*llenborough*] tell him how much I feel obliged to him for all his kindness & thought. I reckon upon his support as essential to the good govt. of the country.

I have written to Sarah. Pray look after Arthur. I am bewildered for the present as to the disposal of that dear boy. If I take him from yr. mother she will feel the bereavement, & yet he must join his regt. I believe the best thing is to keep him at Chatham till Janry. waiting events. I cannot tell you how anxious I am for the next mail.

10. [*To Walter.*] Calcutta. Sepr. 21st, 1844

I am rejoiced to find your dear mother continues in such perfect health. This is a great blessing, but the suspense keeps me in a state of great anxiety on her account. Fortunately I am so urged on by important matters which will not brook delay that my mind is occupied for many hours of incessant labour till at last I fall asleep quite exhausted, but not so during the last 2 nights. I fancy I see & hear you all, & your letters have made me homesick. Then I never can repay your dear mother for all her devoted love to me, to Charles & to all of you.

I find you had not received my letters from Aden. I wrote again from Ceylon & from Madras, then by Ld. Ellenborough, & since by every mail. You must take care when your mother leaves England for the Continent, whether it be for Nice or Alexandria, that the clearest directions are given for addressing letters to her.

I suppose Ld. E. will be in England about the 26th or 28th Sep. He will make a point of seeing your mother.

If anything prevents your mother going abroad, Arthur must resume his studies. When I know your mother's final resolution, I can give directions about Arthur's plans.

Our news from the Punjab is that the Sikh army is on the move, preparing for an expedition agt. Golab Singh, who rules a large portion of the hill tribes. Our information is very deficient, & I am going to remedy it by changing the political agent on the frontier.[85] I don't think I shall be obliged to move up this year. Events in this country succeed each other so rapidly that it is difficult to foresee one day what the next may produce. But I am determined our policy shall be an honest one, & I perceive by Ld. Ripon's letters to me that we have, during the last month, adopted in Scinde & on the Sutlege the very policy he was anxious to pursue, being in some anxiety by letters from Bombay that we might have taken a different line.

We can only move from the end of Oct. till the end of March on acct. of the heat, & 3 weeks ago my instructions have been issued & received by the com. in chief, that is a month *before* they can be executed. It is a great point to be in advance of time, & this remark compels me to be brief, for the mail goes out at 6 this even[in]g.

I cannot allow you, if your mother leaves S. Park, to pay any rent. You know I always felt that event to be so impossible (in which opinion I still remain) that I did not urge what appeared to me empty words. You will do exactly as you like whether yr. mother inhabits it or not—plant, alter & ornament what you like. If the poor require work, I had intended to grub & lay down the rough part of the right of the road going up the hill looking towards Blowers Hill,[86] draining it carefully. That portion is very rough & wet.

My strength in going through the work I do rather surprizes me. I have no headaches or giddiness. I am thin & much the better for it. I don't take hard exercise, because this month is the most trying of the whole year.

[85] Hardinge replaced Lt. Col. Richmond with Maj. George Broadfoot in Oct.
[86] Blower's Hill lies southwest of South Park. (Hasted, iii. 158–9 [map].)

Love to dearest Sarah & the baby. I quite agree in what you say of Arthur. If I were to go up to the frontier, I should like to have him. It wd. expand his milty. mind more than any instruction to see 30,000 men assembled with all their equipments for active service.

11. [*To Walter.*] Calcutta. Oct. 22nd, 1844

I have written to your mother, addressing my letter to Nice. My letters by the former mails will of course follow her. I have said everything I can to dissuade her from the attempt & I can now only leave the issue in the hands of a merciful Providence. If she does not persevere, then Arthur had better come out in the Bentinck. Or if that is too great a sacrifice, he can return with her to England & join me by the Janry. mail. Later will be hot.

I came in from Barrackpore, having suffered from checked perspiration. I was ill for 1/2 a dozen hours, but now [*am*] quite well. My health has quite surprized me.

I have had a charming letter from Sarah, which I cannot answer till next mail. Yr. English mail was received last night & is off this even[*in*]g. I have, therefore, scarcely had time to get through the letters to Ripon & the directors.

Nothing very stirring here except a war between Heera Singh & Golab Singh, that is the plains agt. the hills & which may be long & desultory.

I am on excellent terms with my council &, if I could be secure that yr. dear mother's life wd. be safe, I could be reconciled to my lot & be happy. God bless you & dear Sarah & the dear little baby.

12. [*To Sarah. Calcutta.*] Oct. 22, 1844

I should feel myself to be ungrateful if I did not find a minute to thank you for your dear letter. I still hope the letters I have written will save me from the catastrophe which will happen if Lady Emily perseveres in her attempt.

I have sent my letter to *Nice, poste restante.* I wish I could for an instant drop in amongst you, but I must steel my heart agt. such imaginations. The time will come when we shall be all happily reunited if I can but persuade my dear wife to have more prudence than courage. I am now more fatigued than usual, having had a bilious attack by my own imprudence. But the ins[*tan*]t the post closes I shall go fast asleep, so kind & indulgent is Nature in the midst of all our anxieties & cares.

13. [*To Emily.*] Calcutta. Novr. 23rd, 1844

I cannot say how much I am touched to the heart by all your devoted attachment so affectionately joined by words & acts, for which I never can sufficiently express my gratitude, but you know not how much I am tortured by fears for your safety. Even if you get to Alexandria alive, I fear the exaustion [*sic*] of the short voyage will disqualify you for the rough & longer voyage from Suez to Calcutta. When you get here—ah, d[*eares*]t, in that case I may save you. But God will be merciful to one so fragile in strength & so brave in spirit.

The mail closes this evening. I have just finished a letter to Peel, enclosing him a copy of my scrap dispatch to the Queen. He has written me a most affecte. letter, & I believe we are going on here to his satisfaction.

If Dr McPherson is afraid of taking charge of you from Suez to Calcutta in consequence of yr. sufferings from Italy to Alexandria, then, my dearest wife, you must consider such advice as my prohibition, altho' I hate this word, for I never can prohibit one so dear to me. I can only entreat & conjure you for my sake.

Charles is quite well & so am I, but this is our cool season—the ther[*momete*]r at 80 in the middle of the day! But it is luxury compared to July & August.

I can hardly give you an account of my life. It is getting up at 5, riding about in the dark & working from 11 or 12 hours a day but, I hope, to good purpose; no parties except those I give, which generally consist of 40 persons at Calcutta & 20 at Barrackpore. So day succeeds day in one monotonous circle; at the same time not without its consolations, for I relieve my mind by the reflection that I am doing my duty both to the public & my family.

We expect at the beginning of [*?December*] a Prussian prince Waldemar[87] & I shall give my first ball about that time, which will amount to about 600 persons. Dearest, if I could but see you & the girls in the marble saloon in good health & spirits, I feel it would do me more good than all the applause of the world.

I have taken the field on the subject of education & passed a *Resolution* published in our Gazette promising govt. employ[*men*]t to the most meritorious native students. It has made them very grateful, & the Mahomedans, who have always had a marked aversion to our literature & who from bigotry only teach Arabic, the Khoran & other abstruse religious works, have at once begun to change their system & to introduce English. Conceive some 30 Hindoo boys as black as yr. hat spouting Shakespeare fluently—aye & explaining accurately all the most difficult passages.

[87] A nephew of the King of Prussia, Frederick William IV.

I think I have sheathed the scabbard [*sic*] & hope to keep my promise of a pacific administration in the Punjab. Things look better than they did & I am in hopes my measures may be useful tho deprived of the éclat of military glory.

14. [*To Walter.*] Calcutta. Decr. 23rd, 1844

I have yr. letter of the 3rd & 5th of Novr. I have also one from yr. dearest mother at Nice of the 7th of Novr. She is evidently fearing that I intend to prohibit her coming. As I have repeatedly said, if my entreaties cannot prevail, how can my orders be obeyed? No, if I had prohibited mdear wife from joining me by an *order*, there would have been great irritability & deep mortification &, as you have heard her say, 'If you wish me not to come, I will submit,' I have expressed my wishes in decided terms that she cannot mistake. If therefore the cast of the die is to depend upon my giving *an order*, I can only plead that I never gave yr. mother an order in my life. I never found it to be necessary, & at the end of our lives this act of authority would have appeared to me like a divorce. My horrors of the climate have not changed. If your mother does come out, I must endeavor to keep her alive during the 7 hot months as well as the skill of the doctors will permit. I work hard & sleep sound & have no dreams but of her & the children on b[*oar*]d ship, & I am not relieved by finding her attempt to come is more probable than it was, & in the case of all danger the nearer it comes the firmer it is to be faced, & as I have taken every justifiable step to avert it I must resign myself to the will & protection of God.

The state of things in the Punjaub is very unsettled. Cashmere, peopled chiefly by Musselmen, is in a state of insurrection. Peshawar, at the entrance of the Kyber Pass, [*is*] nearly in the same state, & Moultain, on the western extremity of the Punjab, [*is*] also disaffected. The hill tribes toward the Himalayas [*are*] also struggling for independence whilst the Sikh army is silent & idle [*&*], having extorted the highest rate of soldiers' pay in India, will not move because the season is cold.

Heera S. the Rajpoot has also a Sikh competitor of some importance—a Prince Peshowra Singh, a son of old Ranjeet's but of doubtful legitimacy [*who*] has been outlawed for rebellion by Heera S. The chiefs of the Sikhs who detest the Rajpoots intend to use this prince as their instrument agt. Heera S. Peshowra S. is brave & is now supposed to be making his way across the Sutlege. If he seeks protection from us, we shall afford it but require him to go to the rear & not to make our territory the arena for milty. expeditions & plots agt. Lahore. However, it appears to me that Heera S. can never weather the storm that is gathering around him in all quarters. We observe the strictest neutrality & are determined our good faith shall not be called into question.

The Kolapoor disturbances are at an end but I fear in carrying Punalla by storm the troops behaved with gt. violence to the unfortunate inhabitants.[88]

Then the son of the king of Nepaul has just forced his father to abdicate in his favor. This son is an insane barbarian addicted to sudden gusts of passion & killed 16 officers the other day without any process of trial. The kingdom is independent, & I hope you won't think I am partial to the poor father agt. the son when I tell you I expect an importation of curious pheasants from the old king which I intend to send to England.[89]

Sir Charles Napier[90] is not well but as usual full of energy & is on his march to chastise some murderous Bellouchees who have ravaged some villages near Shika[r]poor.

I am nearly worked to death but in the same breath quite well. Charles is going on an excursion with lance in hand to kill wild boars. I have lent him 3 elephants for beating the jungle. He is so active on horseback that I do not apprehend any accident. Robert Wood is quite well, an affecte. excellent fellow. Love to dst. Sarah & baby.

15. [*To Sarah.*] Calcutta. Decr. 24, 1844

I cannot let the mail close without thanking you for your letter. It has been the heaviest I have yet had, & I have a prince to receive at 4, abt. 16 years of age, to whom I am to present a diamond ring.[91] He has an English tutor & is, it is said, very amiable. When the mail goes, I intend to be as angry as I can & write a Philippic to the son of the k[ing] of Nepaul. I am again very much displeased with the king of Oude. I am called upon to give away a principality as big as

[88] Late in the summer of 1844 a group of agitators called Ghadkaris led an anti-British uprising in the small Maratha kingdom of Kolapur. They rose in reaction to reforms being introduced by the G. G.'s agent in Kolapur through the young raja and his regent. After negotiations proved futile, the British troops, with Hardinge's approval, moved into the principality; the British prevailed and occupied the insurgents' strongholds of Samangarh and Punala, but with considerable loss of life on both sides.

[89] This proved to be merely a passing phase in the turbulent politics of Nepal. King Rajendra Bikram Shah did not really abdicate at this time nor did the crown prince Surendra Bikram Shah take his place.

[90] Lt. Gen. Sir Charles James Napier (1782–1853), governor of Sind, 1843–7.

[91] Mansur Ali Khan, the young nawab of Bengal, 'paid a state visit to the governor general' on that day. (*Hurkaru*, 28 Dec. 1844, p. 727.)

Scotland, & I have not yet made up my mind.[92] And yet, my dear friend, these are *realities*, & I wd. rather be at S. Park with your brown gloves on my hand than deciding upon the fate of princes, if I did not think I would bring to the performance of their duties honesty of purpose & singleness of mind.

I was up before 5. It is now past 3 & I feel in [*my*] *head* as ready to work as I did 10 hours ago, & this I attribute in part to the stubborness [*sic*] of my nature. It is really cold at 5 in the morning but the sun is still fierce at noon, & I am remarkably well but very temperate. No govr. genl. who accepts the office ought to complain, but I never knew what it was really to work until I came here. Ld. E[*llenborough*] has had an offer for Cabinet which he has declined.[93] Probably he will enlist before the session commences.

16. [*To Emily.*] Calcutta. 20th Janry., 1845

I recd., my dst. wife, your letter stating the result of your attempt to join me late last night & I have scarcely closed my eyes, excited by a variety of thoughts which quite banished sleep. Arthur must be in the river, but the Bentinck has not been reported. I long to press him in my arms. You have judged wisely in sending him to me. I shall be able to keep him under my own eye & give him plenty to do. In fact, at this moment such is the state of the Punjab that I may any day be obliged to go up to the N.W. frontier. Once there I should stay the summer in the hills, which wd. suit his health, give him a personal knowledge of India, & expand his mind. His friend, young Pollock, dined here yesterday. How different will be the advantages of our dear boy. With his brother, his cousin, & my staff he will have gentlemen for his companions & my superintendence shall not be wanting.

And now, dearest Emily, let me console you for our inevitable separation. You have given way to a warning which I am convinced spared me, you, & our children much affliction. Even if you have [*sic*]

[92] A succession problem was raised in Indore when Robert Hamilton (1802–87), the Resident, permitted Tookaji Rao Holkar to become the ruler in June 1844 after the death of Maharaja Kundee Rao Holkar. Hardinge rebuked Hamilton for overstepping his power, reminding him that approval for such a succession could only be given by Calcutta. Nonetheless, Hardinge formally sanctioned Kundee Rao's accession on Dec. 28. (Hamilton to Frederick Currie, foreign secretary to the Indian govt., no. 7, 13 Jan. 1845, letter no. 37, enc. no. 7, E.S.L.I., clxxxi.)

[93] Peel told Hardinge in a private letter dated 6 Nov. 1844, that Ellenborough had turned down his invitation to take over the post office or the privy seal, adding: 'His return here has not caused the slightest sensation. There is no curiosity, among this most curious people, to see so great a performer on the Indian theatre' (Peel Papers, Add. MS 40474).

survived the voyage, you would have landed so exhausted that in this climate you never would have rallied. Only conceive me, tortured by the affectionate devotion of watching you in any illness, suddenly required to hasten to the frontier; or conceive us both attending upon a sick daughter, who at Calcutta has no object, no employment, but all the risks of an uncertain climate. When I fancy I see you at Nice by the seashore or in the garden at S. Park, I am happy in the conviction that we shall meet again & close our days in cheerful serenity. Here day by day I should have been kept in a state of fearful suspense. My health is good, my head is clear, & towards you, d[eare]st, my heart is warmer than ever, & I have the presentment that I shall return before 4 years have elapsed a happier & a better man if my actions be regulated by my conscience. I fear no toil, but I never expose myself unnecessarily & I shall be more careful than ever now that I am to return to you never more to be separated. I shall carefully attend to your injunctions in confirming our boys in their religious feelings & observance, & not omitting my own in this respect.

The mass of society is very exemplary & of late years much improved. Tell the dr. girls I will send them shawls before the year is out but not immediately. Yours, d[eare]st, shall be the finest & best, & if I take the *Koh-i-Nohr*,[94] the Mountain of Light, you shall give it to the Queen.

You will see by the papers that the Sikh army, after killing their minister, are in a state of turbulent licentiousness. I may be compelled to move up but I do not expect it. Events, how[eve]r, change so rapidly in Eastern states that we never know where we are in the short space of a week. I adhere to my pacific policy & I feel confident that as yet we have made no false move.

I receive Ripon's praises which, he tells me, he has repeated to H.M. with whom (en confidence [*sic*]) I correspond, but the most encouraging & affecte. letters I receive are those from Sir Robert Peel.

Dearest, I have seen him [*Arthur*], so much grown & improved. His voice is altered but his looks, his dear eyes & his happy countenance, becoming with affection & intelligence, are just the same. I shall go up to Simla in Octr. & take him with me. In the interval I shall take the greatest care of his health & make him work. How happy I shall be to spend my money on his commissions & to give him every advantage. I have already written to Bombay for an Arab [*horse*], but I shall not spoil him. The two brothers love each other most affectly.

[94] This legendary diamond was then in the Lahore treasury.

I have invited Sir R. Sale, Lady S[*ale*],[95] Mrs Sturt,[96] 2 children &
2 daughters to take up their abode here. She [*Lady Sale*] is a clever
woman, shrewd enough to be on her guard in society but from what
I hear very coarse. Mrs Sturt [*is*] very [*?tou de garmson*] pretty.

But dear Arthur has no clothes. He must have grown 3 inches in
the last 8 months.
22 january 1845

17. [*To Walter.*] Calcutta. 22nd Janry. 1845

Arthur has arrived, in excellent health, surprizingly grown, & as
amiable as ever. His voice is the only thing altered. Yr. dearest mother
will have long 'ere this related her attempt to follow me, & I feel
relieved from an intensity of anxiety on her acct. She never would
have survived the voyage, even in Janry. Arthur says it was 90° in his
cabin in the Red Sea. Here, instead of fagging for hours without intermission, I should have had my mind wandering from my business to the
fear & perhaps the agony of seeing her lingering on her death bed.
Thank God! for her safety & the children's, she is in a healthy climate.

I have been writing to her &, amongst other matters, on her income.
She always thinks £2000 a yr. a large income. She will not find it so.
I have therefore told her you will make arrangements with my agent
Cox & Co.[97] for paying to her regularly £500 a quarter or allowing
her drafts to that extent. I have desired her carriage & harness may
be paid by Cox, every bill of any description paid—all donations,
subscriptions & charities to be paid by me—through Cox, & then,
whenever you think you perceive that she would be easier in her
accts., pay her £500 in addition & Cox will repay.

In the letters she has written to me she seems composed and consoled
by having made the attempt, & all feeling of disappoin[*tmen*]t is
assuaged by the fact that the failure was in her own strength & not
by my prohibition. She will now be guided by your advice. I do not
like English girls, whose lot it must [*be*] to marry Englishmen (if they
marry at all), to live too long in foreign towns. The whole life of a
foreign gentleman is idly spent *en se rendant aimable aux dames*, & young
women may get spoilt & dislike their own more sober English society
as forming a disagreeable contrast to that in which they have lived in
Italy. I should therefore advise them not to stay too long in one place,
& I have no doubt, as the intercourse between you & yr. mother is
so much shorter than with me, that you will give her the best advice.

[95] Lady Florentia, wife of Sir Robert Henry Sale (1782–1845), the veteran Indian
army officer.

[96] Mrs Alexandrina Sturt was the Sales' daughter, who, along with her husband, Lt.
John L. D. Sturt, was also taken prisoner in Afghanistan. (Patrick Macrory [ed.], *Lady
Sale* [Hamden, Conn., 1969], p. 159.)

[97] This firm took care of Hardinge's financial matters in England.

I do not expect that affairs in the Punjab, desperate as they are, will take me up to the mountains this spring. My own notion is to go up in Sep. next. About the beginning of May the snows melt in the Himalaya hills & the Sutlege is a torrent till October. All communication by fords across the river is at an end for 5 months. The temptation on either side to make forays & to court collisions is almost impracticable. I therefore expect to keep the peace myself &, in spite of taunts from the army through the press, carry out my views of a pacific policy as long as it is possible.

As a milty. and political question I prefer our present frontier with a Sikh govt. as our advanced guard. If the Sikhs are destroyed, we cannot tolerate Musselmen with Cabool & Persia at their back, but, by affording the Sikhs time to recover & not taking advantage of their misfortunes & their crimes, the vessel of the state may right herself, altho' everything at present is anarchy, weakness, & confusion. I don't think we have made a false move as yet, &, as I am tough enough to bear the taunts of the army & the press, you may, as I have before said, be confident I shall have reason & justice on my side if the problem of the Punjab can only be solved by the sword. Of course I expect to be abused, the lot of all public men.

These milty. preparations don't relax my exertions in making a high road & about a dozen suspension bridges between Calcutta & Benares,[98] in cutting a canal in the upper province, & establishing 101 village schools. I am occupied in devising means of putting a stop to the horrid rites of an aboriginal tribe between Madras & Calcutta, not 300 miles from this capital, of buying children & sacrificing them to propitiate their deities to give them good crops. These savages are called *khonds*. They have never been conquered by Hindus or Musselmen, &, their country being a dense forest of jungle, they are difficult of access. We believe that 1500 innocent human beings are thus sacrificed every year.

I must now, my dear Walter, close this letter & resume the drudgery of official correspondence, for the mail closes in a few hours. I must make the boys write to Sarah. Love to her & all the Ellisons.

18. [*To Sarah.*] Calcutta. Janry. 23, 1845

The packet of letters is closing, but I must thank you for your note. Whilst anarchy & violence triumph in the Punjab, I am all harmony & happiness here. Arthur is in the room, looking so well, so much grown & so improved that it delights me [*to*] look into his eyes, they beam with so much goodness & intelligence. Then I am grateful

---

[98] See no. 20 and note 103.

beyond measure that my dear wife so opportunely failed in her attempt to join me here. A few days ago there was a prospect of my being obliged to go up to the frontier at the very time she was expected here, but not by me. I knew she wd. never arrive. I was satisfied she would either turn back or die on b[oar]d ship. To see her lingering here wd. have killed me by inches.

In the autumn I shall go up the country & spend 1846 in the hills, but he is a bold man here who talks of what he will do a year hence.

Arthur has a very handsome Arab of high caste & he appears the happiest of boys. But when the mail closes, I shall take him in hand & show him he is not to govern the governor. I shall make him copy letters till he writes well. Then he is to have 3 times a week a tutor for history, etc., & I shall make him responsible for some small dept. of my business. In short, he shall not be idle.

I confess I have been beaten about *pig-sticking*, the fashionable phrase here for hunting wild boars with spears. He hardly rides well enough for the roughness of the ground &, if the boar has him within reach of his tusk, I shall be in an agony. We eat the head, to the horror of the Muhommedans who hate the unclean beast. And certainly they are justified if they were generally as unmotherly as the prize lady pig at S.P.

We have our grand piggery here filled by Sir. Robt. & Ly. Sale, Mrs. Sturt, 3 other ladies, relations, & 2 infants. He is one of our milty. heroes seen to most advantage with a sabre in his hand. She is clever & knowing, like a lady here, but entre nous, damning the waiters on b[oar]d the steamer. Your heroines ought to be eccentric, but Florentia coming out with a direct plain oath is in proof of a maxim of mine, that ship-board tries the temper so boisterously, that the nature is displayed before the passage is at an end.[99]

Mrs Sturt [*is*] pretty but unfeeling, the little daughter born in captivity.

19. [*To Emily.*] Barrackpoor. 7th of Febry. 1845

The letters have come up by the steamer but those that I most coveted from you & the dear girls have not arrived. This is the fortnightly mail. I have letters from Walter, & he writes in admiration of Peel's speech. Not so Ld. Ellenborough. He talks of the liberality of Peel's budget as a financial *reform* act, annoying to our friends &

[99] The Sales had travelled with Arthur from Europe to Calcutta and had occupied the cabins vacated by Emily.

conceding to our enemies.[100] I observe the postmaster's dept. is still open, & I hope by some interchange it may, towards the end of the session, be made available for our friend Lord Ellenborough.

I have a short note of 20 lines from Ld. Ripon saying he approves of all I have done. He says I have acted in accordance with my instructions (which I have never received), & [he] takes time to consult Peel before he will answer some long & important dispatches of which he acknowledges the receipt. However, all my acts are approved & that is a great satisfaction. In some discussion with the other presidencies, who thought they were supported by the govt. & the Court, the home authorities have decided in the view taken by me.

George Hardinge has, I imagine, arrived at Calcutta. I shall be able to house him & be a father to the poor boy, & I hope eventually to place him upon the staff.[101]

Altho' Ripon does not give me much information, I make it a point of giving him the fullest information of all my measures & intentions. I presume from what was done in the Cabinet that my private letters are seen by the ministers, & I have no doubt that I get more than my full share of credit.

Walter has sent me a plan of the farm of Mrs Pott's joining into Blowers farm & lying between Stone Wall & Mrs Allnutt's[102] I sent for. Charles put all the papers into his hands, told him what I intended to do for the 3 younger children & asked him whether he wished the purchase to be made. He came back & decidedly said *he did*. Being aware that the return will be less from land than from the funds, I presume the purchase will be about £6000. I suppose he has himself saved £2000, but I do not interfere with his arrange[men]ts, & they are so simple that he does not require advice. I think he is attached to S. Park, & it may turn out that his future income may enable him to live at it with comfort & respectability. With my professional income & yrs. in add[itio]n & the means we have from other sources,

---

[100] After Peel's budget of 1845 containing tariff laws and income taxes was approved, despite protectionist animosity, he buoyantly wrote to Hardinge: 'I have repeated the coup d'etat of 1842, renewed the income tax for three years, simplified and improved the tariff, and made a great reduction on indirect taxation.' Saying that he refused to accept any amendments to his bills, Peel added: 'This was thought very obstinate and very presumptuous; but the fact is, people like a certain degree of obstinacy and presumption in a minister. They abuse him for dictation and arrogance, but they like being governed' (24 Mar. 1845, Peel Papers, Add. MS 40474).

[101] George Nicholas Hardinge was almost seventeen when he arrived in India. He was the son of Hardinge's younger brother, Maj. Gen. Richard Hardinge, by his second wife, Caroline Johnson.

[102] Mrs Frances Allnutt (1772–1868) then lived at South Park Villa on the northern edge of South Park. She was the former Frances Woodgate of Somerhill, Tonbridge, who married Richard Allnutt II in 1793. (Doble, pp. 1–3; Hasted, iii, 228, 246, 261; Newman, p. 460.)

we can always be sure of giving our children a comfortable home. At my death I think he may have enough to live there respectably & if not he can sell the lands & farms for what I am about to give. It may also stimulate him to exertion when he returns 3 yrs. hence to England. Upon the whole, I think it advisable & hope you will approve.

I will now fold up my letter & trust that the same merciful Providence which has hitherto protected us will continue His blessings & that I shall hear from you by the overland mail in good health & cheerful spirits.

20. [*To Walter.*] Calcutta. Febry. 8th, 1845

I send this letter by our half-monthly steam communication, which will also enable you to write twice a month whenever there may be occasion for a more frequent intercourse. Having received no letters since I last wrote, I have only to give you an account of our proceedings here. Charles & Arthur [*are*] quite well, Bob Wood [*is*] 300 miles up the country tiger-hunting, I am in excellent health & quite satisfied that we have made no false move since the Punjab revolution occurred.

Lord Ripon writes that I have given entire satisfaction, not only in the ordinary transactions of the govt. but in those sudden decisions which have been required, such as Colapoor & the Punjab, & that he has reported to this effect to H.M.

I have desired Charles to send you our proceedings in education at the annual report of the progress of the Hindoo College. What I said was not reported but pretty well put down by a gentleman who was present. The essays & answers to questions on literary & historical subjects are taken down in a room in which all the candidates are seated at tables, without books of reference or any previous knowledge of the subjects to be given in the questions part. The result is the substantial knowledge of general information previously acquired. The composition or grammar is not corrected & the students who gain the prizes vary from 16 to 20 yrs. of age. It is quite clear to me that the minds of these black fellow creatures, when properly cultivated, are capable of the highest intellectual attainment. Thus you will perceive that, whilst anarchy & confusion reign triumphant on our frontier, the milty. gov. genl. is engaged in civilizing the native population & enlightening their minds which from pagan superstitions are still darker than their skins.

My great road of 400 miles is all arranged—bridges are building & small posting houses at every 8 or 10 miles on the road with mail carts & small 4-wheel carriages, which will carry travellers at 8 or 9 miles an hour instead of travelling dawk at 3 miles an hour on men's shoulders.

Thus I have silently collected on the gt. trunk road,[103] heading to the frontier & at convenient distances, 500 elephants for our heavy guns & stores, 7000 camels exclusive of minor carriage etc., etc. with 34,000 inf., 2000 artry. & 100 guns, [&] 6000 cav. ready if we make a movement to do it in force. But this *now* is postponed till next autumn, for we shall not be attacked by the Sikhs, & between Febry. & October no man can say in India what may occur. But you will observe we are ready for any event & without any display.

In the interval I am doing all I can to keep the Lahore govt. on its legs, but it is too tottering. The mother of the little Maha-raja is a handsome debauched woman of 33, very indiscriminate in her affections, an eater of opium,[104] & governed by a slave girl[105] who acts as her prime minister. Everything like govt. is, I fear, hopeless. We have offers from various parties to assist in placing the Punjab under British protection. Golab Singh has, through various channels, sent us the same offers which we have constantly rejected & desired all our agents to discountenance. Our treatment of the Lahore govt. has been open & cordial & will bear any scrutiny, for we have written the *truth* to all parties. We desire no acquisitions of territory, & in reply to some offers of Golab S. through Genl. *Ventura*,[106] a French offr. who has served 25 yrs. in the Punjab, I made Charles write a letter, thanking him for some letters making similar offers of transferring the Punjab to us which he, Charles, told the genl. had been frequently made & constantly rejected. This virtuous forbearance in rejecting the offer of the finest kingdom in the East will be communicated to Guizot[107] I have no doubt—at least I intended it should. I have given the general a letter to Ld. Ellenborough & I think you will be amused by his conversation & anecdotes. Call upon him, tell him you are my son,

---

[103] Several portions of this historic road were then in a state of disrepair, and Hardinge took various measures to improve its condition. (Lawrence, p. 334.)

[104] Rani Jindan (1817–63) was in fact then 28. She had been married in the 1830s to Ranjit Singh, who was nearly 40 years her senior. She became regent for Dalip Singh when he succeeded to the throne.

[105] This so-called slave was a maidservant named Mangla, a confidante of Rani Jindan. She was also said to be a mistress of Jowahir Singh, the Rani's brother. (Singh, ii. 35n.)

[106] Jean Baptiste Ventura was born in Modena, Italy, around 1792 and, after the French occupation of Italy, was recruited into Napoleon's army. He rose to the rank of colonel and fought in various campaigns. He arrived at Lahore in 1822. After some initial hesitation, Ranjit Singh took him into his employ, and he consequently rose to occupy high military and civilian positions in the Sikh state. C. Grey (p. 93) calls Ventura 'the most able of all Ranjit Singh's European soldiers.' The chronic political anarchy of the early 1840s forced him to quit Lahore, and he returned to France in 1845, revisiting Panjab briefly in 1848; he was given the title of Count de Mandi by the French government and died in 1858.

[107] François Guizot, the French foreign minister.

ask him to dinner, pump him, & he will tell you all about us. He has a daughter, but from his reserve I suspect she [*is*] not of pure European breed.[108]

The milty. system of the Sikh army—that of delegating all authority to the arbitration of 5 private soldiers, passing by their offs. & even the govt.—is by its example in the East fraught with danger. This is the point on which I am most anxious but still, a possible danger & the inconvenience to which we are exposed by a large army so close to us is no sufficient reason to rob our ally of his territories, &, as I have already told you, I should in policy have preferred the old arrangement as it existed in the time of Runjeet Singh. We had an ally guarding that frontier, so circumscribed by natural impediments that he never could increase his territory or give us uneasiness but who was sufficiently strong to keep off all intruders. The old Runjeet was our advanced guard agt. Mussulmen tribes, performing good service without pay or trouble to us. But if the Sikhs, a small nation not exceeding probably 600,000 souls, cannot hold this country & fall to pieces, what is to be done?

This problem will be solved before this time next year. In the meantime, keep these details to yourself &, if you talk with Ld. E., abstain from repeating them.

When the mail is dispatched, Charles is going a *pig-sticking* (in higher flown terms, wild-boar spearing) of which he is very fond. After his accident, it gratifies me to find him excel in field sports as it convinces me his calamity is not so great as I feared. Ben has a Cambridge tutor for 2 hours every morn[*in*]g from 7 till 9 in mathematics, algebra, & arithmetic except Mondays & Tuesdays when we are at Barrackpore. He is very engaging, & I shall now begin to give him regular work in the secretary's dept. &, when matters are more arranged, make him attend the *orderly room* duties of Fort W[*illia*]m (that is, be an assistant to the adjt. of the 40th Regt.) in seeing behind the curtain how the interior discipline of the regt. is really carried on.

He will, I think, be temperate when he finds it is not manly. At first he was rather disposed to take more mixtures of wine than I liked, but he is such a good fellow I shall have no difficulty.

Love to dearest Sarah & baby.

[*PS.*] I very much wish the *hedge*, from the gravel-pit to the lodge gate

---

[108] In 1825 Ventura married at Lahore 'an Armenian lady of mixed descent, whose father was a Frenchman.' She bore him a daughter, but they were separated after about two years of marriage as a result of his continuing maintenance, like most other contemporary Sikh chiefs, of a zanana, 'and there are certain anecdotes extant regarding his infidelities, which show that she had ample cause for leaving him.' (Grey, pp. 104–5.)

stone wall, to be planted on a firm bank, stout posts, & done in the best manner for endurance. Jones[109] knows the line.

21. [*To Walter.*] Calcutta. Febry. 20th, 1845

The mail will close in an hour, & the over-land very provokingly has not arrived from Bombay. I therefore know nothing of your dear mother's movements. Charles & Arthur are quite well. Charles has had 8 or 10 horses, which he is continually *swapping* in order to gratify his enthusiastic passion for *pig-sticking*, & if a horse will face a pig & chase him he is perfection.

Arthur has the handsomest horse I have seen & so temperate & graceful in his movements that he wd. make a most charming lady's horse. He cost £300 a yr. or two ago & I gave £160 for him, not a high price for Calcutta. I got him cheap, for he had failed as a racer.

He, Arthur, has 2 hours every morn[in]g in mathematics but is very difficult to settle down to his work. How[eve]r, I have him under my own eye & I hope to make something of him.

I divide my time between Calcutta & Barrackpore & am over head & ears in education questions, law & police reg[ulatio]ns, filling up the chinks of spare time (& they are very narrow) with canals, roads & bridges. The exciting portion of my work continues to be the Punjaub where the army is as mutinous as ever, carrying no orders into execution unless they happen to suit the temper & caprice of the moment, but committing, as at Jusrota,[110] all kinds of horrors in burning villages & carrying off 1000 women. These atrocities have exasperated the hill tribes, who now will prefer the oppression of Rajah Golab Singh or at least tolerate it for the present, rallying under the man they hate in order to gratify their vengeance agt. the Sikhs who have dishonoured & plundered them & who are now attempting to renew their barbarities on a larger scale. Golab S. is alarmed. He has written again to us to make terms for our conquest of the Punjab, & none of the parties seems to comprehend that we can be restrained by principles of good-faith. Assuredly our good-faith has shown itself in India under questionable forms; but I am so determined that our reputation shall not suffer that I am reprimanding & probably shall displease one or two of our young politicals on the N.W. frontier who have been dabbling in political intrigues.[111]

[109] A gardener at South Park.

[110] Jasrota, about forty-nine miles from Jammu, was plundered by a Sikh force sent early in 1845 by Lahore to invade Gulab Singh's territories.

[111] Hardinge's ire was particularly directed at J.D. Cunningham (1812–51), an assistant agent, and Richmond, who had by then left India. They allegedly had, in confidential negotiations, led the governors of the Sikh provinces of Kashmir, Rajauri,

The govt. of Lahore under the ranee passes its time in alternations of anguish alarm [*at*] Peshora Singh's cabals & of the grossest debaucheries in which the regent plays a most profligate part. I believe we have saved the poor little maha-raja's life by our threats not to recognize a successor if he be removed by violence. But he is no son of Runjeet S. nor is there now any son of his alive. All kinds of intrigues are going on—forgeries of letters, plots & counterplots—& I have been very hard worked during the last month writing all the most important letters myself, leaving the originals in my hand-writing in the offices so that the extent of my interference can be traced at any future time; & up to this hour, during 7 months of incessant toil & innumerable subjects, I have not had a conflicting Minute from any colleague.

I give abt. 70 dinner invitations in the week & have the best cook & the best wine (thanks to Grant *the Chin*)[112] in Calcutta. I have obtained the most complete control over my temper by 12 hours' perpetual labour which has subdued all irritability, altho' I confess abt. 5 o'cl. I am completely exhausted. If I can but last my time here, I shall go to sleep for the brief remainder of my days.

We have now had three months of delightful weather, & I am ready for the hot winds & steaming rains of the summer. This ordeal passed, I shall go up to Simla for a year &, by traversing India, obtain a local knowledge very useful to a govr. genl. Still, these efforts at my age, within a month of 60, cannot be made without their corresponding consequences. But I sleep well, have no indigestion, & have nearly got rid of the giddiness I had in England.

The climate perfectly agrees with Charles & probably will with Arthur if he wd. be as temperate as Charles.

Give my love to Sarah & baby. Let me have all the Carlton news, all the family details.

20 february 1845

22. [*To Emily.*] Calcutta. Febry. 20th, 1845

The overland letters have not yet arrived & our post closes this e[*venin*]g. We are all quite well. The weather continues cool m[*ornin*]g & e[*venin*]g, & young & old are able to get on horseback.

---

and Jullundur to believe that the British government was prepared to establish direct relations with them. (Broadfoot to Currie, no. 34, 8 Feb. 1845, letter no. 25, enc. 6; Currie to Broadfoot, no. 136, 4 Mar. 1845, letter no. 25, enc. 7, E.S.L.I., lxxx.) Cunningham, however, was not removed from the frontier and he went on to write his impressive *A History of the Sikhs*.

[112] Sir Alexander Cray Grant, a Tory politician, was so called on occasion by both Hardinge and Peel. The term could refer to a prominent chin to distinguish him from the other Grants of the period or simply be a nickname. He was an M.P. from 1812 to 1843 with only one interruption.

Arthur is delighted with an Arab I have given him. It cost £200 2 yrs. ago. I bought it for £160, having failed in winning a race. You must not think I spoil him, for the ordinary class of horses costs £100. Charles cares for no horse unless he will face a wild boar. He is going up the country for 10 days the end of this week. I keep Arthur with me. He has a mathematical tutor & is going on very well. He has promised not to smoke[113] & I have no doubt will be as temperate as his brother. I am up before 5 & at 1/2 past 6 see that he is ready for his tutor at 7. I shall watch his proceedings narrowly when the hot weather sets in, but in Sepr. or Octr. I go up to the mountains & then I shall have no apprehensions as regards his health.

I continue to like my colleagues in the council & all my secretaries. Nothing can be more harmonious. Much of the work I do myself & leave all the Minutes & letters in my own handwriting in the office, as the letters are signed by the secrys., so that my portion of work is known &, I believe, appreciated, & I am in the hands of no favorite who can insinuate that my good decisions are his & my bad decisions my own. Thus the time passes, relieved by the hope that I am doing my duty to the public & looking forward with cheerful confidence in Providence to the day that is to see us all reunited in S. Park.

I am anxious to know what your plans are. I imagine you will return to England so as to arrive in May before the Italian heat has become oppressive. You can return to a warm climate in October &, dearest, pray remember that expense where your health is concerned is no object.

The family details are superintended by an active A.D.C., Capt. Hillier. Charles superintends the accts. and everything goes on regularly. On each Wednesday I have a dinner here of 50 & at Barrackpore on the Monday a dinner of 30, making 80 a week, which exceeds Lord Auckland &, I believe, Lord Ellenborough. I have given one ball [*for*] 600 persons which cost not quite £300. On the Q.'s birthday I give another which is paid by the public. I keep down expense by strict regulations & reckoning by the month. I believe I am a little below Ld. E.'s average. I expect an Arab from Bombay in a fortnight. I have now only one horse whilst my A.D.C.'s have each 3 or 4. But I wait to please myself, & by patience, as in the case of Arthur's horse, I get a treasure of an animal. These trifling details I do not hesitate to give you, for you must be tired of Eastern details of Scinde & Punjaub.

Charles Napier at 64 is making a very active campaign in the deserts on the frontier, chastizing some Belochee robbers & conducting

[113] With a touch of disappointment, Emily noted in the margin: 'What do my young men say to this? Truly that their promises have been pie crust.'

it with his characteristic vigor. The result will, I think, be so far important that, by capturing their cattle & destroying a proportion of their bloodthirsty plunder, he may enable a neighbouring friendly tribe to take possession of their country & gradually prevent the repetition of their forays into our territory.

In the Punjaub the anarchy & confusion remains much as before. The ranee, the mother of the prince, is very, very profligate in every way. The troops despise her sway & only tolerate it because her weakness opposes no obstacles to their mercenary demands. They have marched against a powerful raja of the hills, Golab Singh, & have outraged the feelings of the hill tribes by carrying off 800 women. We have had overtures to take the Punjaub from various quarters, but we are honest in our policy, & no one here knows the ultimate plan of the govt. Come what may, we shall have a case that will bear a H. of Commons scrutiny. To you I will say that I wish to keep a Sikh govt. in power in the Punjaub & not to enlarge our overgrown empire in the distracted state of that country. This is very difficult & I fear cannot be accomplished. If their folly & weakness will not allow of this result, the other alternative may drive us to the necessity of occupation. Having moved up troops silently & from our extremities this season, we shall be in a condition to act according to circumstances next autumn. We are therefore calm & silent & intend to continue so for the next 7 or 8 months, & then fresh events may require fresh combinations. But you will read of no declarations of policy from me. The action of the govt. shall not be crippled by personal vanity in issuing manifestos. I hope every precaution to meet coming events has been taken by me, & in Sepr. I shall move up to the frontier.

We have had a desultory warfare in the Bombay territory which gives trouble & causes expense but otherwise is of no importance,[114] & in other parts of the country we are quite tranquil. The trade & commerce are increasing, & before the public eye I am very busy in canals, roads, & bridges.

I will now throw down my pen but not close my letter till the evening in the hope the mail may come in.

5 o'cl.

No overland mail or letter from you, but I shall write again on the 8th of March & by that time [would] have heard of yr. movements. I have sent £1000 to Cox by this mail to place you quite at ease. Arthur is writing to you & the girls. Give them my best love and now,

---

[114] No sooner had the trouble in Kolapur ended than a new rebellion broke out in the neighbouring state of Sawantwari (then referred to as a part of the South Maratha country), and the Company's troops suffered early reverses. Large reinforcements were sent from Bombay into Sawantwari and peace was not fully restored until May. The rebel chiefs escaped to Portuguese Goa. (See note 160.)

d[*eare*]st, God bless & preserve you in good health & cheerful spirits.

23. [*To Walter.*] Calcutta. March 7th, 1845

Charles is 150 miles off *pig-sticking* & Arthur is positively for the last time to take his chance the day after tomorrow. Wood has not returned, having shot 80 deer & 5 wild buffaloes besides bustards & other game. I am therefore almost alone, but they are all so passionately fond of field sports that until the sun is dangerous I do not forbid it.

Charles writes that a new horse faces a wild boar very bravely; that a large fighting boar attacked the planter's horse [&] wounded him very severely, when Charles came up & speared him through the body—38 inches high, very bristling, with a savage noise between a roar & a grunt which generally frightens the horse in spite of the rider's spurs.

Arthur is growing fast & is up at 1/2 p[*as*]t 6 to receive his tutor for 2 hours. His arms & thighs are muscular & his stamina promises better health than I expected. He is very popular, for he really is very goodtempered & amiable, & he is a great comfort, for he comes in to give me his gossip & his jokes whilst I am dressing—& in this country the necessity of having something to caress is an absolute must. He is gradually adopting Charles' temperate habits & independence of action, for sometimes his easiness of temper induces him to give way to others. I take him up to the mountains this autumn & all 1846, by the end of which year fresh combinations will have arisen &, at 60 yrs. of age, with proper confidence & hope, I need not lay plans in this country of a longer date. I am in excellent health & ride 6 miles at a good pace daily.

I have been attending the annual examinations of all the colleges, distributing prizes & making short speeches, which are very indifferently & very *differently* reported. But the measure is supported by all parties, & the bishop[115] writes me word that my proceedings have gladdened his soul.

We are improving several local laws & the police of Calcutta as well as the provinces.

With the army I can do very little. The force cannot be reduced whilst affairs are in their present condition in the Punjaub & the com. in ch.,[116] who is 1000 miles off, renders any communications on reforms & alteration a very uphill work.

---

[115] Daniel Wilson (1778–1858) was the Bishop of Calcutta from 1832 until his death.
[116] Maj. Gen. (afterwards Field Marshal) Hugh Gough (1779–1869) became C. in C. in India in 1843.

But I work on perseveringly. Nothing depresses me. I begin at 5, can now work till near 6, take a ride till 8, eat a moderate dinner, & fast asleep at 1/2 p[as]t 10. I have committed no acts of despotism to haunt my conscience, & I repeat that up to this hour I have not had a dissentient Minute from any of my council.

The affairs in the Punjaub seem to portend a change. The Sikh army has moved to Jummoo. The delegates from each regt. have entirely taken all power out of the hands of the generals[117] & have themselves (upwards of 100) had conferences with R. Golab Singh, the chief of the hills, who feeds them on sweetmeats & all luxuries, flatters, & cajoles them whilst the army do nothing but plunder & commit all kinds of excesses, exasperating the hill population & serving the ends of this able rascal whose object is to gain time. They have offered him the wazzier-ship which he has, of course, declined, & offered the post of honor & of danger to the illegitimate son of old Ranjeet S. [*Peshora Singh*] whose younger brother, Dhuleep S.,[118] is the poor boy now on the throne. Major Broadfoot, our agent, has distinctly reported that a short declaration of mine, stating to these barbarians that, if they deposed the boy by violence, we wd. not recognize his successor, has saved his life & kept the govt., if it can be so called, on its tottering legs.

The finances will fail, the troops will plunder, & by degrees the population will return to their original trade of district robbers from which they emerged 50 yrs. ago. In the meantime we are waiting as before the progress of events, acting with prudence, I am convinced, but also with energy, for we have a large force in very manageable positions, which has scarcely attracted public attention by means of a very strict system of carrying on the secret service of the army as well as of the political dept.

When necessity spurs & stimulates a man to action, you wd. be surprized at the work I get thru' & the facility of the operation. I am thin but quite well, by *temper* not to be disturbed! What a change! I really have not time to be angry, & all the people about me are so

[117] Since the middle of 1841 the Sikh army's contumacy had reached such a level that they no longer considered themselves responsible to the government but regarded themselves as the true agents of the people. Thereupon each Sikh battalion elected an executive body of its own known as the panchayats, or panches. They administered their own affairs and, through their delegates, negotiated demands with the generals and the government. The panchayats became a most powerful body in the Sikh kingdom, but they often displayed a deplorable lack of judgment and, as Cunningham writes: 'Their resolutions were often unstable or unwise, and the representatives of different divisions might take opposite sides from sober conviction or self-willed prejudice, or they might be bribed or cajoled' (p. 254).

[118] Rani Jindan was not the mother of Peshora Singh. He was thus considered a half-brother of Dalip Singh.

zealous that I have very little cause for irritability. That dear fellow Arthur has quite your temper. Whilst I am writing, an officer who interrupted me on business says Charles has killed the largest & fiercest boar of the season & is the best rider in the field. They make a run at Bob Wood's riding, but I have no doubt there is jealousy at the bottom. For the first time this quarter of a century, I wish I had two hands to pierce a wild boar!

I wish you could see us on the frontier! I shall have 500 elephants for great guns, stores, tents & baggage! When collected, what a pity not to use them agt. an armed mass of the greatest ruffians in the world!

In the meantime, I suppose the Indian policy of Lord Ellenborough & his recall have been before both Houses, unless the Auckland faction should have interposed & prefer anonymous attacks to open warfare.

Give me all the news you can,[119] even of the Penshurst village. On a fine day, the sun setting, walk up to Blowers Hill & place yourself about 50 yards in the potatoe [sic] field: on yr. left, Stone Wall & its woods; on the right, Penshurst Church in a vista. I consider that position for a cottage quite beautiful—windows ranging south & north with a terrace of 200 yds., etc. It is a relief to talk to you of these trifles. It does not make me home-sick or depress my courage. On the contrary, braced by 3 months of cool weather, I am more up to the intense labour of this office than I have been since my arrival.

I have framed your admirable picture of Penshurst Church, which I keep on my table.

We hourly expect letters by the steamer coming in but which, I fear, will not now arrive before I am obliged to close my letter.

Tell Sarah that we talk of you incessantly.

I have been up before 5 & have more letters to write.

24. [*To Emily.*] Calcutta. March 8th, 1845

Charley has come home this morning like David, having with his own spear slain the Goliath of boars in single combat, piercing him at the first tilt through & through &, when his horse would not go up to the savage beast, dismounting & putting him out of his pain on foot. He is the best & boldest rider here, & it is a great consolation to

[119] In his letter of 1 Mar. 1845, not yet received by Hardinge, Peel had partly answered his request: 'Lord John Russell and Lord Auckland wish to prevent discussion relating to his [*Ellenborough's*] recall. Macaulay is bursting with an oration against him. The Court of Directors remain on the defensive, and are decidedly for peace. [*Joseph*] Hume moves for papers relating to Ellenborough's recall. We shall strenuously resist the motion' (Peel Papers, Add. MS 40474). Peel was determined to prevent a full-scale debate as he feared it would further embarrass the Tory government.

me to find that his cruel accident does not disqualify him from excelling
in the most expert & daring of all sports, for when housed on the back
of an elephant the tyger [*sic*] is not so formidable as the hog. Ben came
up to me & said, 'I have another invitation to go to the boar hunt,
but knowing you don't like it I will refuse.' I cd. not stand this appeal
& I therefore agreed he should go on condition that this was to be
the very last of the season. To this he joyously assented, & I believe
he returns tomorrow. He has taken his beautiful Arab, which I don't
quite like, & if he has a fault it is an ignorance or total indifference
to matters of economy. Charles is the reverse & most prudent &
sensible. Arthur is growing taller & stouter. I go into his room at 1/2
past 6 to see that he is up. This I gave [no] thought of before but now
that you have sent him to me as a blessing I omit no pains to ascertain
every point regarding his health as standing in yr. absence in the
double capacity of both parents. I ill replace her to whom we all owe
so much.

I only hope Peel & those whose judgement I respect will be satisfied
with my exertions. For the mass of the public I have courage &
independence to be very indifferent.

Both our boys are very popular—Charles manly, straight forward,
& substantially civil but rarely complimentary; Arthur lively, gay,
fascinating, & goodtempered & demonstrative, amusing to women &
less shy than Charles, & yet in all the essentials of good dispositions
both equally valuable members of society.

The mail goes out by daybreak, that is, [*by*] the steamer; & the
Hindostan, which is due, has not come in, so I have no letters to solace
or comfort me! I have sent 3 warm Persian silk shawl gowns, warm &
comfortable if you go into the mountains. The bearer is a Hindoo[120]
who will leave them at Marseilles & send them under cover to Mr
LaCroix[121] at Nice. He will forward them &, as they go at the same
time as the letter, you can make the necessary enquiries.

I have gone round to the different colleges to their annual ex[*aminatio*]ns & have made a short speech at each. I have established 100
new schools & hope to increase the number. I am making a very fine
road with several bridges which is to be finished in 2 years, & I am
urging the Ct. of Directors to authorize a railroad for 400 miles. Thus
while we have silently collected an army of 30,000 men on the frontier
ready for *defensive* operations, we devote our exertions to useful purposes [*&*] services of peace, but no man can say what may occur with
an army of 50,000 wild barbarians on our frontier under no restraint
& who, when without pay, will disperse & return to their old calling

[120] Probably Dwarkanath Tagore. (See note 128.)
[121] Not identified.

of robbers, a state from which they emerged 50 years ago & to which with their predatory habits they will gladly return. The Sikh army had reached Jummoo in the hills and were negociating with Golab Singh but, falsehood & treachery being a part of their very nature, it is impossible to trust to any arrange[men]ts unless under the compulsion of superior force.

All the presidencies refer to the gr. general their most difficult questions. Then I have the govt. of Bengal which Lord Ellenborough wd. not undertake, being so frequently absent from Calcutta, & I assure you I sometimes wonder that my head stands the great variety of subjects incessantly brought before me. I may again repeat to you, d[eare]st, that I have not had one dissentient Minute recorded since I have been here.

If, therefore, this good fortune should continue, our boys' health stand the climate, & that under the blessings of God you, my best of wives, will derive strength & consolation from my example & not repine at a separation which, borne heroically, will terminate happily, nine months are already struck off the account & on the 8th June a year will have revolved, & if I then hear that you are well & don't fret but are resigned & tranquil, I shall have strength & energy to master my own insufficiencies for so high a station & be able to retire with you to dear South Park contented & happy.

The m[ornin]gs & e[venin]gs are still cool. I ride every e[venin]g about 5 or 6 miles at a good sharp trot. I am rubbed down with horsehair gloves when I come in, dine at 8, & in bed at 10. I repeat these details because I know you like to hear of all I do, but I visit nowhere except a formal dinner with a judge or member of council & I prefer like a state prisoner to be actively devoted to public business.

Love to the dear girls.

25. [*To Emily.*] Calcutta. Good Friday, 21st March 1845

We have just returned from church. Charles & I had intended to take the Sacrament, but there was none. Arthur is in the hands of our archdeacon preparing to be confirmed when the bishop reaches Calcutta in about 3 weeks & we shall after that time take the Sacrament together, & I trust I shall not allow my worldly cares to prevent me from giving to our children a good example in this essential respect. Now that you are absent from them, I think more of these important concerns. I generally mount to the top of this house at 1/2 p[as]t 6 in the morning to rouse Arthur—& stimulate his courage for his morning's study, for which he has no natural genius. But precise studies exercise the mind & rectify the judgement, & he is already overcoming the annoyance of the rudiments. Charles has sufficient

energy to get through his business creditably, & he is so easy of access
& good-natured that as a secretary I believe he is very popular. Arthur
is more giddy, but all the staff are very fond of him & he has the air
of a gentleman. It is impossible not to love him. He came back having
struck one or two or more boars, & they say [*he*] will ride very well.
I lecture him about health & exposure to the sun &, when I get him
up to Simla, I shall let him take what exercise he chooses.

We ought to have our letters & are in hourly expectation of their
arrival. The mail does not go out till tomorrow even[*ing*] so I am not
without hopes of hearing from my dt. wife. The boys are both quite
well, & I am stronger and better, though thinner than last autumn.
Always acknowledge the *date* of my letters, that I may know whether
any go astray.

Early this morning I wrote a long letter to the Duke. It is surprizing
what I can get through by rising before 5 & going to bed at 10, &
the propriety of writing this letter has long haunted me. If I do not
intrude upon his time, I shall now continue to write. He neither likes
to be pestered with letters or to be neglected, & we have so many
obligations to him & to Peel that their good opinion is more encouraging than that of all the [*?world*] combined. Ripon is becoming more
complimentary—such as I give great satisfaction to the Cabinet &
the chairs, etc., but I don't get much assistance from him.

Here as before all is harmony & good-will between me & my
council. I take my full share of Minutes & letters & something more,
I believe, & I am cheered by the hope that in honor & care we shall
be rewarded by a happy meeting & no more separations for the rest
of our lives. Excepting Ld. Tweed-dale,[122] I am the youngest of H.M.'s
offs. in this country in high com[*man*]d: Gough, 68; McMahon, com.
in ch. [*of*] Bombay, 70; Sir George Arthur, 61;[123] Charles Napier, 64.
The latter is an extraordinary man & I admire him greatly. He has
many Napier caprices but he is a fine fellow—able, resolute, & original.
He & Wm. [*Napier*], the historian, are now attacked on all sides
on acct. of Wm. N.'s book,[124] which I like because it defends Ld.
E[*llenborough*] & his brother Charles N. You should read it.

I suppose the Indian field day on Ld. E.'s policy is over. I shall be
glad of it. I have no doubt he has made a brilliant speech & a successful
vindication of his conduct.

---

[122] Maj. Gen. (afterwards Field Marshal) George Hay, 8th Marquis of Tweeddale
(1787–1876), governed Madras 1842–8.

[123] Sir George Arthur (1784–1854) governed Bombay, June 1842–Aug. 1846. He
acted as the provisional Governor General on Ellenborough's recall.

[124] Sir William F. P. Napier's partisan book *The Conquest of Scinde, with some introductory
passages in the life of Major-General Sir Charles James Napier etc.* (1845). (See no. 96 and
note 277.)

Peel writes me over again that, returning from India the maintainer of peace, I shall be better received than if I had conquered the Punjaub. In the meantime, I shall do what is right & be excluded from a peerage, which has no very great charms for me unless the world were unanimous in considering the honor well earned. Your knight will return very well satisfied of his policy. His measures can bear the test of a moral & Christian scrutiny, & with my neighbours round S. Park I shall be more happy than in this palace, which without you is my prison h[ou]se. But I never will repine. I ought to have had the courage to resist the appoint[men]t. I am here & no effort shall be wanting. God is merciful in giving me as clear a head as I ever had, & strong health to bear the tryal, & with yr. encouragement I do not fear the result.

We shall have no warlike operations in the Punjaub this season, & 6 months hence not the wisest man in the East can say what may happen. The Sikhs are attacking their old friend & ally Golab Singh & will probably take his fort of Jummoo, from which in all probability he has removed his treasures. He is a great rascal & has just murdered some vakeels, or envoys, an atrocious crime.

Calculate, d[eares]t, that I shall now remain here till September. Let me know all yr. movements & give me instructions as to the direction of your letters. My letter will take about 40 days to reach Nice, yours the same time to reach me. Consequently you can never have an answer to any question quicker than *3 months*. Clearly understand this point & act upon it. There are mails every fortnight so that we can correspond twice a month, but I cannot answer any question you put to me under 3 months.

Arthur is on the other side of the table copying my letter to the D. of Wellington. I want him to write a good hand, which requires practice & patience. I am so thankful to have him in my sight instead of [in] a hot barrack at some detestable out-station!

You had better pay for your letters to Alexandria to ensure their being forwarded. Charles has got a new leg from Grey which dear Walter sent him. He rides admirably. Perhaps he is too temperate; still, he is always in good health altho' thinner like his papa. He is surprized at the work I can get through. Bob is in rude health. I have just given him the sword Arthur brought from England, & I am giving directions for a very Eastern pattern for our dear boy.

I shall write again tomorrow & hope to answer a letter from you. 21 march 1845

26. [*To Walter.*] Calcutta. March 21st, 1845

We are all in excellent health altho' I think Charles starves rather too much. Arthur improves every day. I don't think he has a genius for mathematics, yet he makes progress & his mind is exercised.

The weather is hot in the middle of the day, & for the next 2 months the cholera is more frequent than during the rainy season. We were most shocked & distressed by W. Lyall's death,[125] an acquaintance of Wm. Gladstone's & son of the member [*of Parliament*] for London.[126] He was our judge advocate genl. & I had invited [*him*] to spend three days with my family at Barrackpore. He sat down to dinner on Saturday, apparently quite well, & after dinner talked till 11. The next morn[*in*]g at 7 he sent for my doctor, who found him very ill from an attack of cholera & who thought so ill of the case that he sent for two of the milty. surgeons of the cantonment. When I returned from church, he was in a hopeless state & at 2 died of spasmodic cholera.

I offered to go to see him, but he was almost insensible & in great pain. His poor wife,[127] a very amiable woman, he had just escorted into the mountains, to whom I was obliged to break this afflicting bereavement & from whom I expect to hear any hour.

In the absence of your dear mother, I cross-examine the boys as to their health & feel more than usually anxious, but in public I scarcely mention the event of poor Lyall's fate; so many amiable men & women are doomed to spend the greater portion of their lives here that by common consent the loss is felt & the cause is not noticed. The disease itself defies human skill in tracing its predisposing causes, & we fall back upon the Bible, that we are wonderfully & fearfully made &, without neglecting precautions, must rise up & lie down, trusting alone in a merciful Providence.

I am expecting our letters every hour. Our mail goes out tomorrow. Before this time I suppose you have had a grand field day or rather night on Ld. E[*llenborough*]'s Indian administration. I feel confident he will make a most able & satisfactory vindication & that Peel will steer through the shoals & shallows of an intricate navigation with his usual tact & success.

Whilst I remain, I will not repine. A post of this preeminence is not to be held without its corresponding risks & sacrifices, & I should be unworthy of myself if, exhausted by the heat of our sultry winds, my courage or my energy gave way. Hitherto I am persuaded I have made no mistakes in the general outline of our policy, & I am calm & collected in the decisions to which I am obliged to come. I expect

[125] John Edwardes Lyall, educated at Eton and Oxford and versed in various Eastern languages, came to India in 1842. His death at the age of 34 was deeply mourned at Calcutta. He believed in advancing Indian education and delivered voluntary lectures on law at the Hindu College.

[126] George Lyall, then M.P. for London, had also been a member of the Court of Directors since 1830.

[127] Julia Davis Lyall. For more on her family, see no. 88.

an answer from the home govt. on one or two important points, but
there is no excitement mixed up with the expectation, & my pulse,
generally 65, is as low here as in England. Thus, my dear Walter, you
may be confident that, as regards any public acts, I shall commit no
caprices under the pretense of talent, but steadily pursue my course
with as much judgement as I can muster, weighing each case by the
moral consideration of its propriety, which generally coincides with
expediency & policy.

Our national education is going on prosperously, & next week I
attend the public examination of the College of Surgeons, whose Hindoos perform the most difficult surgical operations with the greatest
skill. These black doctors I am encouraging by better pay & more
extensive employment. Our friend Dwaruganath Tagore,[128] whom
you have probably seen by the time you receive this letter, very
generously pays for the education of *two* native students who went to
England under Dr Goodeve.[129] The expense to our friend will exceed
£1200. These boys will return skilful men, & a great no. of collateral
advantages will result from the experiment in extending a personal
knowledge of England—its power, wealth, & in many respects its
virtue. When the poor Hindoos compare their present state under our
rule with the tyranny of their Mahommedan conquerors or the annual
forays of the Mahrattas, they bless the change. When I look to what
is passing on our frontier amongst the Sikhs & find the whole of
India tranquil, commerce & agriculture extending, the population
increasing &, with the exception of the native states, tributary to us
but administering their own laws, the whole in a state of progressive
improvement, I can scarcely regret a pacific policy which, altho' it
will exclude me from a peerage, will, if it can be maintained, greatly
add to the happiness & prosperity of this vast empire.

I am in hopes to be able to produce such a case as may induce the
home authorities to lay out 4 or 5 millions on a rail-road.[130] Canals
are out of favor; they produce so much malaria on their banks that
they neutralise the benefit of free transport & cheap irrigation. My
great trunk road will be finished in 2 years, but I can afford to lay

[128] Dwarkanath Tagore (1794–1846), a wealthy Bengali, had various ties with the
Company. An intellectual and business entrepreneur, he was a strong supporter of
western education and became perhaps the closest Indian friend of Hardinge. He had
visited England in 1842, where he was honoured by various organizations and received
by the Queen. Tagore went to England again in 1845 and died there during his visit.

[129] Goodeve, a young surgeon, had become something of a celebrity because of his
pioneer work with Indian students of Western medicine at the Medical College in
Calcutta. At the end of 1844 he resigned his position to take three or four Indian
students to the Royal College of Surgeons in London.

[130] Believing that railways would not only revolutionize travel in India but also serve
the political and military interests of the Company, Hardinge advocated the idea of a

out very little so long as our milty. expenditure is so large & these vagabond Sikhs on the frontier compel me to keep up a very large force. In my last letter I told you the S[ikh] army, by means of their delegates, was negotiating with Golab Singh near the hill fort of Jummoo. Having gained his point for delay, he assented to pay £250,000 to the S[ikh] army. As the vakeels, or envoys, were leaving Jummoo, he ordered them & the treasure animals to be attacked. The envoys were murdered, the treasure brought back, & this barbarous atrocity has raised his character amongst Eastern diplomatists as a great man who will accomplish his ends by any means! I wait for the official announcement from Lahore to express my abhorrence of such treachery & determination never to allow any British authority to hold any communication with such a monster.

At Lahore we are nearly as uncivilized & equally as cruel. The ranee's brother,[131] a drunken brutal sirdar who recently cut off the ears, nose & hands of a Brahmin who had by order of Heera S. arrested him, the other day killed one of his servants in a passion— no Cleitus taunting the proud Macedonian but a mere fit of brutality.[132] Then his sister the ranee is so profligate that the other day the delegates from the army told her publicly that, if she did not behave better, they wd. cut off her nose (she is very handsome) as a woman of loose manners! The poor little boy [Dalip Singh] of 10 years old,[133] laid up in this hot-bed of vice, has just had a serious attack of small pox from which he has recovered. We have up to the present saved his life by letting them know we wd. not recognize a successor set up by violence towards the boy, & the chances are that he will be spared. The ranee has been meditating a flight to our side [of] the river, but she is weak enough to disclose her projects & of course she is betrayed & the attempt prevented. I expect to hear that Jummoo has fallen.

Towards the lower Indus, Sir Charles Napier has been occupied with a small force of 4000 men in an expedition agt. a robber tribe of Beloochees. He is a wonderful fellow! At 64 yrs. of age, he made 3 marches the other day in the desert with [two] 6 pounder guns of 120 miles—the last day's march 56 miles! No other man in India would have attempted such an effort. I should not know how to replace him

---

grand railway line which was to connect Calcutta to the large towns in the Northwest. At his orders engineers extensively surveyed the ground for such a route. The Court of Directors, which had previously been lukewarm to such proposals, was impressed by Hardinge's arguments and began to study how loans were to be made to railway builders. (*Viscount Hardinge*, pp. 66–7.)

[131] Jowahir Singh (ob. 1845) was then about 30.

[132] In 327 B.C. Cleitus the Black was killed by Alexander in a fit of anger. (Arrian, *Anabasis* IV.8.1ff.)

[133] He was then 6.

if he were to retire or to be carried off. He is, besides his warlike qualities, a very fine fellow. He gains the confidence & attach[*men*]t of those under his command, & I find him practicable, good-tempered, & considerate. He is a very superior man.

It is very provoking to be obliged to write before I open yr. letters, which are within 24 h[*ours*] of delivery at Calcutta. Tell Sarah I long to know how my granddaughter's education is going on, how many words she can utter, & every detail which interests you & her. I trust my excellent friends the Ellisons are both in good health & that the Lambtons[134] enjoy the comfort of their affluence.

Give me the concentrated essence of Bonham as to Carlton[135] news & party politics.

The boys will write to you.

27. [*To Emily.*] Calcutta. 22nd March [*1845*]

The mail has arrived & I must close my budget. How provoking that I cannot answer all your questions, know how you are, & respond to all your feelings. How[*eve*]r, we sent you the best news—that we are all quite well. Still, I want to know how & where you are, & remember, the slightest detail is of interest.

My nerves on public matters are so good that I can't say I have ever gone to bed without being in a sound sleep in a few minutes. My greatest anxiety was the doubts in which your attempt kept me. Free from that care, & confident that the policy is served & our preparations secure, I am always calm & as much at ease as at S. Park.

I wish to alter the south windows of the drawing room to convert it into a bay window. Let me know if you approve. If not, I will give it up. I have placed £6000 in the 4 pr. cts. for the younger children. By the end of this yr. I hope to secure to each £10,000 instead of £5000 &, as we don't owe a shilling, I cannot help dabbling in a little brick & mortar. A friend, hearing me talk of transplanting trees, sent me a small b[*oo*]k on *tree lifting*. I read it through before I went to sleep, that I might not intrude on my official business the next morning. So you see, the same fancies & follies have accompanied me here.

---

[134] William Henry Lambton (1793–1866) and his wife Henrietta (1808–83) lived in Biddick Hall, Durham. He was the younger brother of the 1st Earl of Durham; she was the second daughter of the Ellisons (see note 50) and an elder sister of Sarah James.

[135] Francis Robert Bonham, the Conservatives' factotum, helped establish the Carlton Club in 1832; 'Bonham's essential work was done at the Carlton rather than on the floor of the House or in the voting lobbies' (*Politics*, pp. 398, 414).

Ben now & then peeps in & relieves my labour by his joyous eyes, which say you work too hard & I will try & distract yr. attention, & then he tries some joke or innocent gossip. If I am distract, he talks of you, & then we go on fluently. Pray tell the girls I would write, but that Arthur & Charles are so much more in society than I am that I can give them few anecdotes which wd. amuse them.

I send no scarfs till I know where you are to be for 3 months, & the shawls are put off till the autumn—that is, till I go up to the frontier.

I would write, if I were you, occasionally to Ld. E[*llenborough*]. Praise his speech on India. His kindness to me here was most friendly, & Lady Colchester[136] & other *jaseuses* femmes must not weaken the warmth of our friendship. I know his defects, but I appreciate & esteem his high and good qualities.

God bless you & preserve you, d[*eares*]t, & our dear girls. Their pictures are before me & recall many moments of their child-hood & my happiness.

28. [*To Emily.*] Barrackpore. 7th April 1845

I have recd. & devoured your welcome letters of Janry. 12th & the journal closing Febry. 7th. Every word I treasure as the best comfort I receive during our separation, & I console myself that you are in health & safety. Our boys are quite well: Charles is thinner, but Arthur grows & fills out every week. I have sent through Capt. Lyons a small box with 3 daguerreotypes & miniatures. If you would wish for one of me, I will sit. You will find me thin & more in sympathy with you, but I am better than I was last year. The worry of the separation, the anxiety of the undertaking & previous indisposition had had its effects on my frame. Now I am tranquil & satisfied that I have not *killed you* & am about the same size as when we first married 23 yrs. ago. I am stronger on my legs, have no giddiness from stomach &, as I live very temperately & regularly, I am, in spite of hard work, better in health than last year, having passed my 60th year. I assume all the privileges of the old man &, if merciful Providence will give me understanding till I have gone through this ordeal, I shall never again consent to leave you but, in joyful repose at dear South Park, look back upon the past with the satisfaction of having done my duty &, if my own conscience & my countrymen confirm me in that belief, we shall gradually retire to our rest from this world's care in the hope of a happy futurity.

---

[136] Elizabeth Susan, sister of Ellenborough, was married to the 2nd Baron Colchester (1798–1867).

Arthur will be confirmed by the bishop next month. He is a great favorite, but I must urge him to be more attentive to his mathematics. It is no want of capacity but a want of resolution to set to work in earnest. He is drilled 5 days in the week & gets up at 1/2 past 6 & is with his tutor for 2 hours till 9. I am going to give him another horse. I have just recd. one from Bombay but out of condition from the voyage so that [*I will*] keep it for myself, my other favorite Arab being quite equal to my daily ride of 6 or 7 miles. Charles has 3 horses which he is constantly changing, pigsticking qualifications being the criterion of perfection. That amusement is now over & I am glad of it. Latterly the sun has been too hot, & exposure to its rays is the greatest danger to which Europeans can be exposed. For the next 6 months the boys need never be exposed to its influence, & in the autumn we shall all go up the country to a better climate, to more interesting objects, & fresh scenery. For this is detestably dull.

But when I do escape from my imperial prison, I visit colleges & public institutions, make a few short speeches, which are popular, & attempt to advance the interests of the natives by education & every facility to obtain knowledge. One gentleman, on a hint I gave him, has just translated our Saviour's Sermon on the Mount. But before we attempt conversion, we must educate. Their powers of imitation are astounding, their originality feeble, but the population under our mild laws is increasing & exceeds 100 millions, being about 4 times our own European population. We could administer the govt. better if we could afford the expense of more judges, magistrates & civil servants but while we have the protection & control of the whole of India, we have only the revenue of *one half*, having left the various tributary states the internal management of their own revenue. The people of the lower classes desire to be under British laws, but the rajahs and gentry cling to their power, & several years must elapse before any material change can be effected.

The letters I get from England as regards myself are satisfactory. Ripon does not write much. The secession of William Gladstone is, as far as speaking talent is concerned, a great loss, following so soon after Stanley's removal to the upper House. Peel & Graham are the two [*?pillars*] which support the gateway into power. I am confident a Freemantle will not do for Ireland. I understand he did not show aptitude at the War Office. Lincoln will not speak but Sydney Herbert will make, I should say, a good secry. at war & a good debater. Cardwell will do well & [*Clerk*] as a privy councillor will, on matters of business, be of great use. They are determined, & most wisely, to continue the income tax. I expect difficulty on the sugar duties. However, before you read this, all these points will be known to you. Knatchbull was to be created a peer & Bingham Baring reported his successor.[137] The post office is still vacant. I should hope some arrange[men]t might be made to reintroduce Lord Ellenborough into the Cabinet.

We are in daily expectation of our letters & I shall still have the chance of hearing from you before the day is out. I can write by the express, so I hope to be able to say that I have been comforted by your affecte. expressions up to the last moment of closing the dispatches.

[*PS.*] You will observe probably by the papers that Ld. Tweeddale is in some difficulty about a mutiny in the 6th Native Cavry. I think he was right in carrying the sentence on the ringleaders into effect. But I was obliged to write a long letter to him on some points in which in his General Order he takes a different view from Sir H. Gough, thereby showing a marked difference of opinion between him & the c. chief. The Court & the Duke approve of the line I have taken, & for the future all points of difference between the c. chief of the 3 presidencies are to be refer'd to the g. general for decision. I have a good many quarrels to settle between these different authorities. Hitherto I have succeeded, but it occupies a large portion of time that could be better employed. I shall be curious to receive my home dispatches, for it is just possible Lord Ripon may have recd. our Punjaub news of Heera Singh's death.

You would be surprized to find how tranquil I have become. Yesterday a secry. rushed into the council room with a note saying Aden has been surprized by an army of Arabs & the garrison put to the sword, a few Englishmen escaping on b[oar]d ship. I read the note quietly, detected a palpable contradiction by dates, & I don't think I changed a muscle, altho' the disaster wd. have been most lamentable. I have braced up my nerves to be very calm, & I mention the anecdote to prove to you that the responsibility of office does not wear me down. I cd. wish occasionally to get away for a week as public men do in England. Here it is the incessant drudgery which never intermits which tires the mind & body.

Six months hence I shall have a gt. relief in journeying through this interesting country to a colder region, & I hope my return to Bengal will be en route for England: 1846 at Simla, 1847 returning here, &

[137] Hardinge's comments on the political situation in England were prompted in part by various communications reaching him from London, including one dated Mar. 1, 1845, from Peel: 'The loss of Stanley and Gladstone in the House of Commons is severely felt. Sidney Herbert promises well as a debater. Lincoln and he, as probably you know, are in the cabinet' (Peel Papers, Add. MS 40474). The Cabinet reshuffle resulted from the resignation of Gladstone as president of the Board of Trade over Irish Catholic issues. Knatchbull was not made a peer.

early in 1848 again in yr. affecte. embraces. A thousand casualties
may shorten this period; none can prolong it. Five years is the period
& mine shall not be 4 years. I may displease my masters, my health
may suffer, the administration may be changed. But happen what
may, if alive, I shall be with you early in 1848.[138] God of His infinite
mercy preserve you & our children during this eventful period! Thus,
dearest, looking to these dates as the worst side of the picture, that is
the longest absence. I trust that you will fortify me in my resolution
to go through this tryal bravely. Ten months are struck off the long
[*separation*] & when 24 have passed I shall have the buoyancy of youth
in getting through the remainder. If Arthur gets his lieut[*enan*]cy, I
may send him to you earlier to beguile & console you.

In yr. letters to Lady Peel, don't [*?allude*] to these details. We are
very cordial but I am determined never to complain. Nor might I,
for his selection is the most honourable incident of my life, altho'
attended with consequences which few but ourselves can appreciate.

I hope to have a statement of yr. finances. I have £1000 ready to
send home to put you at ease. Oh, if this vessel wd. but arrive!

Walter writes, firmly determined to adhere to Peel. He seems to be
greatly attached to South Park. His visit to Hull was successful but I
wish we could get him into a safer seat. Goulburn[139] has shown me
much affection & Graham is also very cordial, Grant indefatigable &
the best man of business I cd. have had. He is aux anges, having been
again recd. by Sir R. & Ly. Peel. When you go to England, pray
thank him for his services.

29. [*To Walter.*] Barrackpore. April 7, 1845

I have received your letter of the 7th Febry., & we are in hourly
expectation of the Precursor's arrival when I hope to hear from you
& yr. dear mother.

We are all well & in good spirits. The climate appears to agree with
Arthur, but the hot weather has not yet set in. However, with moderate care there is no necessity for either of them exposing their persons
to the sun, which in Bengal is most pernicious, and, as *pig-sticking* is
over for the season, I hope the boys will be as prudent as I am.

I had a long letter, or rather journal, from yr. mother at Nice, not
having then heard of Arthur's arrival. She wrote in good spirits,
assures me her health is better than it has been for some time &,

[138] Emily commented in the margin: 'Good man, he kept his word! Better than the
smokers.'
[139] Henry Goulburn was then the chancellor of the exchequer.

excepting a project of joining me by land, is reconciled to the failure of her attempt to join me here.

In fact, we both derive the advantage of the fortunate termination of her plans. She never would have survived this climate, & she never would have ceased to reproach me as the cause of our separation if I had authoritatively prohibited the attempt. All her letters breathe a pious submission to what she is now convinced is the will of God for merciful purposes, & I hope, when you join her with dear Sarah in the summer, that she will be contented & happy.

I have told her I intend to return early in 1848, when I have completed 4 years instead of 5, but three years in this country to look forward to is a century, & a thousand contingencies may expedite the period. My masters are satisfied at present & laud my prudence etc. etc., but my popularity will diminish, my health may fail, & therefore, in at once fixing the first months of 1848 for my return, I almost feel it at 60 yrs. of age to be an act of presumption.

We shall move up the country in Oct. Charles has taken a great interest in that wonderful discovery of the daguerreotype, & we wish to take one up the country in order to have the most accurate copies of the most remarkable buildings such as the Tage [*Taj*] etc. The invention is making progress, & I understand paper is now employed instead of their metal plates. Will you be so good as to make the most accurate enquiry to be quite sure to have the most simple & most effective of these inventions, to send out 100 plates or sheets of paper with this apparatus *by Egypt,* ascertaining that it bears rough carriage on the line of march, with instructions how to use it &, if out of order, to restore the parts into their places. The great [*J. D.*] Harding will assist you & Mssrs. Cox will pay the cost—I suppose £100. I should also wish the carriage to Calcutta to be arranged in London as goods by the person from whom it is purchased. In elaborate architecture & even in Eastern figures it will be invaluable. I have a group of Charles & Arthur, quite perfect. Let me have yr. classical opinion. I propose to train a clerk to use it under Charles' orders & to bring home an interesting collection of very accurate likenesses of men & scenery. It wd. be a great desideratum to have the means of transferring the impression from the plate on to a sheet of common drawing paper, finishing the sketch in colors, &, to say the truth, I am moved to take this step by my anxiety to prevent Charles from sitting out in the sun. He may take it out when he spears the wild boar & have spirited portraits of the bristly monster. Their bristles are 19 & 20 inches on their back.

I have been going the round of our Hindoo & Mahommedan colleges, but the last [*?one, a*] medical college, was the most interesting. Nearly 200 students were assembled in their theatre from brown to dark black to hear the annual report read & to receive their prizes. I then make them a short address—generally very ill-reported. One ex-student has within the last 3 years performed 18 operations for the stone & has not lost a single patient. They are expert dissectors & last season had upwards of 500 subjects—& these are the people who 10 yrs. ago would not touch a dead body! The mass are dispersed as they obtain diplomas throughout the country. One hundred are brought up for the native army, chiefly the sons of officers, & make excellent assistant surgeons. I have added 20 more & intend to add 50 more paid by the public. The success of this institution is so clear & positive a proof of our desire to relieve the sufferings of human infirmity & do good to the people that it is a most popular institution. We have just sent home 4 black boys—2 at the expense of D. Tagore, who is a prince in liberality. You can see them by inviting Dr. Goodeve, the first man who practically taught dissection in Calcutta. It is a great triumph of reason & good sense over prejudice & superstition, & I trust their boldness in throwing off the trammels of caste will meet with its reward.

In visiting our mint the other day, I found 500 black men & boys employed, each performing his part with great skill. Some were even making the most difficult parts of the machinery, & such is the perfection to which we have brought the mint that we coin 280,000 pieces of copper coin in a day, which is scarcely sufficient for our population & on which we make a profit of 25 pr. ct.

The powers of imitation in the black race are wonderful; their originality is very limited. They seldom ever suggest an improvement.

The paper is so dry the ink will scarcely mark, & I must now, my dear Walter, close my note, still hoping before the mail goes out that the steamer expected may arrive. Love to dearest Sarah & to the baby, who, I hear, can talk a little.

[*P.S.*] The steamer has brought me yr. letter of the 24th Febry. and, *entre nous,* one sheet of *note* paper from Ld. Ripon & not much more by the last mail, approving of my policy which is in *accordance* with my instructions, not one word of which instructions I have ever received. How[*eve*]r, he entirely approves & on the Tweed-dale case of the mutineers & other matters has decided according to the view taken by me.[140] I rely on yr. frankness in always keeping me truly informed of all reports concerning my measures.

[140] Hardinge complained when Tweeddale informed him in a private rather than in an official letter about the mutiny in the 6th Cavalry, feeling that by doing so Tweeddale was raising doubts as to the extent of Calcutta's power over the presidencies in military matters. He also objected to the Madras governor's suggestion that Hardinge and his Council were favouring Bishop Wilson in his dispute with Tweeddale over the working

I have excellent co-adjutors, but Ld. E[*llenborough*] will tell you that Pollock[141] can give me no advice in an emergency, or Mr Millett[142] or any secry., altho' each in their separate depts. understands their professional details. Fortunately a large proportion of the business is milty. & administrative as concerning the army, & here my ordnance & war office & Hse. of Coms. education in estimates is of great use.

With my council I go on very harmoniously, never having a Minute recording a difference of opinion which, during the 8 months which have *already* elapsed, is a novelty. I work so hard & am so exhausted before I go to bed that I sleep from 10 till 1/2 p[*as*]t 4 & am again at work by 5.

I ride in the even[*in*]gs, which tires me less & refreshes me more than the morning exercise. If the press publishes any of my speeches here, you may disavow their accuracy of language, for I decline to revise what I say, & each paper has its own version in substance *correct*.

Love to dst. Sarah. I am in good health & in God's merciful hands.

[*P.S.*] Not a line from yr. mother. I suspect she is not yet aware of the new conveyance.

30. [*To Emily.*] Barrackpore. April 21, 1845

The last letter from you is dated the 18th Febry. which I recd. on the 8th April. The mail has arrived 3 days ago & I thought your letter wd. follow from Bombay. I have no doubt the Marseilles mail was behind its time & that I shall receive yr. letter the 8th May, but it is such a cordial to devour yr. words that I cannot but feel *very very* much disapp[*oin*]t[*ed*].

My letters from England are very satisfactory. Peel says, 'There is universal satisfaction with yr. administration, with yr. views, intentions, & acts.' Lord Ripon says, 'I must tell you how entirely satisfactory yr. proceedings are in reference to the new state of affairs at Lahore. It is useless for us to sit at home & profess to direct affairs of such delicacy & difficulty & presenting such a variety of incidents as now exist in the Punjaub, & we must rely, & do most entirely rely, on yr. discretion & judgement in dealing with them. What you have

---

of the Anglican church in Madras. (Hardinge to Ripon, 20 and 22 Nov. 1844; Hardinge to Tweeddale, 20 Nov. 1844, Ripon Papers, Add. MS 40870.)

[141] Maj. Gen. (afterwards Field Marshal) Sir George Pollock (1786–1872) came to India in 1803 and participated in various campaigns, including those against Burma, Nepal, and Afghanistan. He was the acting resident at Lucknow, 1843–4, and then served as the military member of the G.G.'s Council, 1844–7. He was made Baronet of the Khyber Pass in 1872.

[142] Frederick Millett (ob. 1856) was the civilian member of the G.G.'s Council, 1845–8.

written to me & to Peel is very true.' In another letter, 'Your views of the Punjaub question are most important & appear to me to be just as they are cautious. I am sure the Duke's opinion has always been that the Sutlege is our best line of frontier.' And this was in reply to my opinion differing from Ld. Ellenborough's views on this question. I thought you wd. like to see these passages but don't let them go further. The Queen, I also hear, is pleased with my letters, & from other letters I find that no flaw has yet been found in my proceedings. In various military points of discussion, the Court of Directors have decided in the line taken by me & disputed by others, & now in the other presidencies we shall go on very smoothly, with my council here as usual *couleur de rose*. You know the eagerness of my temper, which age has not yet subdued; therefore you may suppose that approbation gives me fresh courage to do my duty & cheers me in its performance. But I still want, d[*eare*]st, yr. affecte. interest in my fate to make my happiness complete.

I want to know how the bleak winds of March were resisted & that you are well & in good heart. I have sent 800 miles for a small dog from Nepaul. If I find the animal affectionate & pretty, I will, after making him my pet, send him to you.

I send another £1000 home by this mail. You need be under no apprehension of overdrawing Mssrs. Cox & Co's. Instead of urging my wife to be economical I must press her to be comfortable.

The family matters here of dinners etc. etc. are well managed. I give about £500 [*worth of*] dinners a month, including my staff, & have reformed some abuses so that I believe I have done my duty to the office & fairly expend my salary without incurring so much expense as my predecessors. I am quite satisfied on this point & I believe the community of Calcutta & Barrackpore are also satisfied.

In the Punjab an event of some importance has occurred. Raja Golab Singh, the great chief of the hill tribes, having made terms with the Sikhs, came into their camp &, by a bold stroke of policy, threw himself on the generosity of the troops &, after various fluctuations of fortune, one day condemned to die, the next to be wuzzier, he marched with the troops to Lahore & there has been delivered into the hands of the regent, his enemy. The probability is that after extorting from him his supposed immense wealth they will put him to death. This man's fate will not tend to establish a better order of things at Lahore. The army will continue to rule until the finances fail, & then we shall have to be very vigilant in defending our frontier. We had better be without the Punjab, & all my efforts will be to uphold the Sihk [*sic*] govt. For the next 6 months no decision can be required. After that time we must be guided by the progress of events, which are per-petually changing. I do my best. I was up at 4 this m[*ornin*]g *by mistake* and have been working all day but my strength was never greater to undergo sedentary fatigue, & when the day of decision arrives I shall trust to God to give me a just view & shall adopt no line which in my conscience I cannot advocate as the most honourable as well as the best. If my efforts are blessed & that we are both spared, what satisfaction will you not feel for the sacrifices we have both made! If I can preserve peace, I shall prove my sincerity. If I cannot, if a vile democracy in arms compels me to abate so intolerable a nuisance, then I hope by forbearance & a good cause to carry the public voice in my favour. The former I should prefer because it is most advantageous to British interests; the latter wd. have its compensation in relieving thousands of peasantry from the tyranny under which they are suffering.

Lord Ellenborough writes that he supposes I have lost my horses on the road to the frontier. I think he would have been in camp by this time, but he admits we have no case.[143] Peel says nothing of his being in the Cabinet hereafter. Why is Lowther's position not filled up?[144] Knatchbull will be glad to retire. So should I if I had fulfilled my destiny, which will be too honestly pacific to desire any reward.

Our friend Hogg is to be the deputy chairman & one of my masters. He is clever & I expect we shall get on very well together.[145] I regret my friend Capt. Shepherd[146] who retires. Lord Ripon is never in the House from illness, Stanley & Wharncliffe[147] were laid up with gout, & the Duke, being the efficient man, is styled the governor of the *invalids*.[148] Tweeddale's affair will not come before the H. of Commons, I believe. I had had 3 or 4 discussions with him & the decisions have all been given in my favour; we shall now go on very well together. Sir G. Arthur is able, prudent, & conciliatory. I don't think much of

[143] This reaction was prompted by a letter dated 7 Mar. 1845, from Ellenborough suggesting that Hardinge must be prepared to move in a hurry to the Sikh frontier. While Ellenborough urged that, if 'any thing is to be done, you must go yourself,' he nonetheless told Hardinge that 'as yet you have no case for intervention according to European modes of viewing these matters' (Ellenborough Papers, PRO 30/12/14/5 [part 3]).

[144] After William Lowther became the 2nd Earl of Lonsdale in 1844, he asked to be relieved from his position as postmaster general. However, he continued to serve until Oct. 1845 when Peel appointed the Earl of St Germans as his successor.

[145] Hogg, who held various judicial posts in Calcutta from 1814 to 1833 including the office of registrar of the Bengal Supreme Court, became a director of the East India Company in 1839. He served as its deputy chairman 1845–6, 1850–1, and as its chairman 1846–7, 1852–3.

[146] John Shepherd (1791–1859) retired as the chairman of the Court of Directors.

[147] James Stuart Wortley, Baron Wharncliffe (1776–1845), the lord president of the council in the Lords, died in Dec. 1845.

[148] In a letter to Hardinge on 6 Mar. 1845, Ellenborough repeated the current *bon mot*: '[*The*] Duke has got a new office, that of the Governor of the Invalids' (Ellenborough Papers, PRO 30/12/14/5 [part 3]).

Gough's abilities, but this is high treason & I am to be his successor when he retires, but the fact is as I have stated.

The bishop arrives the end of this month & Arthur has been examined by the archdeacon. I shall take the Sacrament with him on the first occasion. Charles always takes it with me. I have subscribed £100 to the cathedral & £50 to some other charitable institutions, £80 to the 4 colleges for prizes, & about the same sum for a village school here of 100 children generally supported by the g. general. Some minor charities make my subscriptions about £300.

Now, d[eare]st, I have told you everything that I think will interest you, & must gallop through some official letters before the mail goes out. Love to Fanny & Emily.

22nd April
[*PS.*] The mail is just about to depart & I open my letter merely to add my last word for Europe & for you. Golab Singh has been delivered up a prisoner & is now in Lahore. The troops seem disposed to take his part & to use him as their instrument in extorting money from the rich chiefs. Plunder & tyranny are the order of the day.

31. [*To Walter.*] Calcutta. April 21st, 1845

I have received your letter of March 6th in 42 days, but I am most disappointed in having no letter from yr. mother. I presume the Marseilles post office was not in time. If she had been ill, the girls wd. have written. These mishaps will occur & I must not repine hearing news once a fortnight from my friends.

Charles & Arthur & poor George [*Hardinge*] are quite well. Wood has had a bilious attack which has pulled him down. He is the best tempered fellow in the world, but very obstinate. He plays racquetts [*sic*] in this climate, comes out into the open air hissing hot, & gets into a buggy to drive home. Dear Ben already has lost his ruddy complexion, but we shall be off for the hills & far away in 6 months & this prospect is a relief for the monotony of a Calcutta life. I am quite well & don't find my mind or body the worse for the incessant toil I undergo—which really has no intermission, but I am gratified by the encouragement I receive. Peel is very warm in his praise & Ripon very satisfactory, but, as to instructions or an idea of the policy I ought to pursue, you would be astonished not at the meagerness but the absolute absence of a bare suggestion.

My senior councillor[149] has been 3 months away. Mr Millett is a

[149] Sir Thomas Herbert Maddock (1790–1870) had been a member of the G.G.'s Council since 1843. He came to India in 1814 and saw political service in Nepal, Bhopal, and Oudh. He would act as president of the G.G.'s Council during Hardinge's long absence in the Northwest.

very good lawyer & amiable man. Sir G. Pollock [*is*] far from well, very modest & diffident &, except on an artry. question, never obtrudes an opinion. I am therefore left to my secretaries, who are clever men, who work cordially under me, but who in any great exigency are not competent to give me advice as Ld. E[*llenborough*] will tell you. I therefore have to rely on myself. In 3 or 4 squabbles with the other govrs. of Madras & Bombay,[150] I have had the entire support of the home authorities, & I wd. send you Peel's words, but they are so strong I am ashamed. How[*eve*]r, whatever is done is my own act. My demi-official letters go before the Cabinet, & in a plain reasonable way I feel on reflection that as yet we have made no mistakes. I feel deeply my responsibility, whilst the question at issue is before me. I go at it with all my strength & won't leave it till I have mastered it & sent it off. Having done my best I throw off all care & am fast asleep for 6 hours till my servants rouse me before 5. I have only been one day in bed after 5—when I had a sort of cholera attack—& my endurance is a great consolation, for last year [*when*] not being well, I had doubts of my honesty in accepting an office for which my strength might prove deficient. Those doubts are gone, my health is better than it has been for 3 or 4 years & I am at peace with myself on this point & relieved abt. yr. dear mother, which made me quite ill. Therefore, my dear friend, trusting always in the mercy of God, have no misgivings about us here. We shall get through our work decently & prudently, &, if warlike operations are inevitable, then you need be under no apprehension, although the very word, the *chances* of war, proves its uncertainty.

We have 6 months of comparative tranquillity before us, & our precautions are all taken. Our forbearance you shall approve, &, if we can contrive to keep up a Sikh govt. in the Punjaub, the effort shall be sincerely made.

When I last wrote to you, the Sikh army was before Jummoo, the hill fort & capital of Golab S. who had, from a personal vindictive feeling, deliberately murdered 5 vakeels, or envoys, returning from him to the army. The army, indignant at this outrage, moved up to the attack. Two days' fighting took place, when the troops again renewed their negotiations & came to terms with Golab Singh as to the division of the property of Heera Singh & his other relatives, almost the whole race having been cut off by assassination. The Raja Golab S. then had a conference, attended by a few followers, with the Sikh genl. They exchanged swords &, after much cant & hypocrisy on both sides, they separated. The next day Golab S. came down &

---

[150] Hardinge had objected to Bombay's desire to augment its army and to some of the policies it had pursued during the Kolapur revolt.

pitched his tents close to 2 brigades of Sikh troops & threw himself
on their protection. This bold & unexpected stroke astonished &
captivated the soldiery. He addressed them & is a perfect demagogue
to a mob; they swore fidelity to him. He distributed money & presents.
The rest of the army were [*sic*] not so satisfied. The delegates assembled
to deliberate: some voted to put him to death, others to promote him
to be wuzzier; and he passed the night in suspense. The next day he
had to appear before the delegates. He explained his views—that he
would pay them, lead them & govern the country better than the
drunkard Jowahir S., & they separated, declaring that they would
not attack Jummoo but return to Lahore with the raja. He remained
with the 2 brigades formerly disciplined by General Avitabile.[151] The
army marched back to Lahore.

But the court at Lahore were of course in the greatest alarm,
expecting that he would, on assuming the govt., punish his enemies.
Every intrigue was at work to rouse the jealousy & fears of the *Sikh*
chiefs agt. a Raj-poot minister. His brother Dyhan Singh had been
minister & murdered.[152] Heera S., his nephew, had been minister &
murdered. His own son had been murdered by the Sikhs.[153] He had
these murders to avenge, he would delight in making Sikh destroy
Sikh in a civil war, &, when rivalry was at its height, deliver over the
country to the English.

The fluctuations in this extraordinary man's march from Jummoo
to Lahore would be *à la Bonham*[154] very exciting. One day he was at
the head of the poll; the next day some adherents had acted on the
other side. Bribes given during the night had rectified the balance
& he was the popular candidate. In his harangues, like another
demagogue, he demanded *justice* for the Punjaub. He denounced the
rich chiefs as plunderers who ought to [*be*] made to disgorge their
wealth for the injured troops robbed by these upstart generals, that
the sergeants & the punchayets ought to rule. He only wanted the
words of Moin, 'Hereditary Bondsmen' etc.

As the army came near the capital, the chiefs, fearing the man, sent
money into the camp &, finding that he had denounced them, made

[151] Paolo di Avitabile (1791–1850), an Italian freebooter from Naples, saw service in
both the Napoleonic and Bourbon armies. In 1827, with the help of Ventura, he joined
Ranjit Singh's army but did not receive the rank of general until the early 1840s.
[152] Dhian Singh rose to be the closest confidant and adviser of Ranjit Singh who in
1826 entitled him Raja-i-Rajgan (Raja of Rajas) and later appointed him the minister
of the Sikh state. Intelligent, charismatic, but cunning, he emerged as the most powerful
man in Panjab after Ranjit's death. His career was cut short in Sept. 1843 when he
was killed by a rival faction.
[153] Sohan Singh, Gulab Singh's second son, died with Hira Singh in Dec. 1844.
[154] Hardinge is comparing the stormy career of Gulab Singh with that of Peel's
manager, F. R. Bonham.

common cause against him. Without going into a variety of detail of generals beaten with slippers because they were [unhurt?], the result has been that the 2 brigades, alarmed by the march of the army to destroy them, promised to give up Golaub S., & on the 8th of this month he was escorted into the capital seated on an elephant, his face covered with a shawl to conceal him from the gaze of the troops.

This man is loaded with crimes but is the boldest & ablest man in that country. He was too confident in his own powers of persuasion & the reckless daring of coming out in[to the] enemy's camp without terms, having recently murdered 5 envoys of the Sikh army, shows the enterprizing character of the man.

They will not kill him till they have squeezed all his enormous wealth out of him. This wealth has been amassed by cruelty & extortion. He ought not to be pitied. His abilities & his winning manners, his eloquence & his good looks, are qualities which command favour, but this man's career is unredeemed by any acts of virtue. He is supposed to be worth 6 or 7 millions. We have now a letter from him beseeching us to attack the Punjab & destroy the army signed by this traitor. But in this country where assassination to gain an end is perceived as decisive of character, &, furthermore, humanity attributed to weakness & fear, his crimes are over-looked & the mass of the people ready to deify him as a superhuman hero. These are the people with whom I have to deal on European conditions & terms of honesty.

The great anxiety is the possible infection of milty. democracy in our army. All democracies are vile but milty. democracy the worst. However, I won't enter upon this chapter. In other quarters we are quiet. Ld. E. recommends me to have my post horses laid on the road! (confidential).

Jones is very slovenly in his farmyard. The secret of fine healthy cows is to keep them & the calves warm and dry in the winter. Jones' system is disgracefully slovenly. Burke[155] wd. say what Crampton's peasant replied to my question abt. his cow looking so sleek & fat: 'Sir, it would ill become the *beast to* look otherwise in the master's field.' They ought to be very clean & taken up early in the autumn into the yard.

The hedge on the high road bounding Blowers Hill should be strongly fenced in by a post & 3 rails, as strong as on the new rail way road from Penshurst to the station. When properly fixed, the bank for the quick hedge should be broad & sound. Some bad oaks which I marked with Jones wd. furnish the timber &, if done at leisure, the quicks could be planted in the autumn.

---

[155] Burke seems to have been a nurseryman who helped landscape South Park.

The oaks from Darjeeling will thrive in England.

I am going to send next year a plant called *Amherstia nobilis*[156] to Mr Wells.[157] I believe the Duke of Devonshire has the only plant now in England.[158] It is very beautiful.

And now, my dear Walter, adieu.

32. [*To Sarah.*] Calcutta. April 21, 1845

Your affectionate note was most welcome. Pray kiss the dear baby for the Indian grandpapa. I know of old how happy you must be when it begins to talk. If you make it like yourself I shall say you are a very good mama.

Since I closed my letter to Walter, a *dawk* has arrived, saying that Golab Singh has been given up by the 2 brigades which had hitherto protected him & that he has been escorted into Lahore seated on an elephant, his face covered with a sheet to conceal him from the gaze of the crowd. The troops have ordered that every precaution shall be taken to protect his life, & they now declare that he is the only able man left in the Punjab. As he has the honesty to offer to repay the sums he has embezzled, they think the rich sirdars should be made to do the same, & in all probability his life will be spared for the purpose of using him as their instrument to extort money from the rich to be handed over to them.

Will you also beg Walter to look at The Friend of India which I send him. He will find under the art[icl]e 'Hindoos,' that the law we have just launched will probably as a measure turn out to be the most important in advancing the Christian religion of any that has yet been passed. We don't attempt to proselytize or to bribe any infidel by reward to change his religion, but we insist on the liberty of conscience & decide that no Hindoo shall be punished by loss of property because he chooses to become a Christian. Half Calcutta wd. lose their property if the Hindoo laws as to caste were rigidly enforced, for loss of caste is loss of property. We therefore say on the score of religion this shall be so no longer. If an Englishman chooses to be a Brahmin we don't take away his property, & we only demand fair protection for those who embrace Christianity.

I only wish I was 40 instead of 60 & could convert the 24 h[*ours*]

---

[156] A plant of Burmese origin which bears large, deep-red flowers with yellow spots and is considered holy by the Buddhists. It was named after Countess Amherst, the wife of Lord Amherst, G.G. of India, 1823–8, under whom the First Anglo–Burmese War was fought.

[157] William Wells, a prominent Penshurst resident living at Redleaf.

[158] William Cavendish, the 6th Duke of Devonshire, collected tropical plants at Chatsworth.

into 48. The subjects are interminable—& then I have to jump from Hindoos & legislation to military precautions on the Punjab (a republican army & all its vile democracy) & to write volumes to London, whilst piles of boxes are heaped up on my table, groaning to be dispatched. How happy I shall be when the day of my deliverance arrives, but in the meantime I am as determined to go through as at any former period of my life, & the will has a gt. effect upon the powers of the body.

Your little friend Raleigh has not seen much service. He is sharp & competent, & I had some difficulty in getting over some adverse points, since which I have had occasion to give him a sharp admonition for not protecting the sepoys of the regt. he commands which is quartered here. To show an example, I took it in hand & diminished the daily duties of his men by 140 unnecessarily upon duty every day. Now we shall be excellent friends. His excuse was that he found the regt. thus fagged & left it so. This is, I find, a common error in India.

His brother has gone home with £60,000 in his pocket made by doctoring. I believe they are in the direct line from a brother to Sir W. Raleigh.

I forgot to tell Walter that I sent to Cox £1000 this mail. He can supply his mother, if she should in her dislike of accts. have made any mistake, by just seeing Cox on the subject, who will act as he recommends.

Dear Ben already looks paler but is quite well. The beginning of October I hope to be on my way to the frontier, & a sharp winter will revive us all from the laxity of Calcutta. My paper is quite damp & my clothes wet, whilst the sun is fierce, beyond endurance. But in the evening I ride every day, & came in from Barrackpore this morning.

The poor mothers here see their children till they are 5 & then lose sight of them for 12 years. What misery!

33. [*To Walter.*] Calcutta. May 2, 1845

Our steamer is going out, & yours is not [*in*] & will not arrive till the 5th or 6th.

I have therefore no news of your mother or her intended movements. On the 20th I shall have recd. yr. letters & also those of the govt., which I am anxious to open as I expect *at last* some opinion as to the course of policy to be pursued. I am confident that they will be satisfactory, but I have so many milty. as well as political arrange-[*men*]ts to attend to, with Gough at a distance & on the *qui vive* in matters of milty. interference, with an Indian staff so superannuated that they afford him very little assistance & me still less, that [*I*] am

2 JUNE 1845   81

anxious to have the leading points which I have indicated decidedly
affirmed by Ld. Ripon. When this is done I shall be more at my ease.
We have also a question with Goa abt. refugees who have escaped
into their country from the pursuit of our troops. [*Sir George*] Arthur
wishes to compel the Port[*ugue*]se govr. to surrender men who have
laid down their arms on condition that Port[*ugue*]se authorities will
protect them. I respect this protection to insurgents & vagabonds
because I feel, if the Sikhs were to demand the surrender of their
refugees coming into our territory for the purpose of putting them to
death, I should refuse to surrender, &, altho' I have authorized our
offs. to pursue our enemies *in arms* across the frontier into the Goa
territory in certain cases, I will not force a Port[*ugue*]se govr. to break
his pledge on my threat contrary to my own practice.

My principle & advice & order to Sir G. Arthur is to consider Goa
as belonging to *France*. What a set off agt. Queen [*?Pomurre*][159] the
French wd. have if we lost sight of humane principles &, because we
are strong, coerced the weak![160]

Raja Golab S. was still a prisoner at Lahore. The genl., Lal Singh,[161]
a paramour of the ranee, was busily occupied in obtaining her consent
to assassinate her own brother Jowahir S., now the wuzzier[162] & a
brutal drunkard. All parties went to the council room with an equal
no. of armed followers. Swords had been drawn & any day may bring
us the news of some bloody struggle.

The boys [*are*] quite well. Love to Sarah & baby.

34. [*To Walter.*] Calcutta. 2nd June 1845

The mail will not arrive from England before ours closes tomorrow
at 3 o'cl., & the same provoking arrangement will prevent my receiving yr. mother's letters, which are a month in arrears. I am anxious
to know what you & Sarah have decided on doing for the summer,
as it would be of the greatest comfort to your dear mother to see you
in Switzerland.

[159] Not identified.
[160] The Bombay governor felt that by an Anglo–Portuguese accord of 1838, Goa was
obliged to surrender the Sawantwari chiefs who had taken refuge there. However,
Hardinge asked G. Arthur not to send troops to capture the chiefs, for the intervention
might be disapproved of by the British government as it could encourage France to
act similarly elsewhere.
[161] A handsome Brahman who had rapidly gained prominence since 1843. He was
made a general and later served twice as the minister. Lal Singh's rise, however, was
said to be due more to his scandalous liaison with Rani Jindan than to his own ability.
[162] He formally assumed the ministry on 14 May.

I read yr. speech in defence of Robert Fitz-roy[163] & was much pleased with it. It was just like you & what it ought to have been. With very honourable feelings & a high moral sense of duty, there is an obliquity & obstinacy in Fitzroy's character & judgement which made me, from observation of his powers of mind called forth in the duel affair,[164] most anxious that he should not accept this New Zealand govt. I am afraid he must be recalled.[165]

I see by The Times I am accused of imposing additional import duties here in opposition to the principles laid down by my master, Sir Robert. The fact is the order came from Ld. Ripon, most positive in its terms, which this govr. is, by act of Parlt., bound to obey, reluctantly passed by me here, altho' in many respects it will do no harm as it taxes the wealthy & not the poor, the European & not the native. It so happens I have, contrary to Ld. E[*llenborough*] & contrary to Lord Auckland's recorded opinion, *lowered* the duty on salt, which is excessively high in Bengal & an absolute necessary of life. My measure has been followed by an increased consumption of the article & a gain to the exchequer, & next April I hope to make another reduction if in the interval the result should encourage us to repeat the experiment.

The necessity of Ripon's increase of duty in imports is to be justified by Ld. E.'s very proper act of abolishing all internal duties in towns of the most vexatious description to the people by which we lose, with a deficient income, £300,000 a yr. & may recover, by a tax on wines chiefly & European luxuries, £100,000 a yr. Knowing the strength of my position on this question, I am very indifferent to the attacks of The Times.[166]

[163] Robert Fitzroy (1805–65), a nephew of Hardinge and a cousin of Walter James, was a grandson of the 1st Marquess of Londonderry on his mother's side. He took over as governor of New Zealand in Dec. 1843 where his efforts to reconcile violent disputes over land ownership between the English settlers and the local people aroused rancorous denunciations in England. Walter James' support of Fitzroy came in a Commons debate on 11 Mar. 1845, in which C. Buller, the M.P. from Liskeard, condemned Fitzroy's governorship in a long speech (3 Hansard, lxxviii. 658–70.)

[164] While campaigning for a seat in the Commons during 1841, Fitzroy became embroiled in a dispute with a former political ally, Mr Sheppard, resulting in a challenge to a duel which, however, never took place. Their feud nevertheless continued and ultimately led to a public scuffle. This affair left doubts in the minds of some, including Hardinge, as to the level of Fitzroy's maturity.

[165] Fitzroy was removed from the governorship in Nov. 1845.

[166] The Company enjoyed a monopoly on the manufacture and sale of salt in Bengal. Although the salt duty was only one rupee and 3/4 of a rupee per maund in Madras and Bombay, respectively, it was 3 1/4 rupees in Bengal. In the autumn of 1845 Hardinge raised the duty to a rupee in Bombay but reduced it to three rupees in Bengal. The G.G. believed that the reduction of the duty would help the poor in Bengal, a move that was fully supported by Ripon. (*Viscount Hardinge*, pp. 64–5; Ripon to Hardinge, 4 Oct. 1844, Ripon Papers, Add. MS 40860.) However, many in England

I have this day completed a short Minute on an interesting subject—
the attempt to abolish human sacrifices in a tract of wild country
about 300 miles from Calcutta, inhabited by rude tribes who are the
aborigines of the country & inhabit a very difficult country between
Calcutta & Madras, in extent 300 miles long by 100 wide. They are
armed with bows & arrows, [&] are brave with a jealous love of
liberty. Their jungles & fastnesses & their poverty have only on one
occasion induced us to enter their country, when the army in 2 or 3
campaigns suffered great losses from the unhealthiness of the climate.

For ages these tribes have purchased victims from the adjacent
countries, boys & girls & men & women, who are kept & well treated
in their villages. When the annual period arrives for the celebration
of these impious rites, the village assembles the poor victims, arms &
legs are broken that no show of resistance may be made, & he is alive
fixed into a young tree split into 4 openings. The priest gives the first
blow with an axe, & everyone present then rushes upon the victim &
strips off the living flesh & carries a piece of it to his field as a
propitiation to the earth god to give them a good crop.

A captain of infantry has been living amongst these tribes & has in
some cases succeeded in persuading them to abandon these cruel
practices. We propose now to pass a law to punish by transportation
& perpetual imprisonment the sellers & procurers of these victims
called Mehrias, to increase the captain's estab[*lishmen*]t by 2 or 3
doctors & other agents both European & native, to give him full
powers as a magistrate & his discretion of bestowing rewards &
inflicting summary punishments, but the exercise of these powers
requires much tact & judgement. If we resort to force & intimidation
in suppressing these abominable rites, we shall force them to practice
them in secret &, if we prevent the Hindoos of the adjacent districts
from kidnapping children & even men for their infamous traffick in
blood, these savages may then, as has already occurred, sacrifice their
own children.

Our operations therefore are to be conducted by 5 or 6 officers,
each in charge of a district, pitching his tent amongst those groups of
savages, dispensing medicines (& I have proposed vaccination), & by
small presents conciliating their goodwill, having no rents or taxes to

---

felt that the reduction in salt duties would damage the export of English salt to India.
The Times repeatedly condemned Hardinge's policies, most scathingly on April 7 (p. 4):
'Sir H. Hardinge is a gallant soldier, but a good soldier may be a bad financier. Does
Sir Henry bear in mind that whilst he is taxing what comes into India, he is taxing
what goes out of England?' Calling Hardinge's position at variance with Peel's anti-
protectionist policies, the newspaper asked: 'Does he bear in mind the financial triumphs
of his master, the PREMIER, and recollect that Sir Robert is reducing and repealing
taxes while Sir Henry is laying them on? Will not the Minister feel that there is a game
of foot and loose going on? That his policy is being thwarted?'

collect, being only known as samples of the white men who have conquered India & whose intercourse with them is shown by acts of benevolence & friendship.

The tribes are governed in the patriarchal system, which is sufficient for the management of each tribe within itself, but there is no authority over various tribes, when feuds occur, of arbitrating in their quarrels & preventing bloody conflicts which are very frequent. This want of an arbitration whose impartiality is to be above all suspicion is very generally felt, & our agent has in some instances successfully interfered. The natural instinct of the people teaches them this truth, that by such means life & property & the blessings of peace have been brought within their reach & that the B. offr. is the agent who, as the dispenser of good & the adviser agt. evil, can mediate between them as a disinterested friend. We have no object in endeavouring to bring them under our govt.—they are too poor to pay tribute— & the satisfaction of extinguishing these unholy rites is unalloyed by any selfish consideration.

The no. of victims is estimated to be about 1500 each year. One district has consented to give up this horrid practice, & the adjacent tribes have been called in to bear witness that the crops are as good as when those cruelties were committed. I should have recourse to a few bags of guano! How[eve]r, to shorten this sketch of what we are attempting to perform, I will merely add that I am sanguine of success, although the extirpation of an ancient usage must of course be slow but, I trust, sure, as it will proceed on the mild & voluntary system of convincing their reason, & that we who take all this trouble are only activated by humane objects.

The Hindoos are a little angry with me at present for the Liberty of Conscience Bill.[167] I never felt in my life so powerfully in the right. It is a step in the right direction, & in 2 months these gentle submissive people will have forgiven me. No Hindoo who becomes a Christian will forfeit his property. The educated classes are already deistic, & this act will do more eventually for Christianity than all the missionary societies. Ld. A[uckland] did not dare to make the attempt, for, notwithstanding the desperate audacity of the Affghan War, he was a timid politician. Ld. E. has a strong feeling that conversion is dangerous & that the black race had better be left to a religion which makes them safe & not unhappy subjects of a foreign power.

I feel that we are bound, as the instruments of Providence, to do them all the good we can, by education, civilization, & a gradual

---

[167] The Lex Loci Act, presented to the G.G.'s council in July 1845, proposed that the inheritance rights of those converting from one faith to another within the British presidencies would not be adversely affected.

participation of the benefits which our Western habits & moral observances can impart. India never can be colonized by Europeans. In this climate an Englishman makes his fortune & retires; his posterity degenerate in mind & in body. By superior energy & good fortune we have established a govt. which for centuries to come will require British management &, if the army remains faithful, there is very little prospect of our power being diminished. But I never can as a Christian subscribe to the ungenerous principle that the mass of this people are to be kept in ignorance in order to perpetuate our power. We must do what our religion teaches us is right & leave the rest to the wisdom of God but not by proselytism & zealous interferences, more especially on the part of govt. & its official agents. Toleration is our profession in matters of religion &, by this truly *Protestant* principle of giving to every man liberty of conscience, I feel that I have incurred a moderate risk in the certainty of obtaining eventually a great end. My only merit is in venturing to pass the Rubicon.

Ld. A. had frequently been pressed to pass the Education Resolution. He was alarmed & wished to gain time. Talk to my friend Dwarganath Tagore—there are hundreds of kindred minds to his. We can't afford European agency to govern this mighty empire. We must have recourse to native assistance &, by proclaiming that the best scholars & best men shall be preferred to govt. offices, we not only stimulate the rising generation to become able & worthy members of the community but we obtain by honorable means & for purest purposes the best instruments that can be found.

I am in stronger health than last year. The weather has been very hot, & I really have scarcely felt it I am so entirely engrossed by business. I am quite thin, my flesh as hard as a board, whilst I ride at a brisk trot for an hour every evening. Charles looks pale &, I think, feels the climate. Arthur is also pale but in good health. In Oct. we shall escape to a colder region.

In the Punjab, affairs are as usual full of disorder & intrigues of conflicting factions & I fear not likely to improve. In Napaul the king has busily murdered his minister,[168] but these are events of quite frequent occurrence that they pass almost unheeded. In the Bombay presidency our S[outh] Mahratta insurrection is at an end.

In Scinde everything is quiet, but I can't say that the *profit* of that conquest is likely to be realized. I rather expect that you have had a recall discussion. Macaulay was bursting for distinction.[169]

Love to Sarah & the baby.

---

[168] Matabar Singh was murdered by his own aspiring nephew, Jung Bahadur Rana. Queen Rajya was a party to the act for, by feigning illness, she tricked Matabar into coming unprotected to her palace where he was killed.

[169] Macaulay, an old political adversary of Ellenborough, had been a frequent critic

35. [*To Emily.*] Barrackpore. 8 June!!! [*1845*]. The anniversary of our separation

I recd. your letter & Fanny's yesterday. I was disquieted & unsettled by so unexpected a communication & flew to business till I came out here, & have now just returned from church more tranquil in judgement. My first anxiety is to relieve you from suspense by a general acquiescence that the proposal is one which, having already recd. your approbation, will be favorably listened to by me. I would fain view this proposal like that event of last year that brought me here as the precursor of future happiness by a present sacrifice. Every rational parent knows that this sacrifice is in the order of nature & must be made. That of last year was required by public duty & that sacrifice has had its rewards. You are, thank God, in better health, & I am conscious of having done my duty & what was right. The year which has revolved this day & been swallowed up in the waves of eternity is a great relief, reassuring me that under Divine Protection we shall have a happy reunion. Reverse this picture &, whenever you are low in spirits, your high sense of duty will feel that our unselfish decision was the most proper & honourable course. To resign my child to a protector only known to me by yr. appreciation of his character & his own straightforward manner of stating his own case is very painful, & it was the apprehension of such an occurrence that weighed heavily upon me when I had to decide on our separation, but this is an unavoidable misfortune & I can, on this as on everything else, only trust to your discrimination & maternal sagacity. I must therefore leave the decision *in your hands, approving of the course you may take*.

The mail does not go out till the 12th but, having relieved my mind from some of the anxiety which your letters had caused, I shall defer writing to you till later on Indian & home affairs.

36. [*To Walter.*] Barrackpore. 9th June 1845

For the last 3 days I have been greatly disquieted by letters from yr. mother, by which it appears that a Captain [*Arthur Thurlow*] Cuninghame [*sic*] has proposed to Fanny & that your mother has conditionally accepted the proposal. I presume before you receive my

---

of his Indian policies in Parliament and undoubtedly enjoyed his dismissal. However, despite the fears of Peel and Hardinge, Macaulay ultimately decided not to pursue the issue of Ellenborough's recall, presumably because Russell and Auckland on the one hand and the Court of Directors on the other decided not to press the matter.

letter she will have written to you. I send you his letter to me, which is straightforward & sensible.

The son of Sir David Cuninghame [*sic*] & the grandson of Ld. Thurlow[170] is connection good enough for any family. His present means are £9000 & his commission—with future sums *settled* of £10,000 on the death of Mrs Genl. Brown[171] (Ld. T's daughter) & £5000 on the death of his father. Of this sum of £24,000, the odd 4,000 wd. be required for the purchase of his com[*mi*]s[*sion*]. He can therefore settle £20,000 &, with Fanny's £10,000, the settlement wd. be £30,000. In reply to yr. mother, I have said I shall give £350 a yr. as the interest but I shall make it £400—& this, with £500 his income, will be £900 a yr. In a vicarage living quietly all the year round this would be sufficient—but a milty. offr. is unavoidably exposed to sudden orders which involve expense, & their present income is certainly very scanty. I have also told yr. mother that I shall throw in the first year's interest as an aid—provided the affair proceeds.

His character, I have no doubt, deserves the praise which yr. mother bestows. He is a nephew of Lady Saltoun's[172] & served on Saltoun's staff in China. He will shortly get his majority &, if he is an honourable & amiable man, I am quite ready to admit that I have no right to be too fastidious in giving my consent to the proposal. Still, my dear Walter, it is a most powerful tryal to resign your child to a man whom you have never seen. This was one of my first objections stated to Peel when the Indian offer was made—that my children were just stepping into life & required my advice & protection more than at any former period. It is quite out of the question that I, who am to be absent still 3 years, can decline proposals because I have not reconnoitered my son-in-law. In this state of things, I have written at great length to your dear mother, not, I hope, adding to her responsibility but giving her all the advice & caution in my power.

If he is invited to return, he must either go to London or send instructions ample enough to enable his sol[*icito*]r in conjunction with mine to draw up the settlements by which his £20,000 & Fanny's £10,000 can be secured by the trustees to the marriage settlement. I propose you & Alick Wood[173] to be the trustees—the settlement

[170] Arthur was David Cunynghame's third son by his marriage to one of 1st Baron Thurlow's (1731–1806) three illegitimate daughters by a Mrs Hervey.

[171] Mrs Brown, an aunt of Arthur, was another of Thurlow's illegitimate daughters. She was married to Gen. Samuel Brown who at one time was an assistant secretary to the commander in chief.

[172] Lady Saltoun was Catherine, yet another of Thurlow's daughters and therefore also an aunt of Arthur Cunynghame. Her husband was Alexander George Fraser, 16th Baron Saltoun (1785–1853), then the C. in C. of the English forces in Canton.

[173] Charles Alexander (Alick or Alex) Wood (1810–80) was an elder brother of

appears to me to be simple enough—that £5000 of the £9000 now in
his possession & the future £10,000 & £5000 & Fanny's £10,000
should be settled on them or the survivor for his or her life & on their
child or children after them in such proportions as the parents by will
may devise, with power to the trustees to advance out of the settled
money sums required for the purchase of com[*mi*]s[*sions*] for a son etc.
If there should be no children, then the survivors to have the income
of the settled money for his or her life, each by will on the death of
the survivor bequeathing their respective shares as they may deem
proper &, in case of no will, to return to their respective families.

Sir David C. lives, I understand, at *Bangor*. Is it quite sure that he
can leave £5000 to his son? That he is entitled to receive this sum I
have no doubt, but it will be necessary to look to this point. I have
no doubt that the £10,000 of Mrs Genl. Brown's, living, I believe,
near Bromley, will be forthcoming. Genl. Brown must be abt. 70—a
clever, gentlemanlike man of the world who, I think Mr Wells told
me, had built an Elizabethan room to his household property at
Bromley, which is the reversion probably alluded [*to*] & is worth little
or nothing as he probably has to pay an annual rent.

I have told yr. mother I insist on the settlement as advantageous
to both their interests. In these days of rail-way & other speculations,
clever but poor men are tempted to improve their fortunes by those
means which prosper with the few & ruin the larger proportion of the
gamblers. The poorer they are, the greater the necessity of securing
this £30,000. I can anticipate no objection on his part, meeting the
case of the purchase of commissions in the mode I have proposed.

Lord Saltoun is a straightforward honorable man, who will, if you
go to him, give you every particular of this young man & would scorn
to gloss over any doubtful points requiring explanation.

Mr Wells knows Genl. S. Brown & I am personally acquainted
with him. He was Peel's second in his first quarrel with O'Connell in
Dublin, where Peel went with Brown to Boulogne. O'Connell was
purposely arrested, & he *then* registered his vow in heaven not to fight
a duel, (a *year subsequent* to his having killed D'Esterre), not from
remorse & praiseworthy courage to obey God rather than man, but
that it was convenient to assume this privilege after the young secry.
had resented some language of O'C. which forced the latter to challenge Peel.[174]

Robert Wood. While in India, Hardinge often turned to him for assistance in attending
to his personal affairs in England.

[174] D'Esterre, a member of the Guild of Merchants in Dublin, was killed in a duel
with O'Connell in Feb. 1815, when Peel was the chief secretary of Ireland. In Sept. of
the same year, after a public exchange of insults, Peel, using his friend Samuel Brown
as a go-between, invited the Irish leader to a duel. The challenge was accepted

Cap. C.'s connections must, I am convinced, agree with me in the propriety of making this settlement, & I have desired your mother to have a perfect understanding with him on this point before the affair proceeds any further.

With regard to my £10,000 for Fanny, Alick Wood will be able to settle this matter satisfactorily. The £6000 in yr. hands & £8000 in the 4 pr. cts. at Calcutta, exclusive of £4500 st. on mortgage in Ireland, make this arrangement easy. The mortgage need not be touched; it is yr. mother's fortune. If you guarantee the £10,000 I paying the interest, that is all that can be required, & in 2 or 3 months I will transfer to Cox £4000 from Calcutta to yr. order, making with the £6000 the sum reqd.

I should therefore prefer this course to any other. In the event of Harden[175] being purchased, Charles has £3000 & at the end of the year will have £4500, & I have promised to lend him the residue, which I shall do without interest in order to make him take an interest in his own affairs. I calculate that I can fairly lay by £1000 a month— giving more dinners than either of my predecessors & *better* wine; & by next Janry. or Febry. I shall be able to give to Arthur & to Emily, including our marriage settled money, £10,000 each—according to the intentions of my will which you read in London. Charles will have S. Park & any savings I may make during my residence here, after his parents' decease—assume £10,000 for 1846—& his own stock of £3000 a year. He may calculate on my savings & his own at £13,000 or £14,000 a yr., but in this climate & at my age I don't presumptuously calculate on these possible results. My first object is to be just & impartial to all my younger children, & that object is near its attainment, giving to the eldest son the preference which our wise laws of primogeniture permit, but not starving the rest from a mistaken ambition. Having a professional income which dies with me, I can afford to give my children their portion without waiting for my death, & it is my greatest satisfaction, next to the successful performance of my duty, that they should benefit by my toil & be aware that their welfare in a pecuniary sense has never been sacrificed for any selfish consideration. I confess when I look back for the last quarter of a century & recollect that I have had a seat in Parlt. & its position to maintain, I wonder with some admixture of pride that I have been able to keep my head above water.

I have hastily & perhaps imperfectly given you my sentiments &

but Mrs O'Connell, fearing for her husband's life, had him arrested. The two men subsequently agreed to a bout in France, but while Peel and Brown crossed the English Channel the English government prevented O'Connell's departure from London by putting him in jail. In 1825, O'Connell ended the dispute by apologizing to Peel.

[175] A farmhouse near South Park across Grove Road.

wishes on this matter, which worries me more perhaps than it ought. It is my inevitable fate to be separated from you all for the next 3 years if I live, & I am aware in these matters that I must be harassed by the perplexity of having to give my consent blind-folded, placing my whole trust in the maternal anxiety & discrimination of yr. dear mother. On all these points on which I have touched, I need not suggest that they are strictly confidential to you & to Sarah. I shall write again when I have got calm on this affair.

10th June

I leave it to you if the affair goes on to employ Wm. Woodgate or Parkinson. I should prefer the former. I don't write to Alick Wood in the uncertainty of the result. I know I can rely on his friendship.

If Cap. C. should come to London, take a judicious opportunity of letting him know that I profess to have no interest at the Horse Gds. or with the minister & that here I am so powerless except in E.I.C. patronage towards those in their service that I cannot do anything for my son Arthur. I have no vacancy on my own staff, that the Punjab policy is pacific. In short, I wish it to be understood, in discouragement of a common error that persons in my position have gt. powers of patronage. I have none & I hate asking a favor of a minister dunned to death by his parliamentary supporters for any place which falls vacant.

I certainly leave it to you & Alick Wood to relax or tighten the marriage settlements. I can only specify the principle—the details I cannot regulate at this distance. In short, my dr. Walter, I cannot write happily to you on this subject. Yr. mother is confident &, as I look to character, honorable sentiments, & good temper, & she has had an opportunity of observing Cap. C. on all these points, I can only rely on her acuteness. To decline when she approves & our child thinks her happiness concerned would not be a justifiable course. It is *one* of the penalties of the greatness thrust upon me. I hope it will not be repeated in Emily's case before my time is at an end here. But, having taken every precaution which prudence dictates, I must now endeavour to throw it off my mind & talk to you on other matters.

Peel is certainly in great danger, but the mass of the Tory aristocracy adhere to him by their sons & representatives, &, if there is a breakup, it looks very much like a coalition with the best of the Whig party. But my own opinion is that he will go through the session, take his votes next year, & dissolve. If by any rough steps our Conservative party turn him out this session, I fear the present generation will never see a Conservative govt. in power. The Reform Bill will be felt by an onward march of liberalism, & Peel at near 60 yrs. of age will decline to head a Conservative opposition. If he next year dissolves, he will lose many of his agricultural supporters & the result will be very doubtful, but the mass of the Conservative party will adhere to him. Public men are not insensible to praise, & the bitterness with which he is assailed on all sides must make his a most painful position. I am confident he acts from the most praiseworthy & highminded motives.[176]

Here we are very quiet except as usual in the Punjab, & the cholera is at Lahore & in several towns, committing great havoc. The factions are pursuing their intrigues, hoping this pestilence will visit our canton[men]ts. I have written to desire that the troops may be moved in such an event &, as the rains will have set in, I have strong hopes that we shall escape this scourge.

Ld. Ripon writes in eulogy of our *Goa* instructions, which differed from the line taken by Sir G. Arthur, &, in strict *confidence*, I have been gratified by a very amiable note from H.M. in her own handwriting, stating that my letters give her much interest & information, that my conduct has her entire approval, & that she is glad to hear my health is so good.

I go on very cordially with all my colleagues, secretaries & public functionaries, &, in some little unavoidable skirmishes with the 2 subordinate govrs. of Madras & Bombay, the home authorities have very decidedly supported me.

Charles complains of his appetite not being good. Arthur is quite well but idle, & I am certainly stronger & in better training for the race that I have to run than I was last year.

Love to dr. Sarah & my granddaughter.

---

[176] Hardinge's concern was caused by the sharp opposition to Peel's proposal to extend the grant to, and to endow, Maynooth College, the Roman Catholic seminary near Dublin. Peel told Hardinge on 4 May: 'When we have ... laid the foundations for a better state of things in Ireland, for detaching from treasonable agitation the great mass of Roman Catholic intelligence & wealth, we shall have fulfilled our mission; and, so far as I am concerned, right glad shall I be to be either compelled or permitted to retire from incessant toil, which is too much for human strength.' Piqued by the attitude of 'the old high Tories,' Hardinge on June 12 responded to Peel: 'They surely ought to see that a Conservative Party after the Reform Bill can only govern on Peel principles, & if they by their faction & folly lose the only man who has [the] wisdom & capacity to govern the country, the present generation will never see a Tory Party in power.' Unknown to Hardinge at the time of his reply, the Maynooth Bill had already been passed by the Commons, thanks to a momentary union of the moderate Tories, Whigs, and the Irish members. Pleased with his victory, Peel wrote to Hardinge on May 27 that 'we cannot by mere force—by mere appeals to selfish Protestant Ascendancy principles—govern Ireland in a manner in which a civilized country ought to be governed.' However, the pragmatic prime minister added: 'We have reduced protection to agriculture, and tried to lay the foundation of peace in Ireland; and these are offences for which nothing can atone' (Peel Papers, Add. MS 40474; Gash, pp. 249–50).

37. [*To Sarah. Calcutta.*] 12th [*June 1845*]

The mail is about to close. I have been up since 1/2 p[*as*]t 4 at work, but I cannot resist thanking you for your note of the 17th April.

My letter to Walter will explain all the worry I am in, & I shall be glad when the mail is gone to have no opportunity of saying more abt. it.

I think Walter has acted quite right & I entirely concur in his wish that the R.C. priest-hood were paid in Ireland, & not out of the Protestant tithes. That principle would lead us to invite attack upon the Protestant church on every favourable occasion. In every other respect I agree with him.

The [*Tory*] party is very much shivered but it will hold on through the session. Here my colleagues are amiable, cordial, & anxious to prove their concurrence. Our differences scarcely ever occur & are very trifling, but I now work harder than I did last year. I have more confidence in myself & by writing the most important dispatches myself, which have been supported at home, I have, I believe, their confidence. My head is free from giddiness & I get through quantities of work by the old W[*ar*] O[*ffice*] system of making the secretaries each transmit his business direct with me.

Charles takes more interest in Indian affairs than he did & has time to himself to read. Arthur is very sluggish but the poor boy is up four times a week a little after 4 to attend drills, from 7 till 9 at mathematics, & then sleeps from 10 till 1. He is growing, is improving daily, & has a ready repartee if attacked. I am very glad to have him under my eye. I survey him at all hours when the dear boy is very unconscious, &, what I was not aware of before, he is not only *neatly*, but *beautifully* formed—as straight as an arrow—&, I agree with the ladies, a charming foot. I would wish to be cheerful but I am ill-at-ease & therefore, d[*ea*]r, I will close my note with love to the dear little baby whom I am prepared to delight in as my eldest grand-child.

38. [*To Emily.*] Calcutta. July 2nd, 1845

Both the boys are well. Poor George Hardinge has been laid up 10 days with a fever & is a good deal reduced. I am so grateful my dear sons are not doomed to an Indian life! Arthur is not thinner but his rosy cheeks are gone. He is to accompany me today in my ride as aide-de-camp for the first time. He has enormous spurs & looks very smart. I am happy to say he has latterly applied better to his mathematics & will shortly pass his company's drill ex[*aminatio*]n. Charles [*is*] a l'ordinaire very steady & quite well. Bob Wood [*is*] much better than last year, & I manage to get through this steam bath of a climate, deluges of rain & a fiery sun very well. My head is clear & I have, I think, by responsibility & practice become a better man of business. If I can go on for 3 *years*, what delight & honourable pride in ending our days together at dear South Park! Charles keeps my accounts which I overlook once a month.

I have proposed to my council that I should go up the country next Octr. or perhaps the end of Septr. They unanimously & cordially concur. I have not had one difference in 11 months. Once in the cold weather of the N.W. Provinces we shall be in camp for 5 months moving from place to place & in the hot weather retiring to Simla. I shall also have less to do. My business will be very much confined to political & military matters. Sir H. Gough is somewhat jealous of his authority, but when we get together I hope we shall go on smoothly. *Having all the power, my maxim & practice is to be moderate* in the use of it. The only piece of extravagance I have committed was to buy 4 guns for my boys & myself, as we intend to sport from our elephants when we are leading our vagabond life. I believe I shall have 150 elephants to carry my camp equipage. The boys are delighted at the prospect of a change & both frequently exclaim, 'How fortunate my mother did not come out. She never could have endured Calcutta.' However, don't abuse India as coming from me. I never do. It mortifies those who are obliged to remain here for 30 or 40 years.

Things in the Pu[n]jab are as uncertain as ever. Cholera has taken off some thousand of the Sikhs & has reached one cantonment on the Sutlege. Here it has, we hope, almost cleared, & we have not had a doz. deaths.

I had a long letter from Peel, very affecte., hoping he may be permitted or compelled to retire, for that the work is more than human strength can support. I think he will be obliged to remain at the helm, altho' his desire is an honorable opportunity of escape, & then these Conservative idiots will have 10 long years of Whig rule as the result of their folly.

Walter has been very steady but I suppose Hull is out of the question after his Maynooth vote, & it is as well that it should be so. It is a most difficult & expensive seat.

I had a very friendly letter from the Duke of Northum[*berlan*]d[177] the other day.

I never will return to the H. of Commons again. *J'ai fait mes preuves* & I shall be grateful to sink quietly into repose with the joyful hope of a blessed eternity. I only think of you all & of the best means of making the remnant of my life useful to my family by the combined influence of a good reputation & a surplus income. Still, I am determined to do credit to the office I hold. I gave on the [*?18*] June a

---

[177] Hugh Percy (1785–1847), 3rd Duke of Northumberland.

dinner to 112 in the Marble Hall. I spoke, of course, of the Duke & of Blucher & the Indian Army. I am seldom satisfied with these efforts but I think I succeeded better than usual &, as our senior member failed in his speech, I had the repute of speaking more clearly & to the point, having had about a dozen speeches to make in the course of the year at colleges & public meetings. I stimulate Arthur by showing him what can be done by perseverance without talent.

I still hope we shall find poor Mr Wells alive, enjoying his garden & a happy old age.[178] Now that one year is over, I feel more courage from the experience of the past to encounter the future &, when *two* are over, still greater vigor to hold on for the remainder. If you, dear wife, on yr. part will be of good cheer & encourage me in this pilgrimage, I have confidence in the mercy of God that we shall be happily reunited.

Love to the dear girls.

39. [*To Walter.*] Calcutta. July 2nd, 1845

Again the mail goes out before yr.'s comes in so that I can answer nothing. Peel seems to me to want an honorable opportunity of retiring into private life. He says truly the labour of office is more than any human strength can bear. I, who have known him in Cabinet where reason & not display is the object aimed it, can fairly state the immeasurable space at which he outdistances all his political associates. I hope he will, for the sake of the country, remain in power; if our Conservative idiots turn him out, the disgrace is theirs & the gain his. But my own opinion is, he will weather the storm.

Here we are quiet & prosperous, always excepting the Punjab. There the mortality [*from cholera*] has been frightful—500 & 600 dying at Lahore every day. The virulence is now subsiding. It has not appeared on our side of the Sutlege in more than a dozen cases & few deaths, & the rains will stop its progress.

In the Punjab, affairs are as unsettled as ever. There are many dissensions & differences in the army but, through the punchayet system of delegates, the army as a body are as ambitious & supreme as before.

Prince Peshora S., an unacknowledged son of old Ranjeet, not having a drop of his blood in his veins, has again been in arms in support of his claims to the throne. For some time he was supplied by the army and a certain portion of the chiefs but the troops on receiving a [*rest mutilated and incomprehensible*].

---

[178] Emily commented: 'That hope alas! was disappointed.' Wells died before Hardinge's return.

40. [*To Emily.*] Calcutta. July 3rd, 1845

The Precursor with yr. dr. letters will be here at 2, the letters delivered at 6, & this will go out by express at 3 o'cl. How provoking that I cannot answer yr. letters.

I feel confident that once in the upper provinces it will be my duty to remain there for 2 years; that is, for [*18*]46 and [*18*]47, returning to Calcutta early in 1848. I shall be able to be of more use on the frontier than elsewhere, & our boys will have seen all Hindostan under the most favorable circumstances whilst the climate will be nearly as good as our own.

I rather expect a letter from the Duke. Ld. Ripon, in his last letter as to the future management of Scinde, says the Duke is of opinion we had better leave the decision to you. I hope you have congratulated him on a grandson. I have done so & written to thank him for allowing Arthur to be my a.d. camp.

I rather hope my confidential reports to Ld. Ripon, to Peel, & the Queen have increased the opinion my antecolleagues entertained of me. I seldom spoke in the Cabinet except on military points &, as my views have during the last year been proved sound as to the course of policy to be pursued, I feel the satisfaction of encouragement & of being equal to my work, & that which I have before me, being more mixed up with military details, gives me no anxiety.

I am very temperate & regular & for the last fortnight have been less worked than usual. When I go up the country I hope to have time to read. Now I can hardly spare time to read a paper.

If Peel goes out of office, I must send the prettiest shawl I can get to Eliza Peel through you. He has been a most constant friend to us & I have a strong affection & respect for so good & great a man. He has been shamefully treated & I wish I were by his side to say so.

Graham has written in very affecte. terms also, & I am flattered that my former colleagues have not forgotten me. Thus, d[*eare*]st, I go on trying to reconcile myself to yr. absence but always feeling a void that nothing but reposing my confidential thoughts in yr. faithful breast can fill up. Don't let us regret the separation, but I should conceal my real longing for yr. society if I did not say how deeply I feel the want of intermixing my thoughts with yours. God bless & protect you.

41. [*To Walter.*] Calcutta. July 10th, 1845

I have very little to write, except to acknowledge your & Sarah's letters & also the printed letter to the clergyman of Hull, which I consider sound in doctrine, logic & good sense, & very well written. With the Hse. of Coms. & ripened years, you have made great strides in the power of embodying yr. thoughts. You give to the reader a conviction that you are in earnest & this, like the same quality in the speaking of the Hse. of Coms., is a great point to obtain.

My friend the Legislative Councillor[179] has just sent me the enclosed.[180] I can't say much, for it is an address to the youth of the colleges in Calcutta, when compared with Peel's & Stanley's discourses at Glasgow, but he is well meaning, a gt. friend of Macaulay's & now professes devoted attach[men]t to me.

Before I go up the country & relinquish the govt. of Bengal, which will devolve on the president in council here, I shall endeavour to establish 3 new colleges at gt. towns & reserve as govr. genl. the ad[ministratio]n of education questions. The encouragement given has given more of a paternal character to the govt. than it ever had before & if we could afford in our civil administration to have the assistance we require, the people would be happier. But our finances are in a low way—India is the poorest country almost in the world, our opium funds which give 3 million may disappear by the Chinese cultivation of the poppy, our army cannot be materially reduced nor the revenue raised &, in short, till the Punjab be settled, we must continue in an unsatisfactory state.

The boys are quite well & are the comfort of my life. They are at present very different, but both very sterling in worth: Charles, steadiness personified; Arthur, fond of gaiety & fun but very careless. In this region where we are thrown so much together every hour, they see how I work, examine the result, & imperceptibly will derive some improv[emen]t from experience & the training they receive.

I have sent by the ship Plantagenet two Cabul guns of brass which I bought as old metal. The wheels & carriages are packed up. They had better be put in a dry place & not be unpacked. I also send male & female specimens of the wild buffalo horns. The skull gives a proportion to the horns & I beg you to place them in the hall. A little lime & water will clean the skulls. The freight is, I believe, paid. The ship goes to the Port of London dock & Captain Dummett, a very worthy man, has instructions to send them to the Dover rail-road Penshurst station to yr. address. Any expense incurred you will pay for me. The guns were originally bought by me for Ld. E[llenborough]. I afterwards offered him a Gwalior gun & he preferred his own better, & I have therefore sent these to S. Park as Indian mementos.

Send me a plan of the rail-way by which a train is to go through Oxford.

---

[179] Charles Hay Cameron (1795–1880) came to India in 1835 and collaborated with Macaulay in law reform. He served as the legal member of the G.G.'s council from 1843 until his retirement in 1848.

[180] Not found.

Tell Burke to look after the quick hedges in the orchard & to keep them strongly fenced in from the cattle.

Love to dear Sarah. At this distance I am farsighted enough to see that you are very happy. Kiss baby for me.

42. [*To Walter.*] Barrackpore. Sunday, July 20th, 1845

I received your ever welcome letters of the 5th & 6th June yesterday &, as this is the only day in the week that I don't work at official business before church, I cannot more satisfactorily devote an hour than by writing to you & Sarah.

The morning is fresh & beautiful and the verdure here exceeds even that of our own dear isle. The view from the window foreshortens the River Hoogly, with quantities of country boats of all classes moving up & down this river.

I came here as usual to dinner yesterday & am enjoying the comparative freedom of escaping from Calcutta, having suffered a little from incessant application—& starved accordingly for 3 days—& am not quite well. I shall try [*?fasting*] once a week, for, altho' I am very temperate & regular, I found I was getting back my flesh, notwithstanding horse exercise every evening & a limitation to 6 h[*ours*] in bed. The severity of the business is a relief to the faculties, & in a word I am better & stronger bodily & mentally than last year.

I read the bill for the suppression of *Mehria* sacrifices a first time yesterday. At last we have dealt with this interesting subject energetically &, before I leave India, I hope to know that 1500 poor boys & girls, now cruelly tortured & put to death for the most horrid superstition on an average of each year, will in future years be spared. A large part of the country belongs to Madras, but we have now placed matters on the most prudent footing to secure success, &, if by God's blessing we succeed, this foul blot within 250 miles of the seat of govt. will be eradicated. But we proceed not by force. These poor savages who are the aborigines of the country believe so implicitly in the transmigration of souls into other human bodies that 6 years ago, when a small party of Khonds went to Madras, a distance of 600 miles, they begged after they had been very well treated to be *killed* to spare them the suffering of toiling their way back to their own country, being satisfied that in 9 months they would reappear as infants amongst their native kindred. With such religious creeds— death being no punishment—force is out of the question. We take doctors, European & native, make presents &, on the annual visits of the govt. agent, he will arbitrate amongst these poor people, who live by clans in villages on the patriarchal principle, which is in full force & enables the chief to govern his clan but is of no avail when feuds & quarrels arise between different clans. These quarrels lead to much bloodshed & our agent, appearing amongst them only for benevolent purposes, raising no tribute & requiring no service but justly & fairly arbitrating between them, is treated with that respect & deference which European civilization & Christian principles will always command in the East when divested of the selfish objects of ambition. In this case the whole aim & scope of the govt. measure is one of unmixed good. We don't want their territory but by persuasion & good officers & in part by serious admonition that, if they persevere in what we deem to be crimes, we may be driven to destroy their villages & cultivated grounds, we have good prospects of ultimate success. The force of this bill is directed against the low caste Hindoo in the plains adjoining the Khond Hills, who kid-knapp [sic] the children & sell them to these savages, who say 'The crime is not ours. We have bought you with a price. Let others look to it.' I would send you my Minute upon the subject, but it is long. As soon as our agent has drawn up a condensed report on these poor creatures, I will send it to you.

I have also been hard pressed upon another subject, which my dilitanti [sic] friend, the law member of council, calls the *Lex Loci*. At Calcutta, Madras, & Bombay, within certain defined limits, the supreme courts administer English law to Englishmen & to any other foreigners, Jew, Greek, Armenian, etc. (except in matters of *religion, marriage & adoption*), but administering Hindoo law to Hindoos and Musselman law to Musselmen, &, when there are quarrels between the different creeds, the religion of the defendant decides by which of the *three* laws, English, Hindoo or Mahommedan, the parties shall be tried. Now it is a curious illustration of the immutable principles of justice, in all matters of property, contracts, & rights (*irrespective of religion*), that these 3 laws are practically found to be as nearly alike that a difference on a point of law seldom arises. This probably is attributable to the fact that *we* as well as the followers of Muhomed copied the Roman law, & even the Hindoo law arrives generally at the same sound conclusion.

In the *mofussil*, that is, in the provinces,[181] there is a law administered by regulations drawn up from Blackstone, etc., which the magistrates are bound to apply to Englishmen in the provinces, & the custom is, that if a Portuguese or a Frenchman or an American is to be tried, the magistrate in this case does not follow the course of the Supreme Ct. at Calcutta & try him by English law but attempts to try him by

---

[181] During the Company period the term 'mofussil' meant the rural areas as compared to the urban centres in India.

the law of his own country. On the other hand, the Hindoo & the Muhommedan are tried invariably by their own law or that of the defendant, which in this latter respect is quite proper. Now we propose to improve the reg[*ula*]t[*io*]ns law in the provinces by a digest of English law without introducing any of its subtleties or technicalities, & to make anybody who chooses to come and live in India subject to English law, always maintaining inviolate the Hindoo & Muhommedan laws, which is the religion of our millions whom we found in the country & the former of whom we emancipated from Muhommedan law.

I have with me for this great &, as I conscientiously believe, beneficial measure the three judges of the Supreme Court, the chief justice, Sir Lawrence Peel,[182] being a very able man. I have all my council except *one*, who took leave before I came to India, but I apprehend at home I shall be met by opposition. At any rate I have done what is right; 12 years ago, the Charter Act desired that these means of improving the law should be investigated.

A law commission reported 5 years ago, a draft act was drawn up 4 yrs. ago. Then came the Cabool disasters & *now* that we have a comparative tranquillity in India, I see no sufficient reason, because my proposal may be rejected, why it should any longer be hung up. Supported by such authorities as these I have quoted, I can afford to be defeated but, after what is passing in England, I am satisfied it is the more prudent course of govt. to make voluntary improvements & not to wait till they are forced by popular clamour.

There is, however, another point in this law which will interest you very strongly. By the Hindoo law, if a Hindoo changes his religion, he forfeits his family property & even, according to some, all his acquired property. In 1832 the Ct. [*of Directors*], pressed by the reform [*?liberality*] of the day, recommended Ld. W. Bentinck to do away with such disabilities. This was done for Bengal &, as Hindoos seldom avow a change of religion, no practical inconvenience has resulted from this change. It is now proposed by me to make this law applicable to all India as well as to Bengal. Two or three petitions *only* have been presented against this part of the measure by Hindoos, none from Mahommedans.

We are for a series of years stimulating the native youths at the Hindoo College & other govt. institutions to cultivate the literature, arts & sciences of the West. We are systematically opening their minds. We have, by my Resolution of last October, offered employment to

---

[182] Educated at Rugby and Cambridge, Lawrence Peel (1799–1884) became a barrister in 1824. He served in India from 1840 to 1855 in various positions including those of advocate general and chief justice of Bengal. After returning home, he was elected a director of the East India Company in 1857. He was Robert Peel's cousin.

the most able & the most worthy. The Court desire me to attend to the enlightenment of the native mind in order to fit the native population for responsible office. This recommendation, urged upon me by the Court in full conclave when I was sworn in, was published for the same of their popularity. I therefore now call upon the Court not to place the govt. in the inconsistent position, & the pupils in the cruel position of being subjected to the loss of their property if they throw off the errors of superstition & become converts to Christianity. It is a perfectly safe course as regards its prudence as a political measure. By extending toleration & liberty of conscience throughout India at a time when it can be done with security, we provide for the day when the number of converts may render the question one of importance. This, therefore, is a point I have strenuously urged. I concur entirely in the wisdom of the Court's instructions that their public servants are to be strictly neutral in matters of religion, not attempting to make proselytes. As a native of wealth & learning has said, whose evidence I quote in my Minute, 'The Hindoo College has done more to shake to pieces the superstitions of my countrymen than all the labours of the missionaries.' The clergy agree with me that the proposed extension of toleration will be a great step in advance. Yet I am not without apprehensions that proposals so moderate will be rejected. The moderation of the whole law is in my view its greatest merit. But those who object, and Ld. E[*llenborough*] will probably be one, will urge the policy of maintaining our Indian supremacy by not interfering in these matters. My answer is, then break up the govt. colleges. Don't recommend me to enlarge the native mind & fit it for responsible office unless you have the justice to protect the youth of the country from the consequences of your measures. I have separated this point from the *Lex Loci*; the appeal to the native population by the publication of the draft act has far exceeded my expectations in proving that the measure will give no uneasiness or shake the allegiance of our Hindoos.

I have thrown these matters together in a very hasty way as the fittest conversation for the day &, as I am at the bottom of my paper & the breakfast bell has rung, I close my letter on this subject.

43. [*To Walter.*] Calcutta. July 31st, 1845

I had no letter from Woodgate other than the notes you sent me.

As Mr Pott is not in a hurry to sell the farm, be so good as to tell Mr W. that about the end of Febry. next, I will let him know *definitively* whether the farm at the price stated, £7000 including timber etc. etc., will suit me as a purchase; that I should now close by acceding to the terms but that, the option of delay being given, I prefer having the money in hand ready to pay for the purchase at the time it is made rather than, by making the purchase now, incur any debt even for so short a period. Tell him I am obliged to him for placing the question on a footing so convenient for me.

Thus much for Mr W.

I agree on the soundness of your advice regarding the acquisition of land around S. Park, but a farm, as a matter of occupation & useful example to the neighbourhood, is an addition to every place: if not suitable to the taste of the occupant, he lets it. And at all events, skirting on to the half of South Park, it is desirable to keep off other intruders which the rail-way will bring, notwithstanding the annoyance inflicted by Mr Green's new cottage.

As a question of finance, I prefer to delay for these reasons. At 60 yrs. of age, my life, harnessed by public business in this climate, must be very uncertain.

I send to Cox another £1000 this mail & I imagine, upon the whole of my acct. with Cox, having a proper balance & also the means to meet your mother's wants, that there will be £4000 in my favor. This, with your £6000, will enable the trustees to Fanny's marriage settlements to place the sum of £10,000 in such securities as they may think proper.

My next anxiety is to secure £20,000 for Emily & Arthur. There is £5000 Irish, or £4500 stg., on mortgage in Ireland. I have £8000 in the 4 pr. cts. in Calcutta. By the end of Febry., if I live, I shall probably have £8000; that is, £1000 a month. Seven thousand of this will go to purchase the farm. Throwing in Blowers Hill to the new purchase, they will together be worth abt. £7000, thus making up £20,000 by the time that I am required to make up my mind to that purchase. If I live 8 m[onths] beyond the month of Febry., then, after giving each of the younger children £10,000, Charles will have S.P. & the land, & any money I may possess after the decease of his parents.

These arrangements are in accordance with my will &, if I should give way before Febry., I am not hampering my executors with the purchase of a farm for which I have not paid. Having paid for the farm, any loss on the re-sale here-after is an ordinary contingency, involving some loss but no embarrassment. The Ides of March '46 being over & my children being then all provided for according to their station & my wishes, I have no anxieties for the future on family finance; & I leave the rest, as indeed the present, to the will of Providence, being determined to do honor to this office by the hos-pitality of my reception as long as I hold it, not despising but, on the contrary, attempting to practice a well-regulated economy by a few general principles which the aides-de-camp carry into effect (& I believe zealously, for I lodge every one in my house &, with wax-lights, linnen [*sic*], refreshment at all hours, my house for these young men is really a very comfortable hotel). Now with the exception of Ld. E[*llenborough*], none of our predecessors ever encumbered themselves with their staff, & I find what he told me would be the case, that I can do what I ought to & lay by £1000 a month. This puts me quite at my ease. I kill a sheep every day (we don't cut the half) & of the 70 dinner covers I give in public every week, the waste is enormous. The extent of the expense being known, & never exceeding a certain average, I am never required to interfere, having in *one hour* last year when I went over the acct., struck off nearly 500 a yr. in such items as these: £270 for truffles from France, £100 for [*?myaux*] for puddings, the finest French brandies £150 (never used but in the kitchen & the A.D.C. rooms), wax candles changed, doubling the consumption, & so on. *One hour*'s scrutiny, & a very resolute order against private dinners & suppers, & a sharp A.D.C. to carry my orders into effect have rendered the estab[*lishmen*]t one of the most punctual & the dinners the best ordered that have been seen in the Govt. H[*ou*]se, & *the Chin* keeps me so well supplied with good wine that my guests always do special honor to its quality by the quantity they swallow. Charles goes over the accts. with the A.D.C. & I never have a moment's trouble. But I know every expense, for every month is a dull copy of its predecessor.

And now, my dear Walter, you are initiated into all my domestic affairs, & from what I have now said you can form yr. own conclusions as to the progressive state of my finances from time to time. The information of course will not be a subject of conversation, but, as you are one of my executors, I have given you these details.

Take care that what is purchased for me be paid for by Cox immediately. When I die I wish to have no debts.

This closes a tedious chapter on finance & I don't intend to renew it unless absolutely necessary.

44. [*To Emily.*] Calcutta. 7th August 1845

I recd. all yr. letters from Geneva at the same time by this mail. My happiness is great to find you in good health, & the more you show yr. courage in making with resolution a temporary sacrifice which cannot be avoided, the more I am reconciled to do my duty with energy & spirit. If I heard you were sick & pining, I should have no strength for the difficulties & labours agt. which I now daily contend with cheerfulness & courage. Your sympathy with me is best shown by your conviction that your husband, in devoting his last energies to the greatest colonial empire in the world, may retire with honor, as far as the opinion of the world is worth having, & by observing a Christian & moral conduct propitiate God's blessing here & pardon for past sins hereafter.

Taking a review of the past year, I am grateful & consider this imperial pilgrimage one of the most fortunate events of my life. If I had remained at the War Office, you might at S. Park have improved in health less than at Nice. Now, being stronger, like a good soldier's wife you bear up gallantly against an inevitable ill. I was full of anxiety on yr. account & am now relieved. On my own account, I felt great anxiety in accepting so difficult a post, altho' confident that I should make no great mistake or I should not have been so dishonest as to have accepted so arduous a task. One year of my Indian administration is over to my satisfaction, & the approval of Peel & Ripon is an encourage[men]t which supports & stimulates me to overcome all impediments, exclusive of a great moral obligation & a political duty not to shed blood for schemes of aggrandizement & personal reward. I have a professional obligation to prove to all the world by my *pacific* policy that a military man may be trusted in great affairs without the risk of being influenced by a professional bias to make war when it can possibly be avoided. If I can retire with honor when my term is completed here, at an advanced period of life when men's faculties suddenly become treacherous by the mind imitating the feebleness of the body, I shall truly have reason to be grateful for my good fortune.

Another advantage resulting from this app[ointmen]t is the satisfaction of watching & guiding the steps of both my sons for 4 years after their first entrance upon their duties as men. This will have useful fruits. At South Park they must have been separate from me, & now they not only daily witness what I do but they perceive by my correspondence that forbearance, justice, a sound judgement, & great industry can remedy many deficiencies. They copy my letters, sometimes of 8 or 10 sheets, & I encourage them to talk over with me what has been done, which is useful for the enlargement of their minds & their practical appreciation of the decisions to which I come on difficult cases.

Then again, in a pecuniary sense, unless I had accepted this office, I could not have provided for my younger children so independently. Next March all will be amply provided for &, if my health lasts, Charles may hereafter keep South Park & respectively perpetuate his race in Kent. His own emoluments are £3000 a year which he can put by. This Rothschild of the family will probably be very well off, & after his accident I have much consolation in knowing that his circumstances as to fortune will be good. But above all these advantages his mind will be well regulated & he will be early initiated into public affairs & know the world. Both he & Arthur are quite well.

The latter end of Sepr. I move to the N.W. Provinces. I shall have a most tedious journey in boats on the Ganges & very monotonous. During the winter we shall live in camp where the weather is cold, dry, & bracing, & in the summer, when it is as hot as the mouth of a furnace, I shall take them to Simla.

Arthur has just written to a brother officer consenting to pay £200 more than the regulation price for his lieutenancy if he gets it within the year. He continues very popular.

I do not expect any events will occur this autumn which will force upon us a collision with the Sikhs. If we could safely & permanently settle this affair, perfect tranquillity would enable me to do many things, which a deficient revenue now renders it impossible to perform. Roads, canals, bridges, education, & the amelioration of our institutions all require money. I am going to send home a regt. of British cavalry & of British infantry, which will be a saving of £100,000 a year. But if we had a strong Sikh govt. instead of a weak queen & a drunken profligate brother as her minister, we might do many things by reducing our military establish[men]ts.

I am glad you have seen Sir G. Napier. He is the least able of the family but an honest man.[183] Sir Charles is bitterly attacked. I do all I can to keep him straight in the course. As a military man he is most able & excellent, but he will write imprudent hasty letters & affects eccentricity in his Genl. Orders. A Col. Outram is now running at him full tilt, but, with the pen as well as the sword, Napier is the abler man of the two. The family of the Napiers are much pleased with my Genl. Order &, as I like the whole brood for their talent, energy, & courage, I wish Napier always to be victorious even in his imprudent sallies upon the civil service.[184]

I will again take up my pen after breakfast.

45. [*To Walter.*] Calcutta. 7 Augt. 1845

I have received letters from yr. mother in excellent spirits. How gratified I am that she did not peril her life by persevering to come here!

[183] Sir George Thomas Napier (1784–1855) saw action in the Peninsular campaigns, and served as the governor and C. in C. of the Cape Colony from 1837 to 1843.

[184] Col. (afterwards Lt. Gen.) James Outram (1803–63), was then the resident at Satara. In 1843, as political agent at Hyderabad in Sind, he questioned the annexation of that state. His differences with Napier broke into an angry debate in the press after the appearance of W. Napier's book. Hardinge, who sympathized with C. Napier, then forbade the Company officials to air their official disagreements in the newspapers. However, the controversy did not subside, and Outram in 1846 responded to the Napiers in *The Conquest of Scinde, a commentary* (Edinburgh, 1846).

The boys are both well. Arthur has been very constant to his mathematics & has got through his reg[*imen*]tal drill. I hope he will get his l[*ieu*]t[*enan*]cy before the year is out. He is a great favorite here, but Charles in the long run will have more constant friends.

I have been writing volumes on law, both as it regards the *Lex Loci* & my own position here as govr. genl. as to his powers when separated from his council.

My council have gone with me most heartily. It is quite a pleasure to be associated with such excellent friends.

I cannot let you off in asking Dwarkanath Tagore to S. Park. He is a most benevolent, generous creature & very clever. I warned him that a man never is so popular a lion on the 2nd as on the first visit.

46. [*To Sarah.*] Calcutta. Augt. 7, 1845

First a small matter of business. I omitted in my letter to Walter to ask whether the £1000 I send home by this mail, with other monies in Cox's hands, will be sufficient with £6000 in Walter's hands to complete £10,000, to be secured by Fanny's trustees in such manner as they may think most proper. If it be not, I beg him or Cox to supply the deficiency & I will, as soon as I know what is required, send home more money. If I don't hear from Walter, I shall suppose the sum is sufficient & *not* send any more money to England for some time.

Also tell him I agree with him, that a lodge is more required than the bow window. We will therefore postpone this affair till *I return*, which is a bold phrase.

I have, at the moment of the mail's departure, been occupied by legal questions as to the powers of the G.G. when separated from his council, & have written volumes. The mail arriving 3 days before the other goes out has not enabled me, by beginning my work at 5 & closing at 6, to get through. I must therefore be very shabby in return for yr. affectionate letters which always cheer & strengthen me in this land where *I* & the celestial emperor [*of China*], my neighbour, govern about one-*half* of the tribes of which humanity consists!

I should be delighted to descend from my throne & have a game of romps with baby assisted by the Skye [*terrier*]. I have still enough hair left to be pulled.

I hope you have seen my friend Dwarganath Tagore. He is the most generous of men.

I have established 101 schools in the provinces for teaching children in their own languages, the books translated from the English, & I want to establish 3 more colleges before I leave my province of Bengal, which has nearly 50 millions of inhabitants! They are such quiet people that I have not one cavalry soldier & not a dozen field guns in the presidency!

When the mind of this people is enlarged, such is their natural capacity (as you will observe in D. Tagore) that they are equal to any student. The climate, however, breeds a love of idleness. With rice & water, fruits & vegetables, the luxury of a native in a hot climate is to be naked, to sleep, & not to work, & I fear at 25 or 30 they fall off in energy. However, we are all instruments of God, to work out His inscrutable ways, & are bound by every moral & Christian obligation to educate & improve them. Having given them knowledge & protection, a great tide of human happiness must flow in upon them in this arid enervating climate where, by a balance of Providence, the same part which weakens human toil strengthens vegetation & supplies the deficiency of labour.

We now make abt. 150,000 tons of sugar which circulates in Bengal, being abt. 122 millions of pounds of sugar. We shall shortly be able to provide all the world! As we have destroyed by our home manufactures all their [*Bengal*] muslin & cotton products, I long by every means of legislation to give them compensation in their agricultural pursuits. If we could make our cotton as fine as that of the southern states of America, we should be very independent of the Yankees![185] How[*eve*]r, I won't get into a statistical prose.

The boys are quite well. I expect Walter's selection of a daguerreotype will be most useful in taking very accurate facsimiles of every fine or curious building we see, but we have no chance of Lewis from Cairo. He is afraid to adventure so far.[186]

And now, d[*eares*]t, God bless you, & give the baby a good hearty kiss for me.

[185] By the end of the eighteenth century India began to supply Britain with about 1/5 of her total imports in cotton for use in its great manufacturing centers. These Indian imports continued to increase during the nineteenth century and ultimately began to provide some challenge to the Americans whose southern-grown cotton was fulfilling a large percentage of British needs, and there was a strong movement to improve Indian cotton by adopting American methods. In the very first months of Hardinge's administration, experiments were begun in India with American cotton seeds. By 1845 the desire among English merchants for reliance on Indian cotton was so strong that a suggestion was made to create a separate East India Cotton Company. There were expectations, too, that the proposed establishment of Indian railways would increase the export of cotton. Nonetheless, the British were unable to remove various hurdles blocking the large-scale production of quality Indian cotton until the mid-1860s. (Lewis Cecil Gray, *History of Agriculture in the Southern United States to 1860* [Gloucester, Mass., 1958], ii. 692–4; Thomas P. Martin, 'Cotton and Wheat in Anglo-American Trade and Politics, 1846–1852,' in the *Journal of Southern History* [Aug. 1935], pp. 293–6; Lionel J. Trotter, *History of India Under Queen Victoria*, 1886, i. 22; *The Times*, 22 Nov. 1845, p. 3d.)

[186] John Frederick Lewis (1805–76), painter of numerous watercolours including the *Harem* (1850) and *Door of a Café in Cairo* (1865), was a friend of the Hardinges.

47. [*To Walter.*] Calcutta. Augt. 18th, 1845

I send you another £1000 to Cox. My wine bill has been very heavy &, as I wish you to pay my expense of every description so that I may not owe a shilling in England, I have made an effort to transmit this additional sum, which will, I imagine, completely enable you to pay Fanny's portion & any other promisory obligation. Let me know how I stand in this respect.

The accts. from yr. dear mother are everything I could desire, &, as time wears away, hope increases our fortitude to bear the remainder of my exile with resignation. Three years with the work I have before me is a long period, but work, incessant work, drives care away, & when I retire to rest, having done what I conceive to be right, I seldom am disturbed by anxious thoughts.

Affairs are more unsettled in the Punjab. A drunkard of a minister is a vicious tool in the hands of those around him. Our moderation misleads him. Our forbearance is considered timidity, arising from orders received from England not to touch the Punjab. This is an error arising from various causes too tedious to enter upon. Our policy is pacific but my power of action unlimited. A few letters speaking the truth plainly will set this delusion right.

Still, the aspect of affairs is bad. With such a govt. the re-establishment of a strong Sikh govt. is almost hopeless. The army abandons its posts on the frontier & marches upon Lahore agt. the orders of the govt. The punchayets, or delegates from the ranks, govern the army & the govt. Peshower, beyond the Indus at the entrance of the Kyber Pass, has been thus deserted by the S[*ikh*] troops. Militarily speaking, it is a position of gt. importance. It has been offered by the prince Peshora Singh to Dost Muhommed & the Affghans. It would bring the Affghans to the very entrance of the Punjab, instead of being at Cabool 400 miles further off with a nonpracticable country intervening, & enable them to establish their depots & magazines at leisure. Now everything must come from Cabool. Politically speaking, the effect would almost partake of a disgrace, to allow Ackbar Khan, the conqueror of the feringees, to occupy Peshower, which Ld. Auckland refused to assist the Affghans in obtaining, a refusal which led to the Affghan War. The dismemberment of Runjeet S.'s dominions & the complete anarchy now prevailing must, I fear, lead to serious events. But forbearance shall be exhausted &, if we are compelled to move, I am determined to have an undeniable, strong & prominent case.

I have a journey of 1000 miles before me, & the heat & malaria in October renders that month the worst in the country, but I am well in the midst of a wet hot atmosphere of 84° & look forward with pleasure to the change of scene. My camp will be formed at Agra—I hope in the *garden of the Tage* [*Taj*]. When fairly on the march, I understand it will consist of 10,000 persons, including guards & camp-followers. I shall live under canvas from Novr. to the end of March &, if we can keep things together in the Punjab, retire to Simla for the summer.

If we have anything to do, I shall have one most serious difficulty & that is my relations with the comder. in chief. He is a good soldier, a good-natured man, but very jealous. As his declared successor, & being a milty. man, any interference in milty. operations will not be taken well &, from what I hear & discover from his correspondence, the arrangements for moving & handling a large body of men will give me the greatest anxiety. I cannot interfere in these details without the appearance of superseding Gough, & he has had no experience in these matters, having jumped from the command of a regt. to that of the Chinese expedition,[187] where the navy transporting his troops & his provisions gave him no practice in attending to these details. This is not my own opinion alone but is entertained very generally here, whilst Ld. Ripon will imagine that our united heads will be able to produce a safe & good combination for milty. operations. I cannot even venture to hint these difficulties &, except to you, I have been perfectly silent.

I have settled all the arrangements of the powers of the G.G. proceeding up the country without his council. They are precisely the same as Ld. E[llenborough]'s. My colleagues in council have behaved admirably. Ld. E. had some doubts as to the Charter Act on this point & referred the case for the opinion of the law offs. in England. They gave their opinion that the Act passed here giving him his powers to act alone when absent from his council was not legal. To overcome this difficulty, not of my creation but of his, we have been obliged to alter the Act in a slight degree & the Ct., entirely agreeing with me, that my powers ought to be equal to Ld. E.'s, have stretched a point or two & have in their Minutes expressed their respect for a judgement, rendering it in their opinion most expedient that I shd. have full powers. These have therefore been conferred in spite of the legal impediments arising out of the opinions of the law offs. of the Crown. We never have a difference & I am most fortunate in being associated with such excellent men.

Two years of Cabinet was an invaluable schooling.

Charles & Arthur [are] quite well. The latter has just bought two horses, one for £160 which I gave him, the other [for] £110, which I made him pay out of his staff allowances. On b[oar]d the steamer I mean to fag him in copying letters. I have found the small selections

[187] Gough was the commander of the Mysore division of the Madras army in 1841 when he was sent to command the British forces in Canton during the Opium War.

from Shakespeare & a pocket Milton which Charles had as a boy
with the passages marked by me in the margin, from which he shall
recite 100 lines a day by heart. He has an excellent memory & at
repartee is very quick. Bob Wood will, I think, get his lt. colonelcy in
his own regt. by purchase before the year is out.

Tell Burke to attend to the hedges of quick in the orchard & to
keep the fences in repair, protecting them from cattle. I also wish the
Blowers Hill boundary line along the high view to be fenced in by a
strong post & 2 or 3 rails & a hedge planted on the most approved
principles. Jones knows my wishes on this point. In dressing the line,
so as to take in the *enclaves* & prevent trampers from bivouacking on
the roadside, he should have the authority of the surveyor of roads.
It should be *aligned* on the most convenient terms for the public road,
taking from the farm what may be required for the enlargement of
the road.

Which of the yews have survived? I hope the tree behind the stone
seat is alive.

Tell Sir Alex Grant how much I am obliged to him for his constant
kindness in attending to my affairs. He has authority to pay all my
wine merchants' bills. You will be so good as to collect all the rest,
pay them, & Cox will repay you. Pay Wilkinson for the swords,
Dale for some gloves etc., & the daguerreotype. In short, as before
requested, don't leave a shilling unpaid.

In this country every expense is paid monthly &, having established
a strict system of acct., I have no trouble.

Give my love to dt. baby if Sarah can make her understand that
the kiss is from the old man of the picture.

48. [*To Emily.*] Calcutta. Augt. 18, 1845

We have just returned from church which our family party always
attend. Our boys [*are*] quite well altho' they were not in bed till past
5 on Saturday m[*ornin*]g, having been to a fancy ball, both dancing
the whole night. I don't think they are the worse for the exertion, for
I wd. not allow Arthur to be disturbed, & he slept till 4 o'cl. on
Saturday & till near 9 this morning. I give you these details to prove
to you how careful I am of them because their dearest mother is
separated from them.

We are all anxious to begin our expedition—1000 miles—& we shall
be much relieved from the monotony of Calcutta by traversing the
whole of India & seeing everything of note. I am sorry to leave my
council, for they have quite spoilt me by kindness, & when I find, by
the Minutes of council of the two other presidencies, the squabbles

that go on, I am, I confess, very fortunate in being associated with such gentlemen.

I have found the little edition of selections from Shakespeare with all the names of the children to the passages they had learned by heart & also the small Milton. Both these vols. I take up, & Arthur promises to keep them in his memory, which is good, but he is idle. His tutor has gone up the country. He has, I hope, profited by his sessions, & I willingly paid £100. Arthur has a horse for which he has just p[ai]d £160 & another [horse for] £110. I am afraid my third horse will cost £200. With small pieces of sugarcane when I dismount I have made them all very fond of me.

Upon the whole, the last 6 months has [sic] been temperate, & I work as much as ever but with less fatigue. The constancy, the ennui, not of idleness but of toil, is sometimes very trying, but I think of my position, my energies revive, & I take up the subject before me & drive it home to a settlement with the resolution of my younger days. I am not diverted from my purpose by amusements. I have not dined out for 5 months nor been to a party, & by great regularity I am able to do a great deal.

In the Punjab, affairs are not satisfactory. The persons composing the govt. are such profligate reprobates that it is in vain we can hope for improvement whilst they remain in power. We are very forebearing [sic] &, being convinced that a Sikh govt. is for the real interest of India the most desirable policy, no inducement shall induce me to draw the sword unless the provocation be such that it cannot in honor be passed over. With such an overgrown empire we want consolidation & not extension of territory. These views & sentiments are not popular with my gallant friends, who wish for honor & reputation, but a House of Commons schooling has made me very tough in resisting taunts & insinuations. If I can but retain a clear head & a sound body for 3 years, the day of my retreat will be much happier than when this great honour was thrust upon me.

I have been writing to Walter & was quite refreshed with telling him what I wished P. Burke to do with quickset hedges & fences, sending the said P. Burke a present of £5. When we are snugly talking over our adventures in the Oak Room, we shall never more like to leave it. I only hope that after Nice you will find the climate bearable. If not, I must flit with you elsewhere, but I shall so long for repose, the essence of old age, that our dear home will be a paradise without the bore of 350 servants & 70 or 80 guests to entertain every week.

I long to hear from you about dear Fanny. It is a gt. consolation to hear so high a character of Capt. Cunynghame. Walter is prepared to place £10,000 in the hands of the trustees to their marriage settle-[men]ts.

Walter is much improved in his writing. I thought his printed letters to the Hull clergyman very well expressed & the arguments pointed & sound. Sarah writes constantly & affecly. I have written a letter to the Queen. These bi-monthly mails greatly increase the public business, but I have the inestimable happiness of writing & receiving letters from you.

The mail is just going out. Lord Ripon [*is*] very gracious, giving me carte blanche.

Love to Fanny & Emily.

49. [*To Walter. Calcutta.*] 18 Augt. 1845

The mail is going out & the other from England has just been recd. Yrs. of the 4th July & Sarah's from dear S. Park have delighted me. You seem happy & well & with a mind at ease because you do your duties & are an honest man.

I cannot send home the £1000 this mail. My expenses for going up the country have been very heavy.

The govt. approves of all I have done in some late transactions, & give me *carte blanche*.

50. [*To Walter.*] Calcutta. 7th Sep. 1845

I have recd. yr. letter & Sarah's & am delighted that you intend to be present at dear Fanny's wedding. That affair has given me much anxiety. It is so difficult to consider a man yr. son-in-law whom you have never seen. It restrains an interchange of thoughts & in fact the stranger is always uppermost in my feelings.

On money affairs I believe I have been sufficiently explicit. At Christmas I shall have £10,000 for Emily in the 4 pr. cts. here, £4500 for Arthur on mortgage in Ireland &, if I live beyond June '46, he will be equally provided for. Any residue will go to Charles.

In a fortnight I embark for Allahabad in a small yacht towed by a steamer, my staff in another yacht, &, after passing through Benares, my camp will be formed at Agra somewhere abt. the 25th Oct.

The state of things in the Punjab is most precarious—the govt. so weak, profligate & unprincipled that I scarcely think the army will allow it to continue in power when the absent men return from furlough. It is a most difficult question to settle. I have determined to go up alone, that is without my council, &, being well prepared for any event, I don't allow this or any other question to make me over-anxious. I do what I think right & omit no precautions.

When I leave Calcutta, an act will be passed giving me alone all the power of the govt. in the political dept., the milty., & the internal affairs of the upper province & Scinde, leaving Bengal, Madras & Bombay in their internal & judicial affairs to be managed by the president in council *here*.

This subdivision of work is precisely the same as in Ld. E[*llen-borough*]'s time, & will suit me very well. I hope I may in camp have less work. I don't complain, but the constancy of the labour, without a day's rest, is very trying. I weigh 9 1/2 stone; in England I exceeded 11 st., but I am well, my head clear, my pulse regular, & [*I am*] able to go through the 24 h[*ours*] with 6 hours' sleep.

Charles looks thin & has not a strong digestion. Arthur [*is*] quite well. He laughs away heat & has an excellent appetite.

I am working very hard at present to clear off all current business before I start. The weather is very hot from 10 till 5 & then cools. I shall, by the time I reach Agra, be in a cooler region.

Lewis has accepted my invitation & comes by Bombay to Agra. He has added to his fatigues & difficulties by not coming at once here. I hope we shall be able to send you a book of Indian costumes by so able a hand, but he is very idle. I have nothing to say to his works. I merely receive him as a welcome guest, treating him as one of my staff.

I shall write to you again before I leave Calcutta. Send yr. letters as usual. I think you had better get rid of Jones. He will never reform. I pity his wife. He must be placed elsewhere. He is, I fear, a leader of mischief at S.P.

51. [*To Walter.*] Calcutta. Sep. 19th, 1845

I am quite satisfied if, whenever the £10,000 contingent on Mrs. B[*rown*]'s life falls in, it be secured as part of the settled money. Milty. men, from their habits of adventure, are apt to be cajoled into speculations (for instance, Sir Robert Wilson[188] lost £10,000 in the American funds), & my object was to place these mishaps out of the power of any man however prudent.

Cunynghame was quite right in securing his majority & ought to have the means at his discretion to buy his lt. colonelcy. I merely act by him as I should in Charles' & in Arthur's case, & I have no doubt I shall entirely approve of all you have done.

This is Friday & I embark in my yacht on Monday & be afloat on the Ganges for 23 or 25 days. I am relieved by the very thoughts of the change. Conceive I have never shaved by daylight. I have worked incessantly. I have never missed a council on the Fridays or Saturdays, or receiving 50 guests on the Wednesday any week since my arrival, & my mind wants a few days' rest from being kept so constantly on

---

[188] Sir Robert Thomas Wilson (1777–1849) governed Gibraltar, 1842–9.

the stretch. I leave my colleagues before I am broken down, & now the very necessity of travelling will consume time & give me repose of mind & exercise of body which I much want, altho' I say nothing about it & leave behind me as good a reputation as I deserve.

I send £1400 to Cox which he will dispose of according to yr. orders. Only beg him to take care of his balance. He is a very generous agent & he allows me to run him too close, which at a distance I cannot control.

I have to give or to receive public dinners the whole of this week & to write volumes home to our ministers, the express going out tomorrow & a variety of points to settle before I leave Calcutta on Monday. I sometimes smile at my own confidence, a sexagenarian going up to the extreme frontier in search of adventures. My colleagues think I shall not be able to avoid war. I think I shall, with Sir H. Gough & all my redcoat comrades panting for medals & glory. Thank God I am well. The only annoyance I feel is an occasional *tic* in my wounded arm, which plagues me for a day & then goes away. Charles & Arthur [*are*] quite well, both delighted to change the scene.

I have sent home the new Art[*icle*]s of War for the n[*ative*] army, the Act having been passed in which are clauses restoring *corp[ora]l punish[men]t*. There is always some risk as to the temper in which the n[*ative*] troops may receive it, but it was so clearly my duty to pass it that I have never hesitated. The whole of my council concur. The governors & their councils at the other presidencies also concur. The *three* comders. in chief concur, & Charley Napier, a radical who wrote a book agt. flogging, ardently concurs in my views; & also my *Benthamite* member of council, a Mr Cameron,[189] a f[*rien*]d of McCaulay's [*Macaulay's*], also concurs, & 99/100 of the offs. of the army. This is one of the most disinterested acts of my life. I incur much responsibility in restoring a punish[*men*]t abolished 10 yrs. ago, &, if I succeed, I shall be abused by the philanthropists as I have been accustomed to be abused on the hustings. The details have given me a gt. deal of work.

So Mahon accepts the vacant office of E. Tennant[190] at the Bd. of

[189] The D.N.B. (III. 471) characterized Cameron as 'a disciple, and ultimately perhaps the last surviving disciple, of Jeremy Bentham.' But some of Cameron's peers were uncertain about the degree of his faith in the utilitarian ideals of Jeremy Bentham. Edward Ryan, the chief justice of Bengal, felt that Cameron was 'to a certain extent a disciple of the school of Mill and Bentham.' William Macnaghten, the political secretary to Auckland, believed that Cameron 'though a Liberal is not, I am assured, half so devoted a Benthamite as Macaulay' (John Rosselli, *Lord William Bentinck* [Berkeley, 1974], p. 322). However, Eric Stokes, in *The English Utilitarians and India* (Oxford, 1959), seems to establish firmly Cameron's credentials as a genuine Benthamite.

[190] Sir James Emerson Tennant was the secretary of the Board of Control from 1841 to 1843.

Control. It is below his reputation & his pretensions in many respects, but occupation will make him happier &, as he does not vacate, he may go out if he dislikes it on tryal.

And now, dt. Walter, good-bye. I shall find a leisure moment to write to dear Sarah before the mail closes.

52. [*To Emily*] Calcutta. Sepr. 20th, 1845

We have had balls, dances & parties every day for some time taking leave, & when I dispatch the post I shall go to Barrackpore, remain Sunday, & start Monday m[*ornin*]g on my long journey, which will be tremendously hot. But I am quite equal to it & in good spirits at the prospect of a change of scene. I am glad Arthur is to leave Calcutta. He is very popular with men & women & I fear their spoiling him. I can only find time to hear him repeat 70 lines of Milton every morning. This will improve him & in camp I shall be able to do more. Charles chafed his poor leg by dancing all night at our ball, which was very brilliant & successful.[191]

Events on the frontier during the last month have not been propitious. We shall have revolutions & invitations to take their country by those who are in fear of their lives & the loss of their property. But still I cherish the hope that I shall not be forced to resort to arms. I leave my colleagues on the very best terms, & Ripon writes to me in cordial approbation. The greatest difficulty is as before in the Punjab. There are not the means of establishing a Sikh govt. We are obliged to keep a large force on the frontier, & the Sikh army becomes every month more ungovernable & mutinous. [*This*] problem I must solve in the manner the most just & politic, avoiding Ld. E[*llenborough*]'s error in Scinde, where the cause of seizing the country has not been considered as justified by the treason & aggression of the Ameers. As I conscientiously believe we are better without the Punjaub than with it, I am most anxious to avert the necessity of military opperations [*sic*]. In the meantime we are ready for any event.

I shall have leisure to read on b[*oar*]d the yacht, & I shall take Charles & Arthur with me alternately, dining on board the larger vessel with the staff. We shall anchor every night &, I fear, find the magnificent Ganges very insipid & monotonous.

The Q. seems very restless. Her absence[192] will give Peel a real

---

[191] The fancy ball hosted by Hardinge on Sept. 11 was, in the words of the *Hurkaru* (13 Sept. 1845, p. 299), his 'farewell entertainment to the community of Calcutta' before departing for the Northwest.

[192] Victoria was in Germany for most of August 1845.

holyday [*sic*] which he must so much require. My admiration for his character has much increased by his bearing during the last session.

The departure on Monday & a heavy mail give me more than usual work, But I shall soon have comparative relaxation & idleness.

Love to the dear girls.

53. [*To Sarah.*] Calcutta. Sep. 20th, 1845

I send by the next steamer a small tin box to your address with a gold ornament for your head, which I expressly desired might be made more substantial as the defect of the Dacca work consists in its being too fragile for use. I rather thought it would suit your kind of beauty, & the choice in works of ornament here is so limited that I am quite at a loss what to send.

We concluded our public entertainment here by a fancy ball, which was attended by 400, & rather more than half in costume. It was really very brilliant, the even[*in*]g cool, the party not breaking up till 4. They drink like fish—180 bottles of champagne besides other wines!

I used the privilege of an early retreat to bed & was as usual up by candle light.

I am glad we are to leave Calcutta on Arthur's acct. The women, old & young, spoil him. I hardly know how to occupy his time & make him repeat 70 lines of Milton every morn[*in*]g, & this he does with surprizing facility.

Charles danced so much he was quite lame the next day. Poor fellow. It is a gt. consolation to hear him described as the best horseman in Calcutta.

We look more warlike on the frontier, which is always the case as the season for milty. operations approaches. I hope to be very *unpopular* with the army & to keep the peace. But barbarians of the East have such an intermixture of astute civilization that it is very difficult to ascertain & take the measure of their intentions. They are keen observers but fail in judgement, & events succeed each other so rapidly in native states that our diplomacy is always very uncertain.

I shall write en route.

54. [*To Walter.*] *Sonamooky* yacht on the Ganges not very far from Mongehir [*Monghyr*]. Sep. 30, 1845

We have now been a week on b[*oar*]d & I have enjoyed the change very much. The mornings are delightfully cool till 8 or 9 o'cl. &, as I am up before daylight, I take plenty of exercise in a pure dry air— very different from the salt-petre vapour of Bengal. I most exceedingly rejoice in the change. The post has not yet overtaken me; I have no

boxes chasing me for orders & suitors pestering for interviews, but
here I am my own master to read a book or write a letter without a
breach of duty. If I were ambitious of power I am now, by an act of
the Indian legislation, with a few exceptions of no great importance—
that is, I now can exercise the whole power of the state in matters of
war & peace & foreign policy; I have the whole of the military power
& undivided control over the upper provinces, Bombay & Scinde,
leaving lower Bengal & Madras to the president & the council. But
I care very little for this accession of authority. My colleagues were
perfect gentlemen & we separated as we have lived for the last 14
months, on the very best of terms.

My time will now be devoted to this Punjab affair. I believe I am
the only European who expects to avoid hostilities this autumn. All
my council, Sir George Arthur at Bombay, Sir Chs. Napier in Scinde,
consider it hopeless. I do [*?think*], if we are insulted, we have the means
of redress in our own hands on our own side [*of*] the river without
inconvenience or risk—that is, by seizing the Lahore estates close to
Ferozpoor on our side. If the Sikhs attempt to make open war upon
us, they must be prepared for the unlimited consequences of an
unprovoked aggression. If this case should occur & a war be forced
upon us, we should make it without any reservation of existing rights.
We should appropriate all the resources of the state to pay for the
expense of our occupation. We should relieve the 5/6 of the mass of
the people from the most revolting tyranny of the 1/6, whose violence
& cruelty can form no justifiable excuse for us to allow their chiefs to
resume their estates acquired recently by gift or by conquest. The
tenants only lease to the Lahore sovereign king: 'Pay me the largest
possible rent, I giving you the right of life & death over every ryot or
peasant on the govt. estate.' I have, therefore, exposed to our govt.
the inexcusable impolicy of hiring out a British army to greedy barbarians for such purposes of tyranny & injustice & which, in its
results, wd. fail. If we interfere, let us have no half measures. Let the
advantages of B. justice in a mild administration of the country be
some compensation for the loss of national independence, if indeed
the 5/6 who are slaves can be considered as having any national
attributes.

I detest, on milty. & political principles, extending our frontier to
the Indus, differing entirely with Ld. Ellenborough, & being satisfied
that our present frontier is a more desirable arrangement. But of the
unnatural proportions of discordant elements of Sikhs, 1/6; Hindoos,
3/6; & Mahommedans, 2/6, the 2 larger proportions groan under the
milty. democracy of the minority. If that system so vigorously carried
on by Runjeet S. cannot be maintained, bad as it was on the score of
humanity, then in my judgement, in plain English, it is our duty &

our policy to consider the best mode of relieving the mass of the people & not one worthless & cruel minority of that people.

Eventually, if they cannot settle down into a quiet arrangement of their affairs, we must be compelled to interfere, but before I draw the sword I am determined to have a case which shall satisfy Europe that conciliation & forbearance had been exhausted, & in this temper & spirit I am treading my way through the mighty Ganges, hoping to be at Agra abt. the 20th Oct. where my camp is to be formed either in or close to the garden of the Tage [*Taj*].

The daguerreotype should be put in requisition, but alas! no Lewis will be of the party. His courage has failed him at the last moment. Charles at this moment is tinting a slight sketch taken of the Musselman tomb on the banks of the Ganges, of beautiful proportions, arabesque ornaments, but the whole in excellent keeping. His style is almost perfect for a gentleman because it is so rapid—3 or 4 hours suffice for a faithful record of a pretty scene.

We are all in high spirits altho' it is very broiling from the reflection of the water from 12 till 5. The mornings & evenings [*are*] cool & refreshing. We are getting the salt-petre out of our pores & are all improved in health.

I have taken a strong step without the Court's permission. I have given orders, with the concurrence of my council, for 5 additional colleges in the great towns of lower Bengal on the same system as the Hindoo College & abt. 15 district schools in connection with these colleges. At the district schools we shall have junior scholarships, sending annually the cleverest boys to the colleges where they can live on these scholarships. Here the district boys will compete with the college boys & may obtain senior scholarships, which they can enjoy for 3 years. At the end of their studies, the ablest youths having been supported by the govt., they will be employed under the govt. according to my Resolution of last Oct. Thus, in 10 gt. towns, including the colleges in Calcutta, we shall have 10 colleges & abt. 30 district schools feeding the colleges with their best pupils, all instructed on the English system & giving to every boy an excellent European education, not neglecting his own language. We make several thousands of Hindoos Englishmen in thoughts & feelings & attached to us, despising by the natural force of common sense their own superstitions. Their first step is invariably to become Deists; a few are converted to Christianity. We deprive them of no consolations which their own religion can afford unless 'ignorance be bliss,'[193] but we make them moral men & most able men of business.

I won't go on. I should write a volume.

[193] Thomas Gray, 'On A Distant Prospect of Eton College,' line 99.

55. [*To Walter.*] Camp Agra. October 21st, '45

I have been here since the 16th & last night came into camp having collected my straggling staff, & for the next 4 months I shall be under canvass [*sic*].

By your mother's last letter you were daily expected, & she was very grateful to Sarah for sparing you, & so am I, for in my absence your presence supplied the deficiency in the manner the most consolatory to my feeling, for you can scarcely imagine the annoyance of giving away your child to a man you have never seen. And yet, so brief is my sojourn in this world that I shall rejoice in each loss I sustain in the hope that those dearest to me will enjoy years of happiness when I can be no longer of any use. The selfish parental feeling ought to be repudiated on principle, & I trust the blessing of God will enable my child to be a good & happy wife, fulfilling her duties in our transitory state until we may all hope to meet in a blessed immortality. And yet, I repine more than I ought at this inevitable decision & I trust, now that it is over, I shall be more reconciled to an alliance in every other respect unexceptionable.

Charles will give you his artist-like opinion upon the Taj,[194] a large mausoleum elaborately worked in white marble, which is so unlike any European building that comparison with European architecture seems to be excluded from the consideration of its extraordinary merits. Its effect is surpassing strange, & upon the whole the lasting impression on my mind is that it is the most perfectly beautiful effort of man I ever beheld. The serene blue sky & the brilliant sun have no doubt some share in the magical effect it produces, but each time I gaze on it, the more perfect I esteem its merit.

In the [*Agra*] fort, there is also a mosque of white marble, very chaste & beautiful in its architecture, named the Pearl Mosque. Its style is so different & the proportions so much smaller, that the superiority of the Taj can admit of no doubt. The one is beautiful, the other wonderfully sublime.[195] Charles is up before the sun & has made several admirable sketches.

Only conceive my mortification! The daguerreotype, after repeated orders, was left at Allahabad & I fear will not be up till we leave Agra on the 28th. Charles is distressed at his own want of precision in not

---

[194] Charles' description of the Taj appears in a letter dated Nov. 5 to Sarah: 'It strikes one as something superhuman—as a building suddenly raised by the wand of a magician. ... At moonlight the scene is lovely. The white marble stands out in such bold relief against the dark blue sky, and the cypresses give such a sombre appearance to the tomb that the spectator can hardly believe that he is looking on the work of man' (Charles Hardinge Letters, ii).

[195] Although the mammoth Agra fort was constructed under Akbar, the Moti Masjid (Pearl Mosque), like the Taj, was built by Shah Jahan.

writing down the order for its conveyance; I have arranged with an artry. offr., the son of Phillips the portrait painter, that he shall take the views pointed out by me, instruct a man here to use it, & then send it on to over-take us.

We are going by Deeg & Bhurtpoor & at *leisure* to show the native states that passing events at Lahore make little impression upon me.

I have been up since 5 & just came in from a 3 hour ride to view the Taj on the opposite bank of the river & had the bracing satisfaction of feeling quite cold. Already I am stronger, & when I ride 12 or 14 miles every morn[in]g to breakfast, I hope to regain some of my former activity, keeping an old frame in practice without exhausting its expiring force. Exercise of the mind can improve the powers of the understanding, or at least I deceive myself in thinking so, for I not only find I can rapidly decide a question which wd. formerly have perplexed me, but that the arguments which my judgement offers to my choice are more readily & better put together than they wd. have been a year ago. Thus I come to the conclusion which stimulates my actions—that labour & pains constitute the means of success & that with a moderate capacity, energy, toil, & incessant perseverance [*I*] may produce a tolerable harvest of good & honest repute.

In this extraordinary position, where I am not only required to keep a watch over my own actions & conduct but to exercise a vigilant superintendence over the judgements & caprices of 3 or 4 other governors & their councils, composed of able men, I act on the principle of controlling them by the most plain & moderate means, at the same time endeavouring to maintain the paramount power of the govr. genl., & never allowing anything to pass un-noticed which I think wrong. I correspond privately with the governors, & it occasions vast additional labour, but it enables me to carry on the discipline of the govt. with authority & with harmony. You may imagine I have some embarrassments with an eccentric able man like Napier, the govr. of Scinde, & so on with others, but up to this hour we are on good terms & I intend to remain so.

The comdr. in chief, Sir H. Gough, is somewhat peevish & jealous. When we meet, I hope to soften down any little asperities, but this upon the whole will be my most difficult task if we *ever* cross the Punjab.

My lt. governor here[196] is an amiable & good man. He attends to his revenue & judicial functions, & I can scarcely get him to risk an

[196] James Thomason came to India at the age of 18 in 1822 as a member of the Bengal Civil Service. During his thirty-one year career in India he filled various positions, including foreign secretary to the Indian government (1842–3) and lieutenant governor of the Northwest Province (1843–53). He died on 27 Sept. 1853, the very day on which Queen Victoria approved his appointment as governor of Madras.

opinion on the state of the Punjab, on which question I have recently written every public dispatch since the events became more emergent. I can most truly say to you that I am on every decision left to my own resources where politics are in question. Hitherto my views have been cordially adopted by my colleagues. Now that I walk alone, I must be more vigilant than ever. I left my council behind contrary to the wishes of the chairs & the Court & I am told in a private letter from the chairman just recd. that he hopes I will take my council with me, for that Ld. Auckland got into this Affghanistan scrape when he left his council, & Ld. E[*llenborough*] when he annexed Scinde had also deprived himself of his advisers.

The inference is direct as to the Punjab, but before I left my colleagues I took care to record my views as to Punjab policy in an official letter, unanimously concurred in by them, & I believe I am almost the only official man in India of any authority who expects to keep clear of war this autumn. But everything in that quarter is as precarious & as bad as ever & the necessity of my presence backed by a large force for defensive measures can admit of no doubt. I sleep soundly, confident that hitherto I have acted rightly.

The new Ar[*tic*]l[*e*]s of War, restoring corporal punish[*men*]t, have been well recd. by 250,000 men who know these laws for their co-ercion are made by a handful of aliens & feringees. What a political phenomenon is our rule over such an army & country! This tryal has been a little nervous. It is, I have reason to think, successfully over &, if I die tomorrow, I shall have done the state this one good piece of service.

Charles is looking thin & is not quite well, complaining of his stomach, but this is the effect of the Calcutta atmosphere. Early hours, plenty of exercise & the finest air in the world for 5 months will, I am confident, set him completely to rights, & in the hot months we shall retire to Simla. Arthur is growing stout. I make him in camp repeat 70 lines of Milton. His admirable temper & warm heart induce him to submit to this tutelage with a good grace. Bob Wood has got his lt. col[*one*]lcy—a great step—& he is so affecly. attached to me that I rejoice in it as if it were the *true* Arthur, whose promotion cannot at present be accelerated.

Say to dearest Sarah how greatly I am indebted to her for sending you to Switzerland. Whenever she sees her excellent parents or sisters, give them my affectionate salāms.

If you have the option of buying either Brambletye[197] or Penn's Rocks,[198] I think I should incline to the former. You have everything

---

[197] A large house at Ashurst Wood, near Grimstead, Sussex.
[198] An estate near Penshurst.

to make, &, at yr. age, good taste employed in forming an English place & in rural occupations is a delightful diversity when you return from the useful but less agreeable duties of a legislator. Both have their duties, but the innocent relaxation of the country to a man of fortune is delightful leisure.

56. [*To Emily.*] Agra. Oct. 23rd, 1845

We have been here some days, having travelled with Charles 6 nights drawn by men, making our beds in the carriage, & laying by for the day to avoid the intense heat of the sun, the thermometer varying as much as 15 or 18 degrees between the morning & the evening. We are now in our tents & braced by the cold air.

I feel some remains of the Spanish campaigning which, thank God, is not likely to be called into existence this season, for affairs in the Punjab since the summary punishment of the minister, Jowahir Singh, are much more likely to go on peaceably than during his lifetime. Other changes will probably take place this autumn &, being near the scene of operations, I feel much more capable of meeting any emergency which may arise than I did at Calcutta, 1000 miles from the frontier. The ranee, or queen mother of the young prince, is at the head of affairs. Her moral conduct is most scandalous but she is considered very beautiful, & when she is in any difficulty with the troops she unveils & carries her point by abuse or tears. When her brother, the drunkard Jowahir Singh, was taken into the camp, accompanied by her in a palanquin, he had the young prince in his lap on the same elephant. To secure his personal safety, the troops made the elephant kneel down, tore the prince from his arms, & immediately dispatched the minister.[199] The poor boy saw the fray & was hurried into the same tent with his affrighted mother. She then declared she would take poison. The troops begged her pardon & gave permission that the body of her brother should be burnt according to custom, 4 of his wives consenting to be immolated on the same funeral pile. As the young victims moved to their fate, the brutal soldiery tore off their bracelets or ornaments, a very unusual brutality. The ceremony is one of the most awful of their horrid superstitions. In this state, seated on their pile, their words are supposed to be inspired, & they cursed the Sikh nation as doomed most justly for their crimes to be extinguished as a nation, & very naturally & safely predicted that the feringees would revenge their lord's murder & the outrage perpetrated upon themselves. The poor creatures met their fate with

[199] Jowahir Singh was killed on 21 Sept. The army had been dissatisfied with him almost since the inception of his ministry. The immediate cause of his death was the troops' suspicion that the minister had instigated Peshora Singh's murder earlier in Sept. Lal Singh became the minister.

the greatest courage. The late minister felt his own position to be preeminently endangered by the impossibility of paying the army & was, as a desperate remedy, anxious to quarrel with us, knowing that, as the uncle of the prince, he would be taken care of. Affairs will now drag on in a state of suspense, & I feel pretty certain that we shall be quiet in the midst of intrigues on this frontier.

I have restored corporal punishment in the native army, &, if I were to be removed tomorrow, I shall have conferred a most beneficial act in improving discipline. This has been a subject of the most anxious care, & I have the satisfaction of knowing that it has caused no discontent & is generally approved by the ablest men, military & civil, in this country.

I cannot tell you how much I admire the Taj, the mausoleum of Shah Jehan & his beautiful queen. Charles has made some admirable sketches, & Agra will have contributed very largely to his collection before we leave it on the 28th when we go round to Deeg & Bhurtpoor en route for Delhi.

We move with 100 elephants, some thousands of camel & bullocks, & the number of souls to be fed exceeds 10,000. Today I give a dinner in my tent to 50 ladies & gentlemen & tomorrow will complete my list by about 40 more.

I am, as you may suppose, very anxious to hear of Walter's arrival & that you got through the trial of parting with dear Fanny firmly. When I receive yr. next letters, I will write. At present I cannot describe the novel sensation of considering as my son a man whom I have never seen, but the more I hear of his character & amiable manners, good sense, & frankness, the more I shall appreciate his worth.

Arthur's constitution seems very strong; nothing comes amiss to him. Charles, like his father, has grown thin. He has not at present a good digestion but regular exercise in the cold weather will soon make him robust, & I think the 6 nights of dawk travelling disagreed with him. His powers as a draughtsman are great, & his discernment & taste in selecting good views very striking. He is becoming a good man of business & is very affecte. to me. I am interrupted.

My dinner in camp of 84 persons passed off well & I have, since 5, been reviewing a brigade & writing letters to the Q., Peel, & Ld. Ripon, & am quite well & fresh at the end of a hard day's work. I am again interrupted &, as the express is going out, I must reluctantly bid you adieu.

57. [*To Sarah.*] Camp Bhurt-poor. Tuesday, Novr. 4th, 1845

I remained two days longer at Agra in consequence of Charles being obliged to lay up for an attack of bile & fever. He joined me on

Saturday, quite well, at Futtypoor Secra, which is a large ruin built
of red stone by the emperor Ackbar, with a wall 80 ft. high extending
for 6 miles in circuit. The gateway[200] is the largest I ever saw—120 ft.
to the top of the arch & including the parapet, 140. There are some
beautiful windows perforated through large blocks of white marble as
fine as Brussels lace, but the style of architecture is very inferior to the
beautiful Taj & the palace in the fort, of which Charles has made
some beautiful sketches.

I got up at ½ p[as]t 3, drove in a light mule carriage for 12 miles
& rode 6, when I got into my carriage, placing the maharaja of
Bhurtpoor on my right hand, & thus, in procession surrounded by
elephants & men mounted in splendid dresses, entered the famous
fort of Bhurtpoor which for several years defied our efforts to take it
under Ld. Lake & was afterwards stormed by Ld. Combermere. We
had the generosity to restore it, or rather to give it, to another branch
of the family, then a boy of 6 yrs. old, acting as his guardians &, when
he came of age, handing over our conquest free of debt & a large
sum of ready money.[201] He is very grateful & very fat but intelligent
& governs his state wisely & carefully—better than any in India. He
escorted me to my tent & in the even[in]g attended at my durbar to
lay at my feet his presents. I remitted his nuzzer or money tribute,
being an acknowledgement of vassalage, as a compliment for the just
manner in which he rules his people.

He makes swords in his fort & is proud of their temper. I therefore
gave him one of Wilkinson's blades, which Walter sent out, to be tried
agt. any of his. He instantly sent for his sword, which out of respect
he had left with his slippers at the door of my tent, & begged me most
earnestly to accept it, being of Bhurtpoor manufacture. My secretary
told me I must not refuse & I shall therefore have to pay the price at
a valuation or to say nothing about it & leave it in the treasury of
presents.

This morning before 5 we were on our elephants, the raja coming
to my tent to escort me to the hunting ground. It was dark, but

[200] Buland Darwaza (high portal).

[201] In the aftermath of the Second Maratha War, Gen. Gerald Lake failed to occupy
the fortress of Bharatpur despite a three-month siege. However, in April of 1805 the
defendants gave up and the two sides signed a treaty by which Bharatpur accepted
British protection. In 1825 Baldeo Singh, the raja of Bharatpur, died, and the right of
his young son Balwant Singh to succeed him was challenged by the late raja's nephew,
Durjan Sal. The upstart seized Balwant Singh and took control of the state. Lord
Amherst, the G. G., sent a force to Bharatpur under Gen. Stapleton Cotton Combermere, and, after a somewhat difficult campaign, Durjan Sal was defeated and imprisoned in Jan. 1826. Balwant Singh became the raja with his mother as his guardian,
and a British resident was stationed in Bharatpur. When Hardinge visited the state,
Balwant Singh, then 25, was still the ruler.

occasional glimpses of twi-light made the scene very picturesque. I dismounted &, accompanied by a gamekeeper, was stealthily conducted to some standing corn in which some antelopes were supposed to be. At abt. 60 yds. with a single ball, being in front of the cavalcade, I brought down a very fine buck & of course recd. exaggerated compliments. Except [for] Robt. Wood, nobody killed any deer (the cheetas having failed) &, the sun getting high, we returned to camp, quite satisfied that we are better sportsmen than these Eastern rajas.

Today I return the raja's visit & dine with him, & am now galloping through my official correspondence for the English mail which will leave the camp tomorrow.

Deeg—20 miles from Bhurtpoor. 5th Novr.

Yesterday even[in]g at 1/2 p[as]t 6 when it was dark, we proceeded to visit the raja, having about 25 elephants, each carrying an officer of my staff, & the regts. in camp. The avenues to the town & the streets were lined with lamps fixed very simply on bamboos horizontally joined together & several very handsome archways erected across the streets of bamboo, giving great lightness of effect. When the raja met me on his elephant at the entrance of the upper fort in which his palace is situated, the brilliancy was equal to anything I saw at Vienna.[202]

There were seated in durbar, the B. offs. in full dress on one side & his Eastern courtiers on the other in gaudy dresses. After the ceremony of presenting presents & the dancing girls, who twirl about & sing alternatively, we adjourned to the dining room where our English ladies were placed &, after a sumptuous display of silver plate, the table groaning under the number of the dishes, we took our leave. But I observed the English manners & tastes are making great progress. In his rooms the pictures & prints are English—the fireplaces & the general distribution. The raja, altho' a Hindoo, sat at table &, I presume by inadvertance, the salted *hunch* of a bullock was placed immediately under his nose (the cow being holy & our name of reproach being that we are cow-eaters—an inexpiable offence). As we returned, we were saluted with very good fireworks & artry. salutes from the fort, responded to from my camp.

At 10 I got to bed & at 4 was again in my carriage drawn by 4 mules over very rough ground & rode a very nice Arab 8 miles to this place, the total distance being 20 miles. It is near 9 o'clock & I am

---

[202] Hardinge's impression of the town, perhaps enhanced by the dazzling illumination, provides a contrast to that of Sir William Sleeman, who was appalled by it on a visit in Jan. 1836. He wrote that Bharatpur was, 'though very populous, a mere collection of wretched hovels.' See his *Rambles and Recollections of an Indian Official* (1844; repr. 1915), p. 361.

expecting the party who have come on with me to breakfast—the boys having proceeded more leisurely & by a shorter road towards Delhi.

Like my horse, I have just been rubbed down & find myself in a Hindoo palace built in a garden, the handsomest I have seen in India & very refreshing to the eye after the sandy deserts we have just left. The garden is beautifully laid out in squares with 650 fountains or jets d'eau which are in tolerable order. Large mango trees surround an immense tank or lake which sweeps round 2/3 of the garden, reflecting the palace & the garden &, as the architectural details are very minute & their beauty consists in their minutiae, it is exactly the view which would suit the daguerreotype but alas! all our ingenuity has failed to make it succeed. The principal of the college, a chemist, & an officer of artry., who is an artist, have been labouring in vain, & for the present I have left it at Agra. I wished to have taken the most accurate perspective views of these curious buildings from the same points as those selected by Charles & then to have published them. I fear it will be of no use.

He, Charles, has just sketched two of the raja's men on horseback in their fantastic caparisons, with the dead antelope & two very beautiful & huge greyhounds of the highest breed. Nothing comes amiss to him, landscape or figures, & his rapidity of execution is really surprizing.

He had not been quite well &, as he has been thoroughly doctored & dieted for the last week, he feels himself better than he has been for the last 6 months. Arthur is quite well but very giddy & good-natured, but I fear the prodigality of a govr. genl.'s estab[lishmen]t is a dangerous education for a milty. younger son.

We march tomorrow for Goverdun [Gobardhan] &, as the mail goes out in 2 or 3 hours, I wish you, d[eares]t, good-bye, & may every blessing attend you & Walter & the dear little baby.

I anxiously await the next mail from Switzerland.

As for me, I am in perfect health with 6 hours' sleep & moderate diet. I find this life has already strengthened me. Of course I have rubs & collisions in public life but, considering the peculiarity of the position & the kind of absolute dictator which I am in these provinces, I am not surprized that able men should have lost their balance & dreamed of projects too ambitious not to be [?deemed] extravagant & ambitious.

The army in the Punjab is more disorderly than ever, but I trust I shall keep the peace this season.

58. [To Emily.] Deeg, formerly a strong fort around which about 50 years ago a Hindoo palace was built. Novr. 5, 1845

Since I wrote to you from Agra, we have been generally on the move. I left Charles for 2 or 3 days at Agra in the lt. govr.'s house because it was cooler than the tents. He rejoined us quite well on Saturday night & is better than he has been for some time. He made 1/2 a dozen beautiful sketches at Agra, one at Futtypore Secree where we halted on the Sunday, which I always do, & on Monday at 1/2 past 3 o'cl. I came on to Bhurtpore, formerly celebrated as having resisted our arms but which was taken by Ld. Combermere about 20 years ago.

The raja met me 2 miles from his town, got into my state carriage, and thus we proceeded, surrounded by a motly [sic] crew of Asiatic horsemen, elephants, etc. etc. through the town to my camp. He took his leave and returned in state at 4 o'cl. to receive presents & offer a tribute of homage, about £150, which sum I remitted, as he has at least £150,000 a year but it is the sign of vassalage, & anything which approaches him to the paramount power is highly prized. Probably he would have given me £10,000 to be released from the offer of the customary tribute.

The next morning he called for me to shoot the antelope in his preserves. We were all mounted on elephants & reached the ground a little before the sun rose. I was put in front of the battle & brought up to a cornfield in which a buck was seen staring at us at about 60 yards distance. I was fortunate enough to hit him, & he proved a very fine animal which Charles has introduced into a sketch. Bob Wood also killed an antelope & the rest of the sportsmen were unlucky. It was indifferent sport but the cool air of the morning, the novelty of the scene, & the mode of managing the chasse was interesting.

In the evening at 1/2 past 6 I returned the raja's visit in state. For a mile the road & streets were illuminated with small cups acting as lamps, & the gateways made of bamboo were also decked out with a variety of lamps. At the entrance of the fort the raja met me on his elephant superbly caparisoned. Thence to his palace lined with troops & courtiers dressed up for the occasion, with thousands of lamps. The scene was really very fine—the night being very dark, the artry. firing salutes, horses neighing, 2 men shouting their national cry till we came to the palace door. The raja seated me on the place of honor & his presents on 24 trays were displayed. One I shall look after as it looked very pretty &, if on inspection I like it, I will send it to Nice. I had given him a proved English sword of no value except its temper. He begged my acceptance of his, made by his workmen at Bhurtpore & I could not refuse. I shall therefore be obliged to purchase it at a valuation or let it remain in the tosheeana,[203] which is the office in the Foreign Department for giving & receiving presents, for no public man or his wife or relation can accept presents from natives. At 10, after some pretty fireworks, I got to bed.

[203] A corruption of the Persian word toshekhana meaning a treasury or storeroom.

I was up again this m[ornin]g at 1/2 past 3 o'cl. & came about 14 miles in a mule carriage and rode the remaining 8 on a capital Arab, getting in here at 7 o'cl. I dressed & walked about the gardens, which are beautiful with 650 *jets d'eau*, &, having been engaged in writing to Lord Ripon, now, d[eare]st, relieve my mind & comfort my heart by talking to you. Charles will have a sketch of the palace & is wonderfully improved in vigor & coloring. Tomorrow we march for Govindurr [*Gobardhan*] 9 miles off, where there are some ruins to be seen, & the following day rejoin the camp, having made these detours in light marches to gratify myself & Charles & the staff. Thus you see, I am up early, work all day & am quite well, & the climate is now becoming so delightful that we all feel greatly invigorated & can daily rejoice in the happy contrast between the bracing energy of this climate at this season & the languid feebleness of Bengal. I am going leisurely on my route & shall next write to you from Delhi.

Everything indicates that this cold season will pass over without milty. operations in the Punjab. Still, in this uncertain & extraordinary country & having barbarians to deal with, a friction may occur producing a rupture, but we are so carefully forbearing that in my opinion it can scarcely happen.

This life is very different & much more agreeable than the slavery of Calcutta. I am my own master & the deference paid is so Eastern that I am not surprized that our friend Ellenborough dreamed a little more of conquests & battles than he would otherwise have done, out of the vortex of adulation which meets a g. gl. more here than when his authority is divided as at Calcutta. The worst part of my public business is in being referred to as g. gl. to settle squabbles & controversies with other high functionaries who appeal to me. This is a bore, but it is one of the inevitable ills to which we are exposed in the risks & collisions of public life, & how can I hope that all my relations in such a responsible station can be carried on in the same smooth current by which the evenings of my life will glide away when we are gently floating down the stream of eternity together. I rejoice that by yr. brave advice I accepted the office & am grateful to God for the blessings vouchsafed under such tryals, but the day I embark to rejoin you will, next to that of meeting you, be the most welcome I can ever enjoy.

God bless & preserve you.

59. [*To Emily.*] Camp near Delhi. Novr. 19th, 1845

I have recd. yr. letters of the 30 Sepr. from Geneva, but the preceding letter, probably giving an account of the marriage, has not yet come to me. You speak of a narrow escape on board a steamer in a letter to Charles which he has not received. I trust it will have gone round to Calcutta & that we shall soon have it.

I have bought the girls some Delhi manufactures but am quite at a loss how to get them to Nice. I shall let you know what I propose next mail. I shall send you by the same conveyance another bracelet. You can keep the one you like best & give the other to dear Lady Peel.

Here we lead a very healthy life—up at 1/2 past 4, riding 10 miles to breakfast, then to work, ride slowly for 1/2 an hour in the e[venin]g, dine at 1/2 past 7, & in bed before 10. Charles is quite well & Arthur [is] getting fat. Bob Wood is in rude health. You may imagine how handsome our tents are when I dined in mine 64 persons, with a drawing room of the same size. Charles makes admirable sketches & is passionately fond of drawing. Arthur goes on with his Milton, but a camp is a bad place for study.

I have letters from Ld. Ripon still approving of what I do. I hope Ellenborough will be brought into Cabinet before the next session. I shall not fear his criticism as to my acts altho' they do not accord with his, but, now that Howick is in the Lords[204] & the Duke about to retire, it is desirable that Peel should reinforce Stanley.

What is to happen in the Punjab no wise man can say. We shall not have a rupture this season as far as I can judge. I am determined to avoid the Scinde scrape. If we are compelled to cross the Sutlege, we shall have a case that will bear the strictest scrutiny. If we can avoid that measure, I shall be much better satisfied because I believe our present frontier to be better adapted to the interests of India than the more extended line of the Indus.

Much of my time is wasted in the quarrels which the Napier & Outram controversy entail but, so far as I have gone, the Horse-guards approve of what I have written. Settling these quarrels where I must dissatisfy one of the parties is the penalty I pay for greatness.

The worst penalty is separation from you. That is not the less grievous because each day is to shorten its duration, altho' in reason I hope I shall be more reconciled when half the period is past. Thank God the boys are both well & prosperous, in good conduct of mind & heart as well as in strength of body. Having missed your letter giving an account of the marriage, I am deprived of what I most longed to hear—the happy union of my first married child. I hear, d[eare]st, you are looking remarkably well. I am much stronger than when at Calcutta & in good spirits as to the state of our affairs in this country.

60. [*To Walter.*] Camp near Delhi. Novr. 19, 1845

I have received your letter of the 4th Oct. & am rejoiced that you found your dear wife & child well. The teething time is always very

---

[204] Viscount Howick, a Whig, entered the Lords as the 3rd Earl Grey in July 1845.

trying & the knowledge of the causes relieves you from much anxiety. There is a letter of your mother's from Switzerland which is missing. However, by the last I find she was quite well & about to return to Nice.

After this winter abroad, I am anxious that she should return for Emily's sake to England. Foreign manners, notwithstanding the well-concealed insecurity of society, make an impression frequently very detrimental to young English people &, with Emily's peculiar pre-dilection for gaiety & trifling, I do not think the risk should be unnecessarily run. She is *au fond* very honest—never concealing her wayward & ungentle mood but liking the frivolous excitement of constant amusement, which English gentlemen do not pay to young girls & for which sensible women must respect them.

I understand that yr. mother draws or does not draw within the year £2000 & that my surplus is at her command. My words to Cox are to pay her £2000 a year whilst abroad, & if there is any misapprehension, which I should not think likely, Alick Wood can inform Cox of my wishes. The sum I fixed upon was *that* upon which with a young family we have lived whilst I was in Parliament &, to render it sufficient for any contingency, I desired, if she required it, that £500 might be added. If she thinks it insufficient, she knows she can have it increased but, having made a great effort to give my daughters £10,000 apiece, I do not think it desirable that her surplus income should be devoted to her married daughter, to whom on the first year of marriage I have made an advance equal to the interest on her fortune. Of course with our estab[lishmen]t separated, my means of making good my intentions for my children must depend on economical arrangements, when they do not interfere with the hospitable receptions I am bound to exercise to do honor to the station I fill as far as outward display is concerned; & in personal concerns I practice the same economy I have been accustomed to in England. Her frank exposition of her expenses shows me that her means are ample. If I thought she had any wish ungratified, I would instantly press it upon her, &, if you can find it out, I shall be rejoiced to persuade her to take it. When I return, I descend to my former station & nearly to my former income. My savings are even forestalled, & at my age in this climate I live on sufferance & am happy to give to my younger children whilst I am alive that which they cannot have augmented when I die. The testamentary arrangement I made before I left England is, I think, just & suitable & in 6 months will be accomplished. The residue after that period will belong to yr. mother for her life & afterwards to Charles.

What is to be done next year with the rail branch of Woolwich to Maidstone? Will it be carried?

Here we lead a much more pleasant & healthy life than at Calcutta—up at 1/2 p[as]t 4, ride 10 miles before breakfast, moderate work compared to Bengal, & at this moment our affairs in the Punjab promise to be peaceable for the next month, & that is something gained. Rely upon it, I will not get into the Scinde scrape. My personal repute in my own estimation will stand higher by preserving peace than by the most brilliant successes of war. The real fact is that the interest of India can best be reconciled by a strong native govt. in the Punjab &, altho' I despair of that result, I patiently shall forbear so long as forbearance is a duty.

The poor old king in his palace here keeps up all the pride & form of days gone bye [sic], & asks after his sister the Queen of England. Charles saw him in visiting the palace. His sketching talent makes progress & I think you will admire his later productions. His figures & cattle are very good & his rapidity is extraordinary.

Give my love to dear Sarah, thank her for her note, &, as my little grand-daughter will inherit your poetic talents, I send her the verses of the poet laureate in my praise.[205] He claims in that line a descent from 50 generations!

I shall send you another £1000 by the next mail. I hear a bad acct. of poor Murray's[206] health. Let me know how he is.

I hope Ellenborough will be brought back into the Cabinet before the next session. Under the advice of the Duke & Peel he will be very efficient.

61. [*To Emily*.] Camp Umballa. Decr. 3rd, 1845

During the last few days we have had reports that the ranee, the mother of the maharaja of the Punjab, in despair at the state of affairs & in fear of her own life from the ferocity of the troops (but above all anxious to save the life of her lover Lal Singh, whom she had appointed her minister), had been using all her exertions to induce the army from Lahore to move down upon our advanced stations & invade our provinces. Thus our ally & friend is endeavoring to cause the destruction of her own army in desperate expectation of saving her own life. Another competitor for power, Raja Golab Singh, is encouraging every kind of dissension adverse to the ranee's power, & the troops are, for the most part, favourable to his pretentions. I feel pretty confident they will not be so rash as to move across the river. I have not allowed a man to move from our cantonments, & in a few days I expect that the troops, being tired of camp & sighing for the

---

[205] Verses untraced.
[206] Gen. Sir George Murray, the master general of the ordnance, died in July 1846.

grog shops of Lahore (for the Sikhs are great drunkards), will move back, probably terminating their foolish enterprize by the assassination of some unpopular general.

I like this climate as well as that of Spain. The boys are in rude health, Charles better than I have seen him since he left England. We had dinner in the large tent yesterday & sat down 84. Sir Hugh Gough & the civil & military authorities formed the party. He is a fine soldier-like looking man, Lady Gough sensible & clever, & I think we shall always get on well as long as we are together.

I have been incessantly writing since 5 o'cl. yesterday m[ornin]g with a few hours' sleep, having a great variety of details on my hands in consequence of this Sikh folly which, in the way of precaution, is as troublesome as if we were at war. I have a levee in an hour, another dispatch to write as the information comes in, & I must, therefore, make the boys write if I should be interrupted, which I am at every moment. Pray tell Cunynghame how I am situated. On the 6th I shall continue my march towards Feroz-poor, the comd. in cf. remaining here, & be very glad when the suspense caused by these foolish movements is at an end.

I rather think I must send the Delhi scarfs & a few trinkets to Walter as I cannot collect them for a month, & before they reach London you will be on yr. way from Nice. I am nearly as strong as in Spain, so bracing is this air. We don't omit our gratitude to God for these blessings, but we have at last got a chaplain[207] in the camp & I shall halt every Sunday.

Mrs Somerset & her husband seem very happy.[208]

I have written to Her Majesty & to Peel & a vol. to Ld. Ripon. He supports me very cordially & I am glad Lord Mahon[209] is at the office. I have now, dearest, to write to the chairman &, if I go on writing to you, I fear I shall neglect him. I feel satisfied you will approve of the sacrifice I make, but I have really had so much to do the last 3 days that, if I had not been very strong, I must have given in.

Love to Emily. Alas! you have lost the other but I am sure from yr. discernment you have acted judiciously for her happiness & that is the main point.

---

[207] James Coley was a clergyman employed by the East India Company; for his experiences with Hardinge, see his *Journal of the Sutlej Campaign of 1845–46, and also of Lord Hardinge's Tour in the following winter* (1856).

[208] In Aug., Maj. Arthur William Fitzroy Somerset (1816–45), an A. D. C. to Hardinge, had married Emille-Louise, daughter of the Baron de Haumbache of Hesse.

[209] He was the secretary to the Board of Control from July 1845 to July 1846.

62. [*To Emily.*] Camp Moodkee. Decr. 20th, [*1845*]. 4 o'cl.

We had a sharp affair with some of the Sikh forces on the evening of the 18th inst[*ant*]. We beat them back and took 17 pieces of cannon. I placed my a. d. camp [*Arthur*] at the disposal of the commander in cf., & he praises our dear boy for his gallantry & intelligence. Thanks be to God he is not hurt.

We marched from Umballa on the 6th & on the 11th the army was ordered to move forward, as there was every indication of the Sikhs passing the frontier & overwhelming Feroz-poor. We arrived at this post on the 18th &, shortly after we got in, the enemy attempted to surprize us. We shall reach Feroz-poor tomorrow & form a junction with Sir J. Littler who has 10,000 men under his com[*man*]d.[210] There never was a juster quarrel or more unprovoked aggression. War has been forced upon us, & we must now do our duty. I wanted dear Charles to retire & keep out of fire, but he said, 'Wherever you go, sir, I will certainly attend you.' They are very fine fellows & both much beloved. I am much fatigued, but we are in excellent spirits & all in the best of health. You have too much spirit as a soldier's wife not to endure this anxiety with a confident trust in the mercy of God & the reflection that those who are dearest to you are doing their duty. I will write again after tomorrow.

63. [*To Walter.*] Camp Moodkee. Decr. 20th, 1845

I believe Charles has written to you & related our first affair with the Sikhs on the 18th. Tomorrow we march with 6 B. regts., 10 n. inf. regts., & 42 guns agt. their army opposing our junction with the forces under Genl. Littler at Feroz-poor. I am so pressed for time & so many duties to perform that I can only say you will be satisfied with the forbearance & moderation I have shown in these transactions.

I shall be up the greater part of the night, march at 4—20 miles— & engage the Sikh army midway. My dear boys are noble fellows. You may be proud of yr. brothers. I have no time for further comments. To you & to dear Sarah, the most true & affecte. feelings will never cease to warm my heart as long as it is the will of God that I should continue in this world.

64. [*To Emily.*] Camp, Feroz-poor. Christmas Day, [*1845*]

We have just said our prayers in our large tent & offered our thanksgivings to God for the victory. I send you the Notification I

---

[210] Maj. Gen. (afterwards Lt. Gen.) Sir John Hunter Littler (1783–1856) was the commander of the British forces at Ferozepur. Hardinge made contact with Littler on 21 Dec. during the re-positioning of British forces before the battle of Ferozeshah, Dec. 21–22.

wrote this morning which will give you the results of our proceedings, & you will have the joy to find yr. two noble sons quite safe, in excellent health, & beloved & admired by everybody. Arthur is universally praised, & I thank you again & again for giving me sons who inherit yr. spirit, combining great personal courage with the moral fortitude of the Christian soldier.

We have captured 91 guns, the whole of the enemy's camp defended by 60,000 men who are in full retreat across the Sutlege. These great results will enable us to be quiet & put the Lahore district on this, the British, side in order.[211] There are a dozen of forts to be taken, the greater part of which will surrender to our summons. But before I say a word more of our success, let me observe that the Indian govt. never had a more just quarrel, never was there a more unprovoked aggression by one neighbour on the territory of the other. Their army was dissatisfied & mutinous, the govt. would not pay it & consequently could not command its services &, being afraid for their personal safety, they instigated the army to such a quarrel with us in order to divert its attention from themselves. The Lahore govt., without any explanations or declaration of hostilities, crossed the river with a large army of 60,000 men & 150 guns. They invested our advanced post of Feroz-poor in which I had placed very fortunately a large force. When I heard of these proceedings at Umballa 150 miles off, I prepared our army to move up, but I never could credit that their audacity wd. go to the extent of moving their whole army across. It was expected that they would cross over with cavalry to plunder & then compel us to interfere, which we wished to avoid. We marched very rapidly from Umballa, took up the Loodiana force on our way, & after the Battle of Moodkee moved past their entrenched camp & joined with the Feroz-poor force, giving us the addition of 5000 men & 21 guns &, thus reinforced, attacked their entrenched camp, took it & 74 guns & are now here, having succeeded completely in our operations.

Sir Hugh Gough is delighted with Arthur & I shall send you extracts of his dispatches if he mentions your dear boy. Charles is equally brave & gallant & insisted on remaining with me but, on going to the attack of a battery, I besought him to go away as he prevented me doing my duty, & at last he reluctantly obeyed my command. I will not give you details of war. The loss of my staff has been great— Munro,[212] Somerset & Herries[213] killed, Wood & Hillier[214] [*wounded*].

[211] Lahore controlled a small piece of territory east of the Sutlej under the Anglo-Sikh Treaty of 1809.

[212] Capt. John Munro (1821–45) of the 10th Bengal Light Cavalry, Hardinge's interpreter.

[213] Maj. William Robert Herries (1819–45) of the 3rd Light Dragoons was the son of the former Cabinet minister, J. C. Herries.

[214] The leg of Capt. Hillier, an A. D. C. to Hardinge, was shattered.

Robert has distinguished himself & is a very fine affecte. fellow. I had
at last only my dear Arthur left by my side &, in a long disagreeable
night that we passed near the enemy, he lay almost in my arms & we
never separated but on horseback. Conceive me 36 hours on horseback, fasting nearly the whole of that time. God is merciful & in His
tryals gives me strength to perform my duty, & our cause is so just
that my conscience is clear & unspotted. I have so many important
duties to perform that I will break off, but on this day & after my
prayers the best offering I cd. make was to write, d[eare]st, to you.

65. [*To Walter.*] Camp Feroz-poor. Decr. 30th, 1845

I wrote to you 10 days ago a hurried note in the midst of the most
stirring preparations for a battle. That battle was fought the following
evening & continued the next morning. The result is the total defeat
of the Sikh army of 60,000 men, with 91 pieces of cannon captured,
the enemy having retreated beyond the Sutlege.

We moved on the 11th & by forced marches concentrated our force
on the 18th at Moodkee &, having repulsed the enemy's attack &
captured 17 guns, our next most important object was to relieve
Feroz-poor which, with 7000 men, was invested by 60,000 & 150
pieces of cannon. We left Umballa with 8000 men, picked up 5000
by the way, running some risk at Lodiana to ensure success at Feroz-
poor, & on the 21st we formed our junction with that garrison, having
written the night before to Littler to come out & meet us.

This combination was successful. We met, his force added 5000
men more to ours, & we attacked the enemy in his entrenched camp
in which he had 108 guns, & now I have the satisfaction to see 91 in
this fort.

I believe Charles will send you confidentially my letter to Lord
Ripon which is only to be read by you & Sarah; & if I have been of
the service which it is said I have, let not your affectionate zeal betray
you into any warmth of approval at the expense of this fine old veteran
the C. C., who is as brave as his sword & a perfect gentleman but not
exactly the sort of general we require in critical times.[215]

[215] Hardinge, in a forty-two-page letter to Ripon dated 27 and 28 Dec., described
the developments on the Panjab frontier from early Dec. to the battles of Mudki and
Ferozeshah and indignantly criticized Gough's military organization and leadership.
The G. G. discovered on his arrival at Ambala on 2 Dec. that 'no supplies had been
laid in on the route to Feroz-poor.' He found Gough's staff particularly inefficient and
wrote: 'It is impossible for the C. C. to preserve discipline & conduct the public duties
with regularity, with the assistance he now has.' Hardinge added that more than once
he had disagreed with Gough's viewpoint at Mudki and Ferozeshah, and in one
instance, in his capacity as the G. G., had overruled the C. in C. (Ripon Papers, Add.
MS 40874.)

The night of the 21st was the most extraordinary of my life. I bivouacked with the men, without food or covering (& our nights are bitter cold), a burning camp in our front, our brave fellows lying down under a heavy cannonade, which continued during the whole night, mixed with the wild cries of the Sikhs, our English hurrah, the tramp of men & the groans of the dying. In this state, with a handful of men who had carried the batteries the night before, I remained till morning, taking my short intervals of rest by laying [sic] down with various regts. in succession to ascertain their temper & revive their spirits. The bravest officers desponded—so different is personal from moral courage. Various proposals for a timely retreat were suggested. I declined peremptorily to listen to such weakness. The C. C. came to me & told me he felt the perilous & critical state in which we were— triumphant on the ground we had so severely contested but apparently surrounded by thousands of Sikhs whilst in the dense obscurity of the night, rendered more impenetrable by the smoke of the burning camp, we could not ascertain where the other corps were posted. My answer to all & every man was that we must fight it out—attack the enemy vigorously at daybreak, beat him or die honorably on the field. The gallant old general entirely coincided with me. During the night I occasionally called upon our brave English soldiers to punish the Sikhs when they came too close & were imprudent, & when morning broke we went at it in a true English style. Gough was on the right. I placed myself & dear little Arthur by my side in the centre, abt. 30 yds. in front of the men to prevent their firing, & we drove the enemy without a halt from one extremity of their camp to the other, capturing 30 or 40 guns as we went along, which fired at 20 paces from us & were served obstinately. The brave men drew up in an excellent line, cheered Gough & myself as [we] rode up the line, the reg[imen]tal colours lowering to me as on parade.

The mournful part is the heavy loss I have sustained in my offs. I have had 10 a. d. c. hors de combat—5 killed & 5 wounded. The fire of grape was very heavy from 100 pieces of cannon—the Sikh artry., drilled by French offs., & the men the most warlike of India.

Dear Arthur has greatly distinguished himself. The C. C. is in admiration of his intelligence & bravery. He was close to me at every moment. I think it made me more desperately resolute. Well, my dear Walter, I won't distress you & revive my own sorrow by detailing the loss of my friends, merely stating that, of those you know, Somerset & Herries are [sic] killed & died bravely. God in His mercy spared me & my 2 boys, for Charles, both at Moodkee & on the 21st, wd. not leave me until at last I told him I could not do my duty if he remained with me. They are indeed fine fellows, & I love yr. mother more dearly for giving me such a worthy race. They are both quite well. Dear Arthur melts into tears when we talk of those we have lost &, as the truly brave are always humane, I admire him more with his face flooded with grief than in the sterner look of facing death with becoming resolution.

Our movement was difficult. Every combination succeeded perfectly—no accident, no disaster, no failure at any point. We have beaten the bravest & most warlike & most disciplined enemy in Asia & given him a signal overthrow, with 15,000 men opposed to 60,000 with 100 pieces of cannon, of which we have taken 91. Compare this success with recent operations in Bombay, where 11,000 men could hardly make way agt. the Mahrattas, & I believe it will be admitted that we have gained a great victory. Our quarrel is just, the aggression most unprovoked &, altho' India has been in danger, I trust our countrymen will appreciate our exertions.

My position has been most painful. My C. C. is an honorable man, amiable, kind-hearted, & heroically brave. I had better not finish the character. The fault of any deficiency rests not with him. He does his best & never spares himself, but it is very critical work.

Keep my letter to Lord Ripon. We are quiet for the present, & I can give you no precise decision at this moment of our future movements. God in His mercy deigns to give me strength in proportion to my tryals. I am quite well—very strong—36 hours in my saddle fasting & equal to the days of Albuera when the chill of age is once well-warmed into the heat of youth, & I find all my youthful phrases to the men come glibly from my tongue &, without seeking their praise, I believe I have obtained it.

Your letter & my dispatches from the govt. have been lost, & also yr. dear mother's letters. Pray make arrangements to have Fanny's £10,000 paid *immediately*. I send to Sarah Ben's praises in an official letter to the Duke of W. from the C. C., also my Notification written on Xmas Day announcing our victory.

I am now writing to you at 3 o'cl. in the morning. I go to bed after dinner at 9, get up at this hour & write 15 hours a day when not in my saddle. I visit the hospital & comfort the maimed by showing them a govr. genl. without a hand & his son without a foot, & these practical illustrations are consolatory to our poor fellows. I am getting sweetmeats for the sepoys &, if I can, plum pudding for poor Bull, whose courage in the field or in the hospital is so superior to the bipeds of any other country in the world.

And now, dr. Walter, adieu.

66. [*To Emily.*] Camp Feroz-poor. New Year's Day, 1846. 3 o'cl. [*in the*] morning.

Many happy new years to us & our dear children round a cheerful hearth at dr. South Park when we may talk over our Indian adventures & contrast the happiness of domestic life with the unhappy strife of Asiatic wars.

My time is occupied during the day in long dispatches, General Orders, & instructions without end, & I am up every morning by 4 o'cl. This morning I was called at 1/2 past 2 o'cl. & have just closed a short letter to the Duke &, by close application till 5 this e[*venin*]g, I hope to get through my correspondence for the mail.

Yr. last letters & my official dispatches, in short the g. genl.'s bag, has [*sic*] been destroyed by robbers on the road. This is most provoking, but order & peace are now restored in our rear & it will not happen again.

I have been visiting the hospitals, taking care of our poor wounded men, & mitigating the honors of war by the most active exertions of skill in the doctors & nurses, & these duties are most pleasing. I show a poor fellow my arm & he is consoled for the loss of his own & so on.

We have no letters or explanations from Lahore. We are quiet & so are they. Poor Somerset died in Charles's arms. His wife is 200 miles in the rear. I would not allow any women to accompany the army. I have written to the relations of all the friends I have lost. I find no labour too great to do their memories justice, but I shall be glad when the mail is dispatched, for I begin to feel the work, which will cease in a great measure when the home papers are finished. I shall make Arthur copy Gough's letter to Ld. F. Somerset. Tell Emily it does not make him proud. He is as playful & gentle as if he had never heard a cannon roar, & I rather have faith in the belief that those who see war & know its horrors have their hearts softened to allay its miseries.

I really wish the mail was off. I write to the parents of the friends I have lost, & it brings the g. gl. under contribution for tears, which flow the more freely when I contrast their grief with my joy in having both our boys sound & safe; The camp is *still* & I like to write to you without the constant interruption to which I am subject. It must console you, now that I am of necessity here, to know that you could not have accompanied me even if you had mastered the sea voyage & outlived the Bengal climate. Thus God Almighty disposes everything for the best &, if in my declining years I may have rendered my country some service, I much more contentedly shall end my days with you at S. Park than entangled in the politics of friends forsaking their leader. Peel's expansive mind will lead the party in the right way but here I believe I can do more service than in England. Our finances are not quite flourishing. Here I keep open house. All the wounded officers are supplied & it is the most grateful hospitality I ever dispensed. Robt. Wood has had a little fever but is now as usual & in a month will be able to walk. I have written to his father.

My affecte. love to dear Emily. I know she will prove herself a treasure to us whether in the single or wedded state. The shawls shall be sent in a month & will be in England in April.

67. [*To Sarah.*] Camp Feroz-poor. Janry. 1st, 1846

A happy new year to you, dear Walter, & baby, & may I next year include in my prayer for your happiness another little stranger to love & live for. How strongly they make one cling to life! And in the scenes I have so lately witnessed, how grateful I am to a merciful God for His protection of my 2 boys.

We have had some very severe fighting—Charles & Arthur both safe, Wood wounded. I have had 5 A.D.C.'s killed & 5 wounded. Arthur was the only unhurt & the dear boy was everywhere, & a more chivalric courage never was shown.

I have sent Walter a copy of my private letter to Ld. Ripon which must not be known & which will give you a correct acct. of what has passed.

I have also written to Peel[216] & officially to the Secret Com[*mit*]t[*e*]e &, as I have now been writing with little intermission since 1/2 past 2 o'cl. this morning, I am nearly knocked up. In other respects I am in good health & as hard as iron.

Kiss baby for me. How I long to play with her!

68. [*To Walter.*] Feroz-poor. Janry. 19, 1846

We are much in the same state as when I last wrote. The river divides us & no movement of any importance is made. We cannot stir till siege guns & am[*munitio*]n arrive. These have to march 260 miles; the Sikhs have theirs at Lahore 50 miles off.

There is no doubt that the cause, the motive, the object of this war was to compel us to interfere by force of arms to put down their

---

[216] Hardinge's strong feelings about Gough were further expressed in a letter to Peel dated 30 Dec. and marked 'secret & confidential': '[*It*] is my duty to Her Majesty, & to you as the head of the Government, to state, most confidentially, that we have been in the greatest peril, & are likely hereafter to be in great peril, if these very extensive operations are to be conducted by the com.-in-chief.' Deeming Gough unfit to direct the Sikh war, he informed Peel: 'I respect & esteem Sir H. Gough, but I cannot risk the safety of India by concealing my opinion from you.' Hardinge recommended that Napier replace Gough in Panjab, but the future course of the war made such a change unnecessary. (Peel Papers, Add. MS 40475.)

mutinous army. We always declined to interfere in their internal affairs. We also refused to be hired to do this unpleasant work. The govt., therefore, instigated the army to attack us in order to make us their instrument in destroying their army. Even now the same language is held: 'Go & attack the English whom you promised to conquer if you recd. 12 r[*upees*] a month. If you cannot conquer them & keep your promise, return to the old rate of 6 r[*upees*] a month.'

I fear I shall not be able to proceed if I am to wait for siege guns & a large quantity of am[*munitio*]n, as the season will then be so far advanced that we shall be in the hot weather.

I [*am*] in good health & so are the boys—both delighted with a camp life altho' a tear starts in dear Arthur's eyes when he alludes to his friends he has lost.

We had sharp work in getting into the enemy's camp—10 offs. were shot close to me, exclusive of men, by grape shot, & the boys escaped providentially.

Of the 1871 wounded, 270 only will be permanently disabled; 1100 will return to the ranks; 600 are now again with their regts. & the remainder in a month. The loss in killed & in men incapacitated for further service in the 3 actions will be abt. 830—not near so severe as Albuera.

It is a noble sight to see 91 fine brass guns in line! But what noble fine fellows are our British soldiers!

I will write more at length on the next occasion. I have been up since 3 this morn[*in*]g & can with difficulty get through. The mail goes out in one hour.

God bless you, Sarah, & baby.

69. [*To Emily.*] Feroz-poor Camp. Janry. 31st, [*1846*]

At about 70 miles from this place & towards our rear, a part of our force detached to Loodiana met the Sikh army,[217] attacked it, & drove them into the river & captured 50 guns. This result has been of much importance in securing our communications to the rear & protecting our ammunition & guns & treasure. We have thus taken 150 guns from the enemy since the campaign commenced.

In 6 weeks it will be over & I shall be most happy to have less anxiety on my mind, for I assure you *confidentially* that the responsibility rests upon me of milty. movements over which I have not the control in military details which belong to the cr. in cf. He is a brave, fine, old Irishman &, altho' I don't always admire his military combinations, I respect him for his intrepidity & many other excellent qualities.

But first let me tell you that our boys are in excellent health, in

---

[217] At the battle of Aliwal on 28 Jan. 1846.

high spirits, & in every quality to be loved by us & respected by the rest of the world. Charles is in the very best of health. He has once expressed to me since the fighting began that he still wishes to enter the army. I discouraged it & he has submitted. The Supreme Disposer of events may interfere in the fate of such worms as we are because we are the instruments of His will, but after his loss of a limb, & having witnessed the reckless courage he shows in action, I think it quite out of the question that he should be risked in the service. Dear Arthur is a contribution I make to the profession, trusting in the mercy of the same Providence which has shielded me from many dangers &, you may rely upon it, I will not allow Charles to wear a red coat excepting in Leicestershire with the fox hounds, for he rides admirably & I assure you I get on very fast—riding 25 miles to breakfast or dinner without inconvenience in 2 hours.

I had an accident the other day in riding a new Arab in the dark. He put his foot in a hole & came down on his side with my knee under him. I had the thigh cupped & leeched & am now quite sound & ready for any exertion. The leeches were very unpleasant, & for the 2 hours they were feeding upon me I thought how much you suffered from them when you sprained yr. ankle just before Emily was born. And then I traced all the children & their dear mother up to the present hour rapidly in my mind &, when paper & ink were brought to go on with my work, I had passed in review several years of our happy union & blessed you & thanked God that this accident was so slight at a time I cannot afford to be idle.

Sunday [*February 1*]

I have just returned from church in my tent. Our dear boys are punctual in duties which their dear mother instilled from their youth. I have been starving for 3 days &, having taken no exercise, it agrees with me. Rely on my taking great care of my health. If I had ridden my favorite Arab, Mianee,[218] he would have borne me gallantly, but the mongrel I was riding was a new purchase, & I had said on the road he goes as if he would come down.

The papers attack me so much for exposure in the battle that the danger will not be incurred again, but it is a curious predicament to be placed in. If Gough were killed, I am the next moment C. Cf. & then I must be in & directing the field of battle & this duty imposed by Her Majesty's Warrant so that I know you will justify me & not consider that I was led away by any heat of blood to do what was unnecessary. To kill a g. gl. or *lord sa[h]ib* would here be a victory, &

[218] Hardinge's favourite Arab horse, named for the battle of Miani in which Napier defeated the Amirs of Sind in 1843. Hardinge rode Miani during the battle of Ferozeshah and brought him home to Penshurst in 1848. (*Viscount Hardinge*, pp. 113, 114, 175; Doble, p. 9.)

if we were fighting, which I do not expect, I should be as prudent as my great master in Spain, who never exposed himself without a necessity. I say these things for your satisfaction. The Supreme Power disposes of all events. I escape a severe hail of grape shot & am laid up by a fall from under my horse which might have snapped my thigh. True piety & wisdom is to rely on a merciful God, not to tempt danger unnecessarily but to be resigned to His will in Whose hands are the issues of life & death.

I have just been issuing an order improving the pensions of our sepoys who lose their limbs or are obliged to leave the service on acct. of wounds. To say the truth, I am rather disappointed in their style of fighting, but they are willing, good troops. But in any difficulty Mr Bull comes forth in great splendour; the blackguard is merged in the hero & he fights to the last moment.

I see by the state of the Corn Law question that our friend is in great difficulty. If he assents to a free trade in corn, I doubt his getting through the session. I shall patiently wait to hear from him. I must go through with this most difficult affair in my hands & then wait events.[219] If I am not fairly supported, I shall resign. The Whigs will be anxious to appoint some friend of their own. They are welcome. If I return with an honorable character, having carried our army victoriously to Lahore under very difficult circumstances, I shall return to you & be a pruner of roses, having fairly given to the public the best years of my life, living for the few which remain in the bosom of my family & grateful if the tryals to which I am exposed shall have been creditably overcome.

I expect every hour interesting news from Lahore after the defeat of the Sikh troops on the 28th Janry., but they are so treacherous & cunning it is impossible to rely on their assurances.

I don't send you the letters of praise I get; I am ashamed to show them. The boys think my nerves on gt. occasions very firm. I hope they will inherit my scanty good qualities & none of my bad. I am very proud of them both.

Febry. 2nd

I have a communication from Raja Golab Singh, which may lead to overtures for an arrange[men]t. He is to be made minister & says he is ready to do whatever we like to order. I am obliged to be very cold & haughty, but I propose to allow him to come here to propose terms & make a beginning. It is indispensable that the Sikh army should be disbanded. Their state of anarchy & mutiny is the cause of

[219] As the Irish potato blight deepened the Corn Laws crisis, a somber Peel had written to Hardinge: 'A cloud is thrown over our actual prosperity and our prospects for the future by the prevalence of a lamentable disease in the potatoes' (26 Oct. 1845, Peel Papers, Add. MS 40475).

all the mischief. India is already so overgrown & large that we do not want territory. We shall keep what we have confiscated on this side, make them pay the expenses of the war, clip their wings & lessen their power, but I have always been averse to annex the territory, [&] I still hope to keep up a Sikh nation that is a Hindoo people as contradistinguished from a Mahomedan.

I don't think well of things on Downing Street, &, if I am to have Whigs for my masters who render my position irksome & uneasy, I shall, if I can with honor, retire after I have closed the war.

Bob Wood is nearly recovered from his wound. He rode with me 30 miles the other day. Hillier is well but still lame; a young officer, a nephew of Sir R. Peel,[220] was on a visit to me & was wounded. Respecting everything of the name, I made him my a.d.camp. George Hardinge is here in camp with his regt. He must serve one year before he can be placed on the staff. I have also placed Ld. Tweeddale's son[221] on my staff.

Come what may, I am prepared for every event. I do not care for popular praise but, if the Duke & Peel, the greatest, wisest & best men of the day, are satisfied with me, I shall retire in peace & happiness.

Tell the dear girls I hope to send them the trinkets when our rear is more clear. I have 150 miles of Sikh country in my rear & every village is a little fort.

What a magnificent sight it is to see 145 pieces of captured artillery! These people were trained & organized by French officers. What do they say to 5000 British & 11,000 sepoys attacking 60,000 & taking 90 pieces of fine artillery? Our total loss in our brave countrymen in all the battles will not exceed 1000 men; by the cholera we lost more in 1845. I believe I must gratify my milty. vanity by bringing home *one* Sikh gun to S. Park for posterity.[222]

I am anxiously expecting news of dst. Sarah. God grant her a son. She is most affecte. & attached to us. Kiss Emily for me. The shawls will be sent next month.

70. [*To Sarah.*] Camp Feroz-poor. Febry. 3, 1846

The day after tomorrow our ammunition will arrive & in a few days afterwards I hope to leave this wretched place where nothing is

[220] William Peel (1824–78), of the 1st Bengal Dragoons, was the son of Peel's younger brother Edmund.
[221] Lord Arthur Hay (1824–78), the future 9th Marquis of Tweeddale, was a lieutenant in the Grenadier Guards. He was Hardinge's guest when the war broke out and voluntarily fought in it.
[222] Emily's marginal notation: 'Posterity has 2 in the hall given by the Court of Directors.'

agreeable except a dry wholesome air, & that I would have in a pleasanter spot.

Another victory & 52 guns captured! This makes 143. I shall certainly like a gun for my share & send it to S. Park. This is a pardonable vanity in my old age.

I long to hear of you, d[*eares*]t. I won't enter upon that chapter— I trust in God!

The boys [*are*] quite well. I expect the mail in the day after tomorrow, & I fear the Peel govt. will be out. As regards my position here, if it induces my recall, I shall not repine. I have my consolation in my family & in turning my thoughts to the great acct. I have to render which this mode of life interrupts. I feel I have acted honestly & uprightly, & no G. G. ever had a more just quarrel on his hands, but we don't want this Punjab territory. We are forced into war & dislike the prize as a nuisance even if it were within our grasp.

The boys are quite well & very happy in their different ways. What wd. I give for one day with you & Walter & baby at S. Park. God bless you. I am lame but shall be quite right in 2 or 3 days.

71. [*To Walter.*] Camp Feroz-poor. Febry. 3rd, 1846

You will be glad to read the dispatches announcing another victory by a detached force of our army under Sir Harry Smith,[223] in which 24,000 Sikhs were completely defeated by abt. 10,000 of our people, driven across the river with loss & the capture by Smith of 52 guns. Our ammunition for our field guns will be up the 6th, our guns for sieges a day or two after, & we shall then commence active operations.

This last business, abt. 70 miles off, gave me much anxiety. If we had not been very prompt in detaching a strong force & ordering Smith to attack, we should have had our am[*munitio*]n, guns, & treasure seized. But the force was splendid—10,000 of our best troops opposed to 24,000 of their irregulars, more than one-half cavalry—& I say this to show that the operation was perfectly safe & not one of chance. Still, it was most opportune, decisive & complete, & will be of the greatest use.

R. Golab Singh has, we have just heard, been declared minister at Lahore; if so, he will apply to us for terms & as we shall be ready to move in a week, I hope that the time for negotiation has arrived. We

[223] Sir Harry G. W. Smith (1787–1860) commanded troops in all four battles of the Sikh War, and is particularly credited with the victory at Aliwal. He was baronetted in 1846.

have captured in the field 143 pieces of very fine artry., & yet this warlike people have 100 guns in their camp 25 miles from this place, within 2 miles of our army.

It is very tempting to attack them in their entrenched camp, [*but*] the loss might cripple us & we cannot replace our precious British materials. How superior to every other 2-legged animal is this flesh & blood of the Pools & Bridgers! What heroes are trained in our pot houses! Is it the climate which breeds the Bull Dog, or what is it?

[*References to the arrival of the ammunition and of Gulab Singh's message seem to indicate that the rest of this letter was written a day or two later.*]

It is into 1/2 p[*as*]t 4 & I have just closed my note to yr. dear mother. I am writing in bed since 3 o'cl. & must go on till 5 this even[*in*]g to get through my task.

Last night I recd. a note from Lahore saying Rajah Golab S. was appointed minister & wished to treat for terms. The communication was private.[224] I hope it may lead to terms if their Praetorian bands can be controlled, but with such a republican army, I have no guarantee that any pledge made by the Sikh govt. will be fulfilled.

However, we have now got ammunition for our 100 field guns & that intense anxiety is over. Conceive Gough scarcely willing to understand that am[*munitio*]n is necessary for artry. We have to replace every shot we fire from Delhi 260 miles off; the enemy can replace his in 24 hours. In this army, rapidly brought together & living almost in an enemy's country from hand to mouth, I have to attend to all these details.

The next fortnight will decide the nature of the terms to be imposed but the disbandment of this Sikh army is an indispensable condition. I am averse to annexation & prefer a Hindoo people as the garrison for our advanced post, but these Sikhs must have their wings clipped, &, as I am equally averse to the subsidiary system which by British bayonets enables a native govt. to grind the people to dust, I see no alternative but the dissolution of their army, compensation for the expenses of the war, retention of the Lahore territory on this side, & a weakening of the Sikh power on two or three other points.

I have to decide upon these measures by myself aided by Mr Currie, my pol. secry., who is with me. My council at Calcutta don't breathe an opinion; Gough has not an idea on the subject. Ripon agrees with me but takes no decided line, & I much fear from what you say & I hear in the public journals, that a Whig ministry will be in before the Parlt. meets.

---

[224] Hardinge confirmed this to the Secret Committee on Feb. 19: '[*The new minister*] immediately put himself in communication with us, proferring every assistance in his power for the furtherance of any ends in regard to the state of Lahore which we might have in view' (F.P.N.W.F., p. 67).

I don't think Peel can stand. I am ready, when some hungry Whig requires it, to retire & I suppose I shall hear from Peel if my suspicions prove to be true.

I wish extremely that you will lose not a day in paying Fanny's portion—£10,000. Borrow if I have not sent enough & pray let me know the state of my acct. with Cox. Grant pays my wine bills, which are heavy, & I therefore never know exactly how I stand, but this is an affair which must be settled immediately; at my time of life & in this region of anarchy & bloody feuds, postponement is most uneasy. I have completed, or shall do so in a month, all those arrangements which are necessary for their welfare & I am in repose on that score. During yr. mother's life she will have a competency & the means of retaining her station with S. Park & £20,000, the amt. of our united fortunes, & thus, my dear Walter, I am at ease on worldly matters of a pecuniary nature affecting my family. The life I lead teaches me much philosophy, but late in life I have severe tryals, but thank God my nerves are good.

My horse, a new Arab & not a favorite, fell down & lay upon my knee & thigh. The contusion was severe. I have had the limb cupped & leeched & it is nearly well, & I shall be able to ride in 3 days.

My other horses are very good & safe.

And now, my d[ea]r f[rien]d, with my affecte. regard to dr. Sarah & in confiding trust in the mercy of God that you & she will have a happy deliverance from your great anxiety.

72. [*To Walter.*] Camp Kasoor. Febry. 16, 1846

We have had another decisive victory, by storming the enemy's entrenched camp at Sobraon,[225] driving him with immense loss into the river & capturing 67 guns!

The enemy's force at least were 35,000 with 30 guns on the opposite side of the river, exclusive of the 67 which we captured on this [*side*].

Our inf. force, which was all we had, did not exceed 14,000 inf.

The enemy's loss is estimated at 10,000 killed & wounded, ours to 2,000. Our brave countrymen behaved nobly.

The same even[in]g, the 10th, we passed 6 regts. across the river into the Punjab, the following day laid down our bridge, & this day the whole of the army with few exceptions will be concentrated here. The 18th we march onwards, & on the 21st I expect to be at Lahore & dictate the terms of a treaty.

The maha-raja will come in all probability into my camp, make his submission, & rely upon the clemency of the B. govt.

---

[225] The last battle was fought there on 10 Feb.

The S[*ikh*] army is in a shattered condition, with about 30 guns left, & may attempt to seize Lahore, plunder it, & disperse. I shall insist on a cession of a portion of country which will render our frontier more secure, &, as it is rich, will weaken the Sikhs as a nation. I shall insist on the disbandment of the army & its limitation in inf., cav., & artry. Every gun *pointed* agt. the B. army shall be given up. We have taken in the field 200, & I believe at no period of our Indian history have we had so warlike a people to act agt. or so well prepared with warlike means.

I shall insist on the keys of Lahore & Govindhur [*Gobindghar*]²²⁶ being surrendered in token of the enemy's complete submission.

I shall require, exclusive of territory to be ceded, 1 1/2 millions in money as a compensation for the expenses of the war.

I then propose to attempt to re-establish a Sikh govt. instead of annexing a large country & a warlike population to our overgrown Indian territory. I detest the subsidiary system of having a British force at the capital with a native administration to coerce & plunder the people by British bayonets, & I really see no other means than to clip the state which has shown itself too strong, punish & disband the army, & give the Hindoos another chance. This Hindoo dynasty at the gates of India as our advanced post agt. the power of the Mahommedans is important.

Ld. Ellenborough will not approve of this forbearance & I have no instructions from England, except their, the ministers', concurrence that annexation & the subsidiary system are both bad. I have no council but one sensible man, Mr Currie,²²⁷ abt. me. Gough has not an idea of these matters but is a gallant soldier, extremely sensitive on the score of my milty. interference, & therefore I have to rely on my own judgement aided by Currie, who has been a long time in the country & is an able man.

With regard to Gough, he consults me, adopts generally my suggestions, & with variations makes them his own. For instance, in the late affair at Sobraon he, as you will see by the correspondence, adopts my plan & in his dispatch calls it his own of which I approved. But we get on very well. I have my own way in essential matters, altho' sometimes I am almost in despair at his want of method & combination & discipline. He has a great many fine qualities of bravery & kindness of heart & is a gentleman but very jealous.

However, we have, I think, between us brought this very difficult affair very nearly to a satisfactory conclusion, & by the end of March

²²⁶ A well-known fort in Amritsar built by Ranjit Singh in 1808.

²²⁷ Frederick Currie (1799–1875) had held various financial and legal offices in India from 1820 to 1842 when he became the foreign secretary to the government at Calcutta. He was with Hardinge both during and after the Sikh war and became his close adviser.

I hope to be on my way to Simla, through the *Jullundhur* Doab, a district comprised between the Sutlege & Beas rivers, giving us a much better frontier & a people inhabiting the district who hate the Sikhs.[228]

I suppose Peel, having resumed the govt., will be able to stand.[229] On patriotic grounds I desire it & on personal grounds I feel sure of his friendly support whether he be in the Ministry or in Opposition. These great events here, on which during the last 2 months the fate of our Indian empire has been wavering in the balance, make me indifferent to all public matters, &, altho' my nerves are good & as yet no symptom of declining years, still I shall be delighted to conclude my treaty & march this brave little army back to its quarters before the hot winds set in, which will prostrate all of us.

I have seen Golab Singh, the ablest man & the greatest rascal in the East. I told him publicly, when it was stated that a horse with a gold saddle has been sent to me & another with a silver saddle for the C. C., that I could not forget the blood of my countrymen, so perfidiously spilt, & I only admitted him to my presence because he had had the prudence not to be a participator in these atrocities; that I should demand submission & atonement, indemnity for the past, & security for the future. I refused the gold saddle for the hall [*at*] S. P. These things are said by me in a blue coat & star, seated on a gold & crimson chair of state & translated by my pol. secry., my A.D.C. & officers in full dress, & the man who is dressed in a blue frock coat & a little brief authority utters these things in the tone of the Speaker from the chair. Arthur smiles when I cast my eye towards him; Charles in a blue & gold coat looks grave & demure.

I have, how[*eve*]r, great difficulties still in my way but I shall get through them. The S[*ikh*] army may rally, declaring the terms to be degrading, & shut themselves up in their fortified towns.

I have very scanty means for one or two sieges, & the season is far advanced. If I cannot subdue the turbulent spirit of the army &, after I return to Hindostan, they rise, there is no remedy but the conquest of the country—a great misfortune in my view of its interests & which I must accomplish next autumn

My fall still makes me very lame—the horse laid upon me. Fortunately it was in the sand or my thigh must have snapped. I long to ride with ease, having become so active that I make nothing of 30

[228] It is difficult to comprehend why the people of the Doab, a significant percentage of whom were Sikhs, would be anti-Sikh.

[229] About this time Peel, who was busy advocating his free trade policy in a series of speeches, wrote to Hardinge with cautious optimism about the future: 'I am fighting a desperate battle here—shall probably drive my opponents over the Sutlej—but what is to come afterwards I know not' (24 Feb. 1846, Peel Papers, Add. MS 40475).

miles, & am now on my couch having managed in some pain to ride
for 3 hours on the 10th.

It was nothing compared to Feroz-shah in the way of danger but
a very daring exploit, bravely executed, & in its results most important. Your brothers [*were*] both with me under fire, which is distressing.
You can scarcely conceive what I have gone through in the anxious
case that India is lost or won if I make a false move. By the blessing
of Providence I hope to satisfy you & my friends that moderation has
been united with just considerations for the security of India & the
vindication of the national honor.

I am doing all I can to get my poor wounded heroes who have lost
limbs sent down the Sutlege to Bombay to get to dear old England
before the hot weather sets in. How I love these brave men!

I have just sent off a Genl. Order relating to the battle. You
will see Charles & Arthur mentioned. I have gone into great detail,
which in principle as a practice is bad, but I think the 10th will be
our last battle, & I was anxious to record the names of the most
deserving men. If we settle matters satisfactorily at Lahore, I will
give the army a donation of 6 months' batta & pay it out of the Sikh
indemnity.

My love to dearest Sarah. Let me know every detail abt. Penn's
Rock. Pay Fanny's £10,000—I have £3000 to send but Charles says
the rate of exchange is ruinous.

I admire Peel for accepting, or rather offering, to continue [*as*]
minister when Ld. John [*Russell*] failed. Depend upon it, he is a fine
fellow & of great moral courage, which is after all the most difficult
courage to have.

I am in the midst of eternal references on siege trains, pontoons &
all kinds of pot hooks & hangers, but in excellent spirits for a poor
fellow tied by the leg.

73. [*To Emily.*] Kussoor, about 32 miles from Lahore. [*17 February
1846*]

When our ammunition & siege trains arrived, it was necessary to
strike a blow & pass the Sutlege River & endeavor to terminate the
war before the hot weather set in.

On the 7th & 8th our guns & ammunition arrived from the rear,
& the force under Sir Harry Smith, which had been detached to
Loodiana and had defeated the enemy, returned to camp on the 8th.
On the 10th we determined to attack the enemy's entrenched camp.
We first cannonaded it for 2 hours, then let loose our brave infantry,
& in 2 hours we had gained the camp, destroyed the enemy &
captured 67 pieces of artillery. This was a great exploit for 14,000

infry. to achieve agt. 35,000 of the enemy's regular forces, covered by breastworks & defended by so large a number of guns. The enemy's loss is 10,000, ours 2080. You will be glad to hear that in an action of this nature the staff were not much exposed & that both our boys are well & unhurt. Charles was in the midst of the fray as eager as Arthur & very useful. I have written a Genl. Order, thanking the troops, & that document with the cr. cf. dispatch will give you all the details of these proceedings.

We passed the river the same night & are now on our way to Lahore where I hope on the 21st to dictate terms of peace. Golab Singh the minister came to my camp the day before yesterday. I recd. him in durbar, seated, & merely rose as he came up. I desired him to be told that he was a welcome ambassador because he had had the prudence not to participate in the atrocities perpetrated against the British government.

The sirdars then offered me presents from the maha-raja—a horse with a gold saddle for me, & another with a silver saddle for the cr. chief & so on. I declined to receive presents or to place myself on a footing of friendship till the Sikhs had submitted themselves to the clemency of the British govt., until the blood of my countrymen, so treacherously spilt, had been vindicated by punishing the army, by disbanding it, by taking a portion of the Sikh territory as indemnity, by making the nation pay 1 1/2 million pounds sterg. for the expenses of the war, & several [other] austere & rigid conditions.

These I speak in an authoritative tone in English. They are repeated by the political secry. in Persian, the staff & officers of state being present, &, after a certain degree of public representation, these barbarians with the most polished manners retire. The secry. & the political agent[230] then meet the wuzzier & his divan & the real business is done. Tomorrow we march 12 miles on the road to Lahore, & on the 21st I expect to be there.

The maha-raja or king is to come into my camp tomorrow to submit himself to my generosity & will proceed to Lahore with me. I shall require him to present the keys of Lahore & Govindhur [Gobindghar] & to surrender every piece of cannon that has been pointed agt. the British army. I take from them a fertile district which improves our frontier, 1 1/2 million of money &, as they have shown themselves too strong, I hope to take away Cashmere & the hill districts, declaring them independent of Lahore. The army shall be limited in number

[230] Bvt.-Maj. Henry Montgomery Lawrence (1806–57), one of the more reputable Company figures, had come to India in 1823. A veteran of the Burmese and Afghan wars, he eventually held various political positions in India. He served as resident in Nepal and, upon Broadfoot's death at Ferozeshah, was appointed the agent on the Sikh frontier.

& reduced in pay & various conditions imposed which may enable the govt. to keep it in order. We have captured 220 very fine brass guns & we must not allow of such immense estab[*lishmen*]ts in future. Thus, without annexing the whole of this immense territory to our over-grown empire, already too large, I hope to re-establish a Sikh govt., that is a Hindoo nation, as our neighbour keeping down the Mahomedans, weakened by these concessions of territory, & by the mode adopted to get rid of what is termed the subsidiary system— that is, keeping an army at Lahore to coerce the people, ill-used & plundered by their native rulers who, when by their oppression have excited the people into rebellion, call upon us with B. bayonets to put down the insurrection. This is a detestable system.

I propose to punish them once for all & not be required to interfere in their affairs. If this arrangement, so moderate & forbearing considering the enormity of their offence, does not answer, then on the next occurrence, we must annex the country, which I consider a great misfortune as far as the true interests of India are concerned.

I know not how far my policy may be approved at home. I act for myself. Gough is a mere soldier & can give me no opinion, & my only aid is in the prudence & ability & experience of my political secry. Mr Currie. I have a thousand things in hand. I will close this letter when I have seen the prince.

74. [*To Emily*.] Lullianee, 24 miles from Lahore. [*18 February 1846*]

The prince, or maha-raja, is to come to my durbar at 4 o'cl. this day. I have just come in from Kussoor—the tents not pitched & writing in my little carriage, for I am still so lame I cannot ride. The tendon of the knee pan has been hurt by the weight of the horse lying upon me & I shall be obliged to be quiet for another week, but I walk pretty well & am getting on slow & sure.

We shall march again tomorrow morning & be at Lahore the 21st. Thus in less than 3 months we shall have closed the most active campaigns ever made in India. I hope our European friends will be satisfied. I have had much cause for anxiety, but, when I am convinced I have done my best & have omitted no labour or precaution, I trust to the blessing of Providence, & certainly the Almighty's mercy & protection have been vouchsafed to me & mine in an especial manner. I hope I am sufficiently grateful.

We have around us 20,000 troops & 80,000 camp followers noncombatants, thousands of camels, horses, ponies & bullocks. These are all encamped in a sandy plain, not a potato or blade of grass for man or beast, & yet we live luxuriously for a camp.

Arthur is near me looking very interesting in a cap with a white shawl wound round it as a turban to keep off the sun, for the heat is great already. Charles has been writing to Walter & so have I. At 3 o'cl. this morning I wrote 5 sheets to the Queen before we marched. If I put off the mail for a few hours, I will write to you at 3 o'cl. on the 19th before we march. I require very little sleep. This attitude at full length on the carriage is rather awkward. I shall wait to see my prince before I proceed further.

75. [*To Sarah.*] Lullianee. Febry. 19th, 1846; 5 o'cl. a.m.

We are in all the noise, dust, & bustle of striking our tents & I am writing on my camp bed, laid up with a bruised knee which prevents my walking or riding, but it will be well in 10 days.

After a sharp & decisive action on the 10th, we passed the river & entered the Punjab & are now on our way to Lahore, having taken 220 of the enemy's guns & shown him the style in which the white man can fight. At the same time I must say these black Sikhs fought well, & their artry., which is French,[231] is bountiful & fought obstinately.

Well, I have the ablest scoundrel in all Asia close to my camp—the wuzzier R. Golab Singh—a good-looking clever-eyed man of about 50, & yesterday he brought the little maha-raja to my durbar tent to make his submission & pay tribute.

Conceive a beautiful little boy of 8 years old, brought into the midst of cannon & feringees, amongst strangers represented as monsters who eat cows & destroy Sikhs by thousands. The brave little fellow showed no fear; I coaxed him & made him laugh, a great Eastern indecorum, gave him a musical box with a bird & trays of presents, which he looked at with curiosity. The talk was diplomatic, of old Runjeet his father (who was not his father), & after an hour the boy retired with a salute of 21 guns from our loud barkers the 24 pounders, & now I am about to dress & proceed to Lahore.

The Sikh army of abt. 20,000 men is not far off. If they act with spirit, they will throw themselves into Lahore & give me great trouble to drive them out.

We have had an anxious time both as regards the boys when we fight & the risk which must attend the issue of any battle, but particularly when 14,000 men, of which 4000 were British, attack 35,000 in a fortified camp with 67 pieces of cannon. You will be tired of these details. When I see the ranee, who is very handsome, I will give you

---

[231] Some of the best cannon in the Sikh arsenal were cast by Claude Auguste Court (1793–1861), an 1813 graduate of the Militaire Polytechnique in Paris, who served the Sikhs as an ordnance officer from 1827 to 1843.

an acct. of her. I shd. like to have a picture of the maha-raja. These black children are like little pigs—pretty when young & horrid when grown up. But then, Sikhs are very fine people with large hooked noses, tall & well made & very resolute.

76. [*To Emily.*] Khana Cutch [*Kacha. February*] 19th, [*1846*]

We have just marched in here 14 miles from Lahore. The maharaja came to my tent yesterday e[*venin*]g. He is a beautiful boy of 8 years old & a very brave little fellow. He was brought through the throng of troops in arms. I embraced him & he smiled &, when seated in a fine chair next [*to*] mine, we became very good friends. The talk was of Runjeet S. & good advice & a few political maxims, then 50 trays of presents, he having thrown purses of money at my feet as a recognition of his submission, &, after a long sitting, presents, & compliments, we parted, giving him a salute of 21 guns from our 24 pounders.

We had heard more firing near Lahore since we came in, but whether it is a salute or a quarrel between contending factions we do not know. I have told them we shall make them pay 1 1/2 million for any battle or siege & I hope the last shot with ball was fired at Sobraon on the 10th.

I hope to be on my way to the hills on the 20th March. My knee is easier today & I shall be quite right in a fortnight. I must, d[*eare*]st, close my letter & am ever, in the midst of all this turmoil, your affecte. & devoted husband.

77. [*To Emily.*] Camp Lahore. March 1st, 1846

We have just said our prayers in my large durbar tent & I am grateful to God for the important successes which have attended our arms & for the safety of our dear boys in the midst of such severe conflicts.

I hope to sign the treaty on or before the 10th & on the 12th to be on my way to the hills at Simla.

I cannot say whether my policy in dealing with the Sikh nation will be approved or not. I had already explained to the Cabinet that I considered the annexation of all the Sikh territories to the Indus a great misfortune & that, if possible, it ought to be avoided. I had also explained in the same letter upwards of a year ago that the subsidiary system of hiring a British force to coerce the people, driven to desperation by the misrule of a native administration, a most cruel & dangerous policy on our extreme frontier, bad & wicked everywhere but perilous here. I also had explained that the native states to

be kept up in these frontier countries ought to be Hindoos & not
Mahometans. The Hindoos act as our advanced guard agt. the Maho-
metan tribes, who have for ages invaded India by this very country
of Lahore as far back as the time of Alexander. For Porus was a Sikh
king[232] & the river which we have passed is in the Greek histories
called the Hyphasis. Our safest policy is, therefore, to uphold Hindoos
& not Musselmen.

We have given these Sikhs a great beating & taken from them 220
guns, & 36 more are to be surrendered because they were fixed at us.
We think they may be more submissive after this trial of strength. I
have not only confiscated the Sikh territories on the left bank of the
Sutlege but I have annexed a very rich district, bounded by the River
Beas, to the Indian empire, chiefly to improve our frontier as well as
to weaken the Sikh nation by the loss of so valuable a district. I have
insisted on the payment of 1 million & a quarter of money to be paid
down & the rest in a few months. I have made all the hill tribes
touching our hill frontier independent of the Sikhs for nearly 300 miles
in extent, touching up to Attock on the Indus, taking in Kashmere,
& I have placed all these countries under a Rajpoot dynasty or chief
called Rajah Golab Singh, who is by religion a Hindoo. Thus I
have punished the Sikhs for their unprovoked aggression upon us by
stripping them of 1/3 of their territory & making it over to a Rajpoot
who is to be independent of them. This territory it would have been
most inconvenient for us to occupy with troops. We occupy their
citadel, their prince has come before me in durbar & implored pardon,
the expenses of the war will be defrayed by Sikh money, our new
territories are useful to our frontier, & the revenues from our conquests
will pay all expenses. We give the Sikhs another trial. If they can
control their army with 1/3 of their territory taken away, they are
still strong enough to beat any native power that can assail them but
too weak again to invade us.

I propose to march our 220 captured cannon through India down
to Calcutta. The sight will convey a much stronger moral lesson than
the gates of Somnaut.[233]

Lord Ellenborough may object to this policy, that, having conquered Lahore, I have not made the Indus our boundary. The govt.
at home—Whig & Tory—would be, I believe, averse to this annexation of Ld. E[*llenborou*]gh's. With my small means it would have been
impossible at this season of the year. I have acted with moderation &
I believe my policy to be the best.

[232] He was a Hindu.
[233] Ellenborough's action in 1842 of bringing the gates of Somnath back to India
caused a political furore in Britain.

Fighting one day & negociating the next is very capitivating, if I had not 2 boys by my side. In spite of good nerves, I have gone through much anxiety & have had many difficulties to contend agt. which at some future time I can explain.

Sir Hugh Gough is a fine old veteran ready to fight on all occasions with many very excellent qualities. Sir C. Napier will be here on the 3rd but too late, which I much regret, for all out operations are over. When the treaty is signed, I shall retire to Simla & endeavour to employ myself in internal improvement after rewarding the army in every way that justice & policy can devise. I hope Peel & the Duke will be satisfied. You & Walter will see that our quarrel was most just & was a case of self defence & that victory & power have not made me depart from the line of policy which before the war I considered most expedient for the true interests of India. If the Peel govt. cannot stand, I shall be quite ready to return, but, if I am honourably treated & my recent conduct approved, I should not be justified in sacrificing the public service to gratify party feeling or my extreme desire to return to you. My strength, my head, my frame, & nerves are equal to the service I have had to perform in this campaign at this the cold season of the year. But any long residence in a hot or moist region like Calcutta wd. be very prejudicial.

The reflection that I shall leave our children in circumstances suited to their station & comfort relieves me in the midst of my labours, & I think of them & of you the first moment I awake & call for lights, which is at 4 o'cl.

78. [*To Emily.*] Lahore. March 2nd, [*1846*]

I am in the midst of negociations & movements of troops, but by being regularly called at 4 in the morning I get through a good deal of business, but when I return to you I shall do nothing but lounge away my time in yr. service.

We have paid off the Sikh soldiery, or rather the minister is doing it, & we hope to reorganize 20,000 men before we go. I do not intend to leave any garrisons in the Sikh territories but a strong force on the frontier.

I wrote to H.M. last mail. I don't think I have gossip enough for another letter this time. Charles & Arthur are flourishing, my knee is very nearly well, & I am in good health.

When Napier arrives I [*will*] give the C.C. a gt. dinner at the durbar tent which will hold 150 guests. I am afraid the campaign has been unfavorable to economy. My camp has been a large hotel, but it is proper to be hospitable on these occasions, & at Simla I shall be very quiet. On my way there I have a dozen princes to receive at

Loodiana—some to chide with words of reproach, others to praise & reward—& yet with all this power, which I endeavour to use with honesty & impartiality, I should be delighted to be in the tangle or the Oak Room receiving my neighbours instead of these rajas. If I had been a bachelor & not humanized by a wife & children, I am sure I should have been very ambitious, but my opportunity occurring late in life, I am discreet & moderate & somewhat of a philosopher. I rather like diplomacy when regulated by integrity & I am in every step anxious that the mode of accomplishing my object should be above all suspicion.

The man whom I have to deal with, Golab Singh, is the greatest rascal in Asia. Unfortunately it is necessary to improve his condition because he did not participate in the war against us &, his territories touching ours, we can protect him without inconvenience & give him a slice of the Sikh territory which balances his strength in some degree agt. theirs, &, as he is geographically our ally, I must forget he is a rascal & treat him better than he deserves. However, having, by force of arms, complete power, I have used it leniently but, in language that cannot be misunderstood, I have proclaimed to all Asia that any further relapse on the part of the Sikhs will be their destruction.

Let me know what you think & what you hear of all my proceedings, 'nothing extenuate,' &, if the 1st Lord of the Admiralty[234] condemns me, bear it patiently.

Love to dear little Emily.

79. [*To Emily.*] Lahore. March 3rd, [*1846*]

I have nearly settled the treaty & expect to get away the 10th or 12th. The army will return about the same time, & war's alarms will now be turned to mercy meetings. I have liberally rewarded the troops, &, without seeking their applause, I believe my measures for their welfare & my presence amongst them in danger have tended to make them consider me as their friend. By no other means do I seek popularity, & my training in the House of Commons has made me callous to censure unless applied by those I respect. Our field operations must be approved. My diplomacy satisfies my conscience & gives me very little anxiety. Upon the whole I am satisfied that by the blessing of God we have brought this affair to an honourable & satisfactory conclusion.

Charles has made some sketches of Lahore & some of those he had

---

[234] i.e. Ellenborough, appointed to that office in December 1845.

lost have been found. His collection to his family & himself will really be very valuable.

Your neighbours at Penshurst will be surprized that your old man should so suddenly have changed the pruning knife for a sword & have taken an active part in all this turmoil, but I shall now have a peaceful govt. of two years, carrying out my plans of education & interior improvement without interruption.

Providence has protected & guided me & given victory as the reward of my previous moderation & reluctance to draw the sword. Our quarrel was most just, & the atonement I have exacted is lenient compared to the offence.

I much wish to see the ranee, but I fear I shall fail. I intend that the little maha-raja & his ministers should come to my tent & sign the treaty, my officers, generals & staff ranged on one side & the black sirdars on the other.

The only point on which I am not quite satisfied is the turn which affairs may take when we go away. This is inevitable—we leave the govt. & the nation independent, &, if a severe moral lesson be disregarded & our advice slighted, they must take the consequences.

This campaign of 60 days is an interesting epoch in my life. I forget my fatigues & responsibilities, but I gratefully remember every day the infinite mercies of the Supreme Governor of all nations, & I am confident I shall die a better man than if I had toiled out the remainder of my days in the heat & anxiety of party strife.

I got on my horse this morning for the first time since the 10th & bore it very well. Everything is prosperous with us &, now that all yr. alarms are over, I hope to hear that you are happy, enjoying our triumphs & grateful for the merciful interposition by which our puny efforts have been rewarded by victory.

80. [*To Walter*.] Camp Lahore. March 4th, 1846

My treaty is nearly ready & I hope to be on my way back to the hills on the 10th or 12th.

I took territory from the Sikhs on both sides [*of*] the Sutlege to improve our frontier, in value abt. £400,000 a yr.

I demanded 1 1/2 million compensation for the expenses of the war. Half a million is to be p[*ai*]d in 2 days.

I took Cashmeer & all the hills between us on the Beas River in lieu of the million which they could not pay.

I then give all this territory which we cannot conveniently occupy, being 200 miles in advance of our frontier, to Raja Golab S., who, as a tributary of Lahore, has not made war upon us, in consideration of his paying £750,000 down in gold. Thus I obtain the money to pay our war expenses by stripping the Lahore state of a large tract of country & their exchequer of considerable revenue & create an *independent* Raj-poot sovereign over this extensive territory in order to have this chief, the Raja Golab S., as a counterpoise to the Lahore state, leaving the latter quite strong enough to defend itself agt. all enemies except the British &, as its power as put forth during this campaign has been very formidable, I have taken this mode of weakening & of punishing it.

Annexation was not our policy. I have only 25,000 fighting men. Peshower alone, 250 miles off, requires 10,000 bayonets. I shd. have 15,000 left for the subjugation of this immense country, which in a war might collect 50,000 men in arms.

The subsidiary system is also condemned & I have adopted the present policy as a *juste milieu* system which, if it be approved at home, will, I think, answer all the substantial purposes of the B. govt.

I propose to march 250 of our beautiful Sikh guns through Delhi, Agra, Benares & Patna to Calcutta. This procession will demonstrate the feats this army has performed, & the procession will be better suited to Asiatic taste than that of the gates of Somnauth.

If the Sikhs will not be quiet neighbours we must take other measures, but they will never never again attack us. The Cabool Disaster had given them a notion that they could beat us, & their black men certainly fought as well as our black men—many think better—& their artry. is excellent.

In 60 days we have fought 4 battles, captured 220 pieces of artry. & occupy [*sic*] Lahore.

By the bye, I have 36 pieces of large artry. now coming in which had been pointed agt. us & which I demanded should be surrendered to make [*clear*] the perfidious character of their aggression. Except [*for*] this piece of humiliation & making the maha-raja ask pardon in full durbar, paying tribute, etc., I have, according to our English notions, not pressed upon a beaten adversary.

Our fighting is now at an end & we shall quietly retire to Simla where I shall resume my plans for education, canals, & roads. If the Whigs come in, I am quite ready to retire or, if they offer honorable treatment, I should remain. If they shd. disapprove of my policy in the Punjab when I have been left to my own inventions, I should, of course, desire to be recalled.

The opinion of the Peel govt. & that of the British legislature in coming to a judgement will, I have no doubt, be a just one. I am in my conscience satisfied I have acted right & I care little for Indian opinions because they are to a certain degree influenced by personal considerations—that is, a constant desire to annex territory & increase offices.

The milty. take much the same view & hope more regts. will be raised to garrison the new territories.

The fact is we have only the revenues & the control over one half of India & we have the protection & peace of the whole thrown upon us.

We have had a very difficult campaign in some respects. We have made & concluded a great war in 60 days on peace establishments. We have run some risks, any one of which, if it had failed, wd. have lost India, & this is the tenure of a govr. genl.'s official position. I have had other professional difficulties, but now the business is all over & I am grateful to God for His mercies in giving victory to the right cause & in sparing my two boys where so many of my officers have fallen.

81. [*To Walter.*] Camp Lahore. March 11th, 1846

As soon as the treaty was signed, the Lahore govt. signified its earnest hope that a British force might be left in Lahore till the end of the year in order to give the govt. time to reorganize the army.[235] Otherwise, they were convinced the disbanded soldiery would return, pillage the town, murder the prince, & throw the whole country into confusion.

This was a most trying question for me to decide thus suddenly & forcibly put, for, pending the negotiations, the chiefs prudently concealed their fears, apprehensive that we should take advantage of their confession of weakness & increase our demands. After the Cabool disaster, a detached force in a large town filled with an armed population was an unpleasant question to solve.

I felt that the apprehensions of the S[*ikh*] govt. were likely to prove true & that it would be an incomplete termination of the campaign to leave this country a prey to a worse state of anarchy than any that has yet befallen it &, being most desirous to re-establish a S[*ikh*] govt., I at once determined to give the aid solicited. The danger may be great, but I don't fear it with the precautions I have taken. The moral effect of saving the nation which had without provocation attacked us, of proving to all Asia the sincerity of our conduct by our moderation after our victories, the good faith of withdrawing from Lahore when we have effected a friendly object, the exercise of B. generosity as contrasted with Sikh perfidy all concurred to render this a great political question which must be decided without delay, exclusive of the gt. question of annexation. I therefore decided to take the course

---

[235] The peace treaty with the Sikhs was signed at Lahore on 9 Mar. The supplementary articles, which were added on 11 Mar., stipulated that a British force was to be stationed at Lahore until the year's end.

of supporting this govt. & of giving it an honest assistance as the last experiment in solving the problem whether a Hindoo sect, a minority in the population of the Punjab, can continue to govern a mixed population of which a large proportion are Mahomedans.

The com. in ch. & Sir Chs. Napier, who is here, are very anxious as to the result, fearing treachery from a ferocious & revengeful soldiery. I must take the risk & parry such a blow by vigilance, but I could not be satisfied to leave this town & country a prey to discord & plunder, & I have left 1 B. regt., 8 n[ative] i[nfantry] regts., 22 guns, & other proportions of troops. I feel already the reward of acting a decided & an honest part; the fears decrease daily &, by rousing my energies to meet the contingencies of danger, I think I have applied a remedy to all, & I do not fear the whole S[ikh] army. I only wish as a young officer I had such a command.

We have arranged that R. Golab Singh shall have Cashmeer & all the hills & be independent of the Sikhs.[236] He comes into our camp this night & will march across the Beas (I should say the *Hyphasis*, which is now our boundary), being in fear of assassination. 'Uneasy rests the head that wears a crown.'[237]

The treaty having been settled, I determined that it should be publicly ratified by me & the little maha-raja in my tent. I invited all the genls. & offs. com[mandin]g regts. & some native offs., altogether 300, the street leading through the camp to my huge tent being lined by our soldiers of all arms.

The tent was 210 ft. long—the C.C., Sir Chs. Napier & Prince Waldemar & their staff & all the B. offs. on one side, the Sikh chiefs and officers of their army on the other.

I mounted a monster of an elephant & met the little prince 200 yds. from my tent. Without any fear he got into my howdar [*sic*], smiled, & was quite confident. He was led up to a chair on my right in the midst of cannon, muni[tion] & milty. noise. [He] seemed to like the excite[men]t & has undoubtedly very good nerves. After some forms & ceremonies, I ratified the treaty by my signature & the little [*prince*] signed his Persian name very well.

I then had to address the S[ikh] chiefs, which was translated to them par[agraph] by par[agraph], which you will see in the enclosed paper.[238] A brief reply was made by the minister, when presents were given by me to the maharaja & all his chiefs, &, after an hour consumed in these trifles, I led the boy to the end of the tent & disappeared.

[236] The treaty which made Gulab Singh the maharaja of Kashmir and other mountain territories was signed at Amritsar on Mar. 16.
[237] Shakespeare, *Henry IV*, III.i.31.
[238] Untraced.

The effect of the tent was very beautiful. I spoke short sentences in a strong tone, well translated by my secry., & the whole affair went off admirably.

Yesterday I went to the palace in the citadel to congratulate the maha-raja on my elephant accompanied by 100 offs. on elephants & squadrons of cav. & h[or]se artry. The maha-raja met me outside the walls, got into my howdur [*sic*] again & we then passed through the town to the palace through lines of milty. troops, when he conducted me to his durbar, pointed to a gold chair, & then seated himself in another by my side. The room was very oriental & beautiful &, altho' different from a tent, still very striking. He was covered with jewels, &, when we asked to see the *Koh-y-Nor*, the g[*rea*]test diamond in the world, I admired it & put it on his arm. He was pleased & then took it off that the offs. present might see it. He then wore it during the rest of the ceremony, which ended in his giving me, in return, bags of money & presents &, amongst others, a shawl tent, & in it a silver bed, or rather 4 bedposts, which is so pretty & old-fashioned that I think of buying it for a boudoir room as a curious relic of Lahore to my posterity.

The return was in the same fashion &, as I had reviewed the troops in the morning & am still lame, I was glad to eat my dinner & go to bed. But I was up at 4 this morn[*in*]g as usual & am now going a short march to the palace gardens abt. 5 miles off & tomorrow continue my march to Umritsir. Thus in one month after the victory of Sobraon, we have signed our treaty, leaving a B. garrison in Lahore, having received 1 million & 1/4, sent to Delhi 256 brass guns taken in battle, created a Sikh tributary into a hill Raj-poot sovereign independent of Lahore but paying a nuzzur to us, whose kingdom is as large as Nepaul.

We have weakened a warlike republican power by depriving it of 1/3 of its territories. We have proved to all Asia that the most powerful state, with the bravest army organized by French officers, cannot successfully oppose us, & we have finished our operations by protecting with a B. force the govt. so lately in arms against us.

Our quarrel was most just. I have no reproach on my conscience &, altho' I have been severely tried by circumstances to which I will not advert, I am happy in the confidence that my countrymen will not be ashamed of my policy nor of the conduct of its brave troops.

I march across the Hyphasis through our new district to Loodiana, there to meet all the B. protected Sikhs & to speak my mind to some of them, & thence to Simla for the summer.

In the midst of the late trying events I have trusted to my own judgement of what was just & right &, by the mercy of God, our affairs have terminated to my satisfaction, & I must now patiently await the fiat of my superiors & the verdict of the public.

Charles went to the palace this morning & has made a very pretty sketch of the little prince, of Lal Singh the minister, & a view of the durbar buildings.

We shall have Golab Singh in our camp for some days, & I shall request a sitting[239] as the only favor I have asked for giving him Cashmeer & making him a king. I believe I might have had £50,000 secret presents from the raja for the services & favors he has received.

[*No closing*]

82. [*To Walter.*] Simla. 5th April 1846

I have written so much about Lahore, the Sikhs, & our milty. operations that you must all be surfeited.

I saw 50 chiefs at Loodiana on my way up & am now a private gent[*lema*]n perched up on a high hill 2000 ft. from the stones of the watercourse below, into which I could roll a 6 p[*oun*]d shot.

As to scenery, it is fine, with the snowy mountains in the background, but the shapes are those of hills, made up of stiff clay & shabby rocks, not the great massive slabs of rock which Salvator Rosa[240] delighted in.

The rhododendron trees, twice as big as my body (& since my fall I have grown fat) & several above 50 ft. high, [*are*] now full of deep crimson blossoms, each flower rather longer than a peony. They seem to like the n[*orth*] side of the hill best, but I hope to get away 50 miles towards the snowy range, believing that I shall best succeed in sending home seeds from trees which flourish in a climate as severe or more so than our own, for it seems to be a law of nature that the trees bud & flower in the colony to which they are transported at the same period of the year. Thus this region, being more temperate than England, the plants would flower in March & be cut off by our early frosts, & I suspect those near the snowy range, by blooming later, will do better for our climate. I send you a small packet of deodara [*sic*][241] seeds from a famous tree abt. 40 m[*iles*] to the northward, 200 ft. high. Give Burke half & desire [*him*] to raise them. The rest [*are*] for Penn's Rocks.[242]

I have no doubt your English papers expecting annexation will be

---

[239] The sketches of Dalip Singh, Lal Singh, and Gulab Singh all appear in *Recollections*.
[240] The seventeenth century Italian landscape painter.
[241] Deodar is a Himalayan tree similar to cedar.
[242] Apparently Hardinge felt at the time that Walter might buy this estate.

disappointed & abuse me. As long as Peel & the Duke are satisfied, I care little for the press.

My hope is that yr. dear mother will be in England when this mail arrives. I send my letters for her addressed to White Hall Pl., & also a small box with a bracelet. She may expect some scarfs by the next mail.

Having in 70 days dictated terms of peace at Lahore, made a king of Cashmeer, & sent 256 guns to Delhi & then through the gt. towns to Calcutta, I am now obliged to return to red-boxes & the humdrum business of the state. I am remarkably well, confident that I have acted right, though abused by the press, & gratified by the confidence of the offs. of the army I have just left. I therefore sleep in peace, with a conscience void of having given cause of the late war & having, I hope, justified my professions by my acts that *my case* should be a good one.

Love to dr. Sarah & baby.

83. [*To Walter.*] Simla. April 6, 1846

The course you took with your constituents was honest, manly, & judicious. I do not think it will be an easy seat for you in future; in what direction are you looking out?

What have you determined about Penn's Rocks?

Where is my chronometer?

Have you heard anything more of Hillman's farm being for sale? Pray tell Woodgate to buy it. I have £10,000 in the 4 pr. cts. here.

I have lived at a ruinous expense in camp—serving all the world & giving milty. dinners in my state tent to 150 guests. I shall now be quiet & am not sorry to have a little repose, but the red boxes are arriving in upon me very fast.

Here in this h[ou]se[243] Ld. A[*uckland*] signed his Simla Proclamation. Ld. E[*llenborough*] signed his also at Simla, which will never be forgiven by the Whigs.[244]

Mine have been signed in my camp & are plain matter-of-fact compositions, & I am prepared for the abuse of the press, satisfied if my masters Peel & the Duke approve. You who know my irritability would never have discovered it during our campaign.

Well, the 70 days are over my head & I hope honorably. The next

[243] Auckland House, as it began to be called, was built in 1839; Hardinge was the last G.G. to occupy it.

[244] i.e. Auckland's announcement of 1 Oct. 1838, divulging his intentions to invade Afghanistan, and Ellenborough's proclamation, dated 1 Oct. 1842, condemning Auckland's policies and his readiness to recognize an Afghan government committed to peace.

autumn will, I hope, be tranquil. I am not exhausted by this hard work because I sleep soundly under any circumstances, but no man in India can say from week to week what may be his form of tryal. Still, it is a great position & a glorious empire for England.

84. [*To Walter.*] Simla. April 19th, 1846

We are quiet at Lahore & the presence of our troops enables the govt. to detach its own Sikh forces to any district, having more reliance on our regts. than their own.

The govt. wd. stand if a man of ordinary abilities & honest intentions were at the head of the govt. This, however, is not the case. The ranee is a profligate woman & the minister Lal Singh,[245] her paramour. H.M. [*Jindan*] is in great danger at this moment from a *fausse couche*. The other ministers are devoid of patriotism & seem more bent on plundering than saving the state.

My policy at Lahore, I find by a letter received from Ld. Ripon by the last mail, is in strict accordance with his views.

I see I am denounced by the London press as unfit for my high office. This will all be set right if the correspondence be published. After the Ferozshah dispatches there will have been a fortnight of anxiety, when we were of necessity inactive, followed by 2 mails of successive victories & the 3rd mail, dated from Lahore, announcing the signature of peace.

I shall know the verdict of my masters at home about the beginning of July; in the meantime it is true philosophy to be patient, & I am now fagging to bring up the arrears of business which, I am rejoiced to find, is not near so heavy as at Calcutta, whilst I am enjoying a hill climate.

I send you 2 small bags of deodar seeds. Pray have a large bed prepared in the slip with instructions to Burke to raise as many as he can. Some that Bob Wood sent home are coming up.

With regard to Hillman's farm, I request it may be secured, giving *something more* than a fair agricultural price. I see Woodgate says it is valued at 13,000 & may only bring 6000. I have no objection to go [*sic*] as far as £7000.

I believe Chas. has sent home £4000 since, making £8000 now at my command by discounting the bills at a very low rate.

I have £10,000 in the 4 pr. cents here (in Calcutta). That £10,000 is (in a mem[*orandu*]m I will give to Charles) to be considered as belonging to Fanny; in the meantime I request that Cox will pay

---

[245] Lal Singh reclaimed the ministry soon after the Kasur negotiations.

Arthur Cunninghame [*sic*] the interest quarterly or half-yearly, as he seems to prefer that arrangement.

I will remit £1000 home in May & another in June. Insist upon Cox paying his own balance out of my remittances. He is too liberal.

Having 8000 at command I need not yr. assistance, my dear Walter, to repay the 6000. That sum & the Irish mortgage of 4500 will belong to Arthur at our decease & need not be pd. before.

Emily will have the value of the lands to be purchased until I can collect 10,000 in money. After purchasing Hillman's & Pott's farms, say [*at*] 14,000, I have 8000, it wd. appear, at home, & about the end of the year I shall have remitted 6000 more.

Come what may, if I remain here till next Christmas, the fortunes of the younger children will have been secured:

> Fanny—10,000 in the 4 pr. cts. [*at*] Calcutta
> Arthur—10,000 secured by you, Irish mortgage
> Emily—10,000 secured on land bought.

Charles is very prudent. I dare say by the end of the year he will have put by 5 or 6000 of his sal[*ar*]y.

This being the state of my affairs, I anxiously wish you & Woodgate not to lose Hillman's or Pott's farm.

If a Whig govt. comes in during the session & they recall me, I am quite ready to go home. My conscience is at ease as to my acts, & I can make out a strong case. The Chronicle may abuse me in anticipation of a change of govt. to lay grounds for my recall & the appoint[*men*]t of a Whig successor.[246] These are vicissitudes which don't affect me. I return to a happy home grateful to God for His mercies vouchsafed, & past 60 a wise man ought not to tempt his fortune too long. I only hope to be entitled to the merit of having been a governor genl. who has succeeded in what he has attempted in a plain business-like manner. And if I am ill-treated, rely upon it, I have energy left to vindicate my conduct.

I remember the Duke of W. abused in the Hse. of Coms. by the present Ld. Fitzwilliam for the Battle of Talavera, which that lord

---

[246] The pro-Whig *Morning Chronicle* carried on a relentless barrage of attacks from Jan. to Mar. on Hardinge's Northwestern policies. He was accused of incompetence, irresolution and timidity, which had permitted the Sikhs to cross the Sutlej: 'it would at once be a great blessing to India and to England if it were thought advisable to relieve [*Hardinge*] from a task to the performance of which it must now be evident he is unequal.' Arguing that a 'corrupt, aggressive Panjab' should have been punished earlier, the *Chronicle* demanded that Hardinge ought to annex immediately the whole Sikh kingdom, including Kashmir, and added: 'In our humble opinion he has slumbered too much already, and had better remain wide awake for some time to come' (20 Jan. p. 4; 6 Feb. p. 4; 7 Feb. p. 4; 12 Feb. p. 4; 14 Feb. p. 5; 16 Feb. p. 4; 23 Feb. p. 4; 24 Feb. p. 5; 26 Feb. p. 4; 27 Feb. p. 5; 2 Mar. p. 4).

asserted he had fought for a peerage & from no patriotic motive;[247] & I think in the Lords, Ld. Erskine said it wd. be more humane to shoot the B. soldiers on the parade in St James' Park than to send them to be massacred in Spain.

I am accused, I see, by the Sunday Times of inveighing 50,000 Sikhs across the Sutlege in order to cut their throats & am worse than the French in Algeria in stifling the Arabs in a cave.[248]

The editor cheated the Election Comm[itt]ee of 1000. I met him in the city when the selection of an artist to make an equestrian statue of the Duke was to be discussed. He sided with me in voting for Chantrey & presumed to address me. I turned my back upon him as a swindler & he has on all occasions attacked me.

I imagine Peel is very anxious to retire. I regret it but am not surprized.

Charles & Arthur are by this time near Cashmeer in company with Ld. Elphinstone[249] & my surgeon.[250] It will emancipate them & enlarge their minds. They are really fine fellows.

It is a bore to be writing to England [when the mail] is daily expected. I hope yr. mother will be in London before this letter arrives.

Nothing can be more cordial than Peel's & Ld. Ripon's letters. I am extremely anxious that the merits of my brave old colleague Sir Hugh Gough should be amply brought forward in any debate. I have a sincere regard for him &, as people attempt to make mischief, I express my own wishes to you very strongly. Pray attend to this.

I deeply commiserate dear Sarah & her poor father & mother in their great affliction. I wish I could say anything that would console them, but my sentiments of admiration & affection for so perfect a creature would only increase their distress in losing her. Before I could be of any use to her boys, I shall be in my grave. I hope her dear little girls will be the reflected image of their mother in mind & every virtue. I should very much wish you wd. convey to her the affectionate regard of one who will cherish & respect her memory & take an interest in anything that belonged to her.[251]

What weak mortals we are! I am quite upset by these thoughts. Probably a better Christian with a more lively faith in the transitory

---

[247] There was no universal praise for Wellington in 1809 for Talavera because of the furor over his approval of the Convention of Cintra the previous year.

[248] *The Sunday Times* (15 Feb. 1846, p. 4) had, in fact, angrily reacted to *The Times*, which had reported and condoned Hardinge's supposed 'plan for massacring fifty thousand Seikhs' after tricking them into crossing the Sutlej.

[249] John Elphinstone (1807–60), the 13th Baron Elphinstone, governed Madras, 1837–42. He travelled extensively in India from 1845 to 1847 as a private citizen.

[250] Dr James Thomas Walker (1826–96) of the Bombay Engineers.

[251] Sarah's elder sister, Laura Jane, died on Feb. 26, 1846, at the age of 35; leaving three sons and five daughters; she was married to 3rd Baron Kensington (1801–72).

vanities of this world through which I am toiling would be more composed. I will not write by this mail to dear Sarah.

[*P.S.*] When is my chronometer to be sent out?

85. [*To Sarah.*] Simla. 5 May 1846

I trust in God that you are well through your troubles, but I am so nervous that I have been delaying to write till the last moment, being in hourly expectation of the mail from England.

I grieve most sincerely for the loss you have sustained. It was impossible to see & hear her without loving her for her admirable qualities. Make my affecte. condolences to your dear father & mother. I was much touched by a note of yr. father's to Walter in which, in the midst of his affliction, he begs to be remembered to me.

I am very messed & dull after my life in camp, awake 5 or 6 times a night to write letters, having the lives of thousands in my keeping, & now here I am with red boxes from East & West on all subjects but not the excitement of whether we shall get to Lahore this season or not. And yet how grateful I am to a merciful God that the boys are safe & unhurt. And now I think we have closed the Book of Fate as long as I remain in India—as regards fighting.

When I say remain in India, it may indeed be for a very short time. If Peel with-draws, my office is very much at their [*the Whigs'*] service & a gentlemanlike limit will be quite sufficient. Let me know what is said. I am not a volunteer but a conscript soldier, & I was much obliged to Peel for telling the world so, for I have always [*been*] ashamed of appearing to give myself airs, but I shall return contentedly to my roses & you will all find me very little altered. The grass has not grown under my feet, or rather the quill has scarcely been out of my hand, since I arrived, but I have seen enough & am in that happy state that if I stay, it will be in the performance of my duty, & if I return, I have a happy fireside for a contented old age, for you see I have no intention of leaving my bones in India.

In 6 weeks I shall have the verdict of my masters on the Lahore treaty &, as they have supported me manfully & honorably so far, I know they will do me justice in the difficult position in which I was placed. I ask no more than justice & am quite at ease about the result, not from a callous insensibility but because on reflection I really have nothing to alter.

I send to Lady Emily a packet of letters from Charles, which will give you views of yr. brothers. Both write well, Arthur rather the more quaint of the two. God bless you.

86. [*To Walter.*] Simla. May 5th, 1846

I have been most impatient to receive the mail before this goes out in the hope that I might congratulate you & dst. Sarah on her safety & the presence of a little stranger who will welcome home his old grand-father when his pilgrimage in this distant land is over & above all be the comfort of your old age when you arrive at my period of life.

I miss Charles & Arthur more than I can express. A thousand little confidences pass between us, & I long for their return.

Tell me everything you remark concerning your dear mother, how she looks & whether she is reconciled to my absence till the end of 1848, *if* the Whigs should not turn me out. Here as at home the Whig papers attack me,[252] as I believe, in the hope of having a vacant office at their disposal. They are most welcome.

The debate, from the rancourous tone of the speakers, looked very like a breakup of the Peel administration. In its effect personally towards me, it may be unfortunate, or the reverse, as regards any discussion on my Indian policy. As to the recent campaign, the public never will know the extraordinary position in which I have been placed. My desire to forbear as long as it was possible before I drew the sword is one point, & the prudence of the policy at Lahore is the second great feature. The intermediate points are more or less milty. On the first, Peel has already said all that is necessary, & on the policy I expect his govt. will equally give me its support. I have nothing to fear from the keenest scrutiny & Court investigation—not that I am free from errors, but that I have, in accordance with my own views, carried out a policy approved by the govt. when it was submitted to them.

We have had a riot at Lahore originating in a soldier on duty wounding 2 cows with his sword, which instantly was exaggerated into the report that the English were killing cows. The barbarians raised a tumult which was put down by the Lahore authorities. One Brahmin hung by the Sikh govt. & the place is as quiet as ever. This is one of my responsibilities which will stick to me till next Decr., &

---

[252] More than one Indian newspaper, at least initially, denounced Hardinge's postwar arrangements. The Whig-oriented *Hurkaru* (27 Feb. 1846, p. 229) favoured full annexation, adding: 'There appears to us to be no alternative consistent with the security of our territory from aggression between this complete and ... justifiable and politic measure, and subsidizing the country.' But criticism was not confined just to the Whig newspapers.

The Friend of India, generally pro-Hardinge, criticized the stationing of British troops at Lahore, fearing it could lead to another collision (April 2, 1846, p. 210). The conservative *Englishman* (28 Mar. 1846, p. 2) condemned Hardinge for permitting the Sikh state to continue, however much reduced, suggesting that this gesture of good will would earn no gratitude: 'In this country the friends of one season are enemies in the next, and we may have to contend against combinations already planned, or hitherto frustrated by the fortune of Providence which rules our British destiny in the East.'

on every rippling of the waves Cabool is shouted out as if 9000 soldiers could not protect themselves. Nothing will occur & it does not disturb my repose.

We have a fort which holds out[253] & is inconvenient to take at this season, but it must be done. We have recd. a million of money under the treaty which, with 250,000 more, will pay nearly all our war expenses. As my boxes now come in very fast, I am trying after an active campaign to settle down to the drudgery of office, looking into every detail & doing a great deal of slavish work. I confess I buckle to very reluctantly.

The country is perfectly quiet. The smaller independent states rejoice in a policy which they translate, 'The B. govt. will not swallow us up on the first decent pretext for annexing our territory—look to the Punjab.' It has, I think, had this effect of producing more confidence & attachment in n[ative] powers towards the B. rule, & the milty. success of capturing 256 guns & marching them through the country is giving an importance & reality to our victories which the great mass of the people know nothing of through newspapers & gazettes.

In my letters to your mother, I have sent all those recd. from Charles. He likes his tour & I am confident it will improve him. I shall still be without him for a month.

The day after tomorrow I am going 40 miles into the mountains. I hope to get some rhododendrons, which blossom in June, & I shall send them to you for Burke.

Let me know how the plants in the tangle thrive. I suspect the old [?land] below the tangle is too low & wet for any plants. How have the fruit trees blossomed? Are the strawberries of a good kind? How does Niven's asparagus bud answer?

Let me know what you hear of India if Peel goes out. Do you ever speak to Jocelyn?[254] or Mahon?

What is become of Bingham Baring?[255] Peel quoted Lord Ashburnham in his speech as if they were not on terms.[256]

And now, my dear Walter, goodbye.

87. [*To Sarah.*] Narcondah. May 10th, 1846

I wish in the happiest anticipations that God in His mercy has twice helped you & Walter in tender pledges of yr. happiness, & I pray that

[253] The Sikh commander of the Kangra fort refused to surrender; Hardinge sent a British force with heavy cannon over difficult terrain, the fort being taken on 26 May.

[254] Viscount Jocelyn was a secretary to the Board of Control from Feb. 1845 to July 1846.

[255] William Bingham Baring was paymaster general of the army.

[256] Bertram Ashburnham, the 4th Earl of Ashburnham, opposed Peel's free trade policies.

these dear little strangers will be self-reflected likenesses of their parents
& that I may live to see them.

Tomorrow we return to Simla, having, after the last mail left Simla
for England, determined to play truant for a week, getting rid of
boxes & papers, & unbending the mind by idleness & fresh mountain
air.

This beautiful spot is about 40 miles from Simla & is a high pass in
the mountain from which you look upon the great snowy range which
divides us from Chinese Tartary.

I also have the satisfaction of seeing the Kooloo mountains, lately
acquired by my treaty at Lahore. Bold black mountains are backed
by still higher mountains of ice & snow, some of them 18,000 ft. above
the sea. This pass is 9000 ft. above the sea, & Simla 7,500.

The whole horizon is one mass of glittering mountains abt. 60 miles
off, clothed in snow except when the black precipitous sides of the
mountain prevent the snow from remaining. These black streaks
act like the bold pencil of the artist in bringing out the shapes of the
hills & guessing what their shapes must be when surveyed 60 miles
off.[257]

The first burst of this massive barrier of rock & ice is very grand. I
never saw anything so sublime in nature. Those who have travelled
over Switzerland prefer this infinitely. It is gigantic.

Fron the tent in which I am writing we look down into steep ravines
2000 ft. deep. We look up to masses of ice & rock, which frequently
appear to be suspended in the sky, for we often see a blue haze lower
down which intervenes, on which the snowy hills seem to rest.

I was tired when I came in after a very craggy road of 14 miles,
but when I rode my pony through the jaws of the pass, I was so
enchanted I could not be at rest till I had explored the best points of
view for dear Charles, but others more alive to the refreshment of the
body sent messengers to say the breakfast was ready, & certainly the
sentiment of the picturesque is very compatible with a good appetite
on these high mountains.

During the heat of the day I had to write a very long political
Mem[orandu]m on the state of the Punjab to Ld. Ripon, & that kept
me quiet from 10 till near 5. But we walked & rode, picking up *blue*
primroses & *blue* as well as red strawberry plants in full flower. I found
in the tangles a beautiful little yellow rose, very fragrant, which I shall
endeavour to send to S.P. On the top of the mountains I found
the creeping Cotoneaster with its pretty white flowers enjoying the
mountain breeze but clinging for safety to the rocks, which reminded

---

[257] Hardinge is probably referring to the lofty mountain ranges of Hatu Dhar,
Chwaurtu Dhar and Gansai Dhar.

me of Red-leaf[258] & its excellent master, dear Mr Wells. I found the rhododendron arboreum high up the hill & now in full flower, a month later than at Simla. I intend to send home seeds from these trees which, from the increased elevation, are 2 months later than those at Simla, & they may take after the parent tree & be more hardy. They all grow on the sides of steep banks & are well drained. I have 4 of a different kind which flower in June & July. If the flower is beautiful, these will answer for our climate. Pray remember me most kindly to our excellent friend Mr Wells.

The next morning we set off to breakfast on the top of a mountain 5 miles off. The view after a climbing ride on hill ponies was very good, much finer than from the pass. I found some magnificent fragments of rocks standing almost upright 50 ft. high & 30 broad— fit pillars through which to survey this wondrous view.

I was so restless from excitement that, altho' Robt. Wood had letters of some interest, I declined to open them till I had gratified my eyes with the view of this scenery from various points. A good deal tired, I sat down in the shade & read a letter from Chevr. Bunsen,[259] conveying to me the acknowledgements of the king of Prussia for the notice I had taken of Prince Waldemar, & others relating to the king of Cashmeer on whose head I placed a crown at Lahore. But in the midst of such scenery as this, I could not help moralizing on the insignificance of man.

Scarcely 2 months had elapsed since I was engaged in professionally hunting & being hunted by our fellow man according to the *noble* art of war! And here, after all this turmoil, I am enjoying, posted on the centre of the globe, the more innocent beauties of nature.

Still, in the midst of these wild scenes, when carried in a chair by 4 men over precipices where a false step wd. leave my bones 2000 ft. below, I am forcibly reminded of years gone by, when 50 yrs. ago I used to be strung round the waist by a rope from Durham Cathedral to rob the rooks' nests & in my middle age to shoot old London Bridge. And now I confess I look down the abyss below without giddiness & something like pleasure, delighted to escape from the drudgery of red boxes & the cares & deep responsibilities of this empire. The latter, how[eve]r, follow me here if important. During the campaign I was repeatedly roused to write letters in the night after a hard day's work. I am blessed with health, happy in the renovated strength & spirits of Lady Emily, & my children promise to be estimable members of society, able & willing to do their duty. Nevertheless at 60 years passed, I must not tempt fortune too far.

[258] A large house located on the western outskirts of Penshurst.
[259] Baron Christian von Bunsen (1791–1860) was then the Prussian ambassador in London.

Everything looks like a breakup of the Peel administration. I am willing to stay to superintend the Punjab policy or to return at a moment's notice. I have seen much during my short administration of 20 months. I have done nothing of which I ought politically to be ashamed, &, come what may, I am prepared to take my line with temper & decision.

Tomorrow I go through a wild forest, which will bring me within 25 miles of Simla, &, like a boy returning to school, I confess, dearest, I do so rather sluggishly, being very tired of official papers.

Kindest regards to yr. father. Give my love to Mrs Ellison & Mrs Lambton.

88. [*To Emily.*] Simla. May 20th, 1846

I was very much pleased with the scenery around the Narcondah Pass. I returned here on the 7th day, the exertion & the life in the air having done us all much good, & the stiff knee by constant exercise has nearly recovered its former size & suppleness.

I have not heard lately of the boys. The further they penetrate into Cashmeer, the less frequent are the opportunities of conveying letters. By the last notes recd., which I enclose, they were going on very prosperously.

On the 25th, the Queen's birthday, I give a ball, which will be attended by all the world, & some large dinners the following days. But in this quiet place I live prudently, & I shall recover from the effects of an extensive hospitality during the campaign, when I seldom had fewer than 25 or 30 to meals, & [*at*] one dinner at Lahore [*I had*] 150. It has always been my creed that public men are bound to do credit to the position they occupy, & we have this month secured £20,000 for the 2 girls, Arthur having £10,000 of our marriage money & Charles S.P. & anything which may be at our disposal hereafter. He [*also*] lays by of his own salary [*of*] £3000 nearly £2500 a yr. so that he will be very well off. And as this Eastern adventure in my old age has enabled the boys to prove their merit, neither you or I must ever repine at sacrifices to ourselves so useful to them, & I am delighted to find by yr. letters that you take this sensible view of our position.

I have a great many letters to write in reply to the congratulations of old friends. This is grateful labour. I have a note from poor Mrs Lyall, whose husband died in my house in 7 hours of cholera, a son of the M.P. for London & very good people. She says she wrote to you. Her brother, Sir J. Davis, is govr. at Hong-Kong. They are deeply connected with the Court of Directors & I hope you have answered her letter. Her brother has just vacated the office of chair-

man & has behaved well to me. Mr Hogg is now the chairman. A
few civilities to the family wd. be advisable.

Have you received Sir Hugh Gough's extract of a letter to Ld. F. R.
Somerset about Arthur? I think I sent it to Walter.

You don't notice my Genl. Order issued on Christmas Day. The
scene was so different from those which you & I have spent together
on that festival for 25 years that I thought of you repeatedly during
the service. The subsequent scenes were full of interest & anxiety, &
now everything has subsided into peace & repose.

                                                          21st May

The mail came in yesterday & I find by the Gazette that you are
a viscountess. I have received a very flattering note from Her Majesty
& one from Peel, which is, in warmth of approbation & acknowledgement of my services, more than I deserve.

I have no promise of any public remuneration to maintain the
dignity of the title, altho' some letters contain hints to that effect. It
will not alter my mode of life, but for Charles' sake it is a necessity.

I am glad Walter & Sir Robert agreed to preserve my family name
because I really believe I am the descendant of a Danish corsair or
pirate who was settled near Bristol when William the Conqueror took
possession of England. And Walter did right to attach King's Newton
to the title. Whether the foreign addition be Lahore or Sutlege is
immaterial.[260]

I told you, dearest, not to mind what the press said. I was confident
I had exercised a right judgement in making the treaty I did, & the
press, which so ungenerously assailed me without knowing the facts
of the case, have the gentlemanly candour to do me justice. Sir John
Hobhouse's speech & Ld. John Russell's were particularly gratifying.
I rather fear I have given offence in some unknown way to the Duke.
I love & venerate him too sincerely ever to have any other feeling
than regret. I have had 2 or 3 letters—very cold & official.

Ld. E[*llenborough*] does not say he approves of my policy; the treaties
had not been received, but Lord Ripon is very frank & cordial &
ready to give me credit for everything I do. We have completely
crushed the Sikhs as a milty. power but the tranquillity of a horde of
barbarians after a century of plunder & rapine is not to be expected,
& I shall have a good deal of nice steering in my political arrangements
next autumn. God be praised no more fighting, for you cannot conceive the anxiety of having the dear boys by my side. As to Arthur's

[260] The G.G. was now to be addressed as Viscount Hardinge of Lahore and King's
Newton. The lineage of his family, which once lived at King's Newton in Derbyshire,
can be traced back to the Stuart period. (See nos. 90 and 96; notes 265 and 282.)

going into the cavry., it wd. be very prejudicial to his advancement, & as long as he is on my staff it is unimportant to him whether he is in the cavalry or infantry. When he is a captain & has in 1849 gone to the Milty. College & passed his examination, I will then consider of his being a captain of horse, but he must qualify himself for the higher branches of his profession & always look to the future without losing the enjoyment of the present.

Charles, when I am no more, will have a public duty to perform in the House of Lords, & if, whilst a commoner, he can be employed in public life, so much the better. It may stimulate him to great activity, & he has a very good judgement. Lord Gough's son is going to marry an heiress with £50,000.[261] The Honble. Charles must make a prudent alliance. I hope these new honors will contribute to his means of being a useful Englishman & that you & I may live in the memory of our children as parents whom they love *not* as a duty for bringing them into the world but as friends who have made their welfare their first object.

I think it not unlikely that Gough may in a few months return to England, & if so, I may have the opportunity of doing something for Cunninghame [*sic*], but I must not write on the subject because it is a delicate affair as regards Gough & myself. I believe the govt. know the true state of affairs during the late campaign, but it is my duty to carry on the public services with perfect cordiality & I therefore wish all my family to speak of him with cordiality. Rely upon it, it is for my honor that we should separate by being on the best of terms with him.

Emily may amuse herself with cutting out scraps of news-papers discussing the Punjab war, & they can be pasted afterwards in a scrapbook, as I may want such reflections of the present times if ever I have time & courage to put my papers together.

By the tone of the Whig leaders in both Houses of Parlt., I presume they do not mean to recall me if Peel is obliged to resign. I must, dearest, go on with this great affair in hand on which my reputation is in some degree at stake, & I think you will admit that the encouragement of the peerage & possibly a pension from the Company are not very good reasons for deserting my post. What a space the 2 last years have covered in my eventful life! & how devoutly grateful I ought to be to the Supreme Disposer of all events for the mercies vouchsafed!

23rd May

I have just read the last line of the preceding sheet & I must say I anxiously wish my public course was run. Here I have cool air &

[261] Early in June, George-Stephens Gough (1815–95) married Jane, daughter of George Arbuthnot of Elderslie, Surrey.

exercise & am master of my own time, more than at Calcutta. It is probable I shall pass the whole of this year in the N.W. Provinces, &, if it be consistent with the public service, I shall hope to be here & in the plains during the whole of next year. To look beyond the next year is vain. Here no cholera or liver affects its inhabitants & our boys will be safe. Still, I confess the desire to be with you is stronger every day, & I long to see Walter, Sarah & their babies. How happy they both must be!

I am going to write to Walter this evening. I know how happy he is that this difficult campaign has been terminated to the honor of our country & my credit & that the policy I have adopted is received in England with my general approbation. Ld. E. knows the difficulty &, in my free & confidential communications with him, he has never cut the Gordian Knot. But you know my determination was fixed to have a righteous cause before I drew the sword & then a moderate course towards the enemy. This course is supposed to be different from that pursued in Scinde, & therefore I shall never discuss this matter with him or risk the interruption of our friendship by a tone of comparison as to measures, which wd. annoy him. My common sense has extricated me from many difficulties, & when the Chronicle & Whig press were calling for my recall, I never had any apprehensions of the result because I had kept within the bounds of moderation & mercy. I beg you, therefore, to be most attentive to him. He is a sincere friend, has a good heart, & a better opinion of my abilities than I deserve— therefore, cultivate him.

25th May

I send you a copy of Peel's warm-hearted letter to me. It is better than the peerage. Also for yr. private perusal & Walter's, a copy of the letter from the Queen,[262] which glows with good feeling & breaks through the cold formality of a court announcement of H.M.'s pleasure. Even the Scotch ice of Aberdeen is melted, & he is *eulogistic*.[263] In short, I have letters from the great men of the day, quite sufficient to make me loose [*sic*] my ballast [*as*] if I were 30 instead of 60. As you are not very far from that demure & respectable period of life, you must moderate yr. enthusiasm & let everybody give me praise except my family, & on the subject of Lord Gough you must be very discreet.

[*No closing*]

---

[262] Both letters untraced. However, excerpts acquired from V.A.P. and Peel Papers appear above in the introduction.

[263] Aberdeen conveyed to Hardinge 'the most cordial congratulations on the splendid deeds you have performed.'

89. [*To Walter.*] Simla. May 26, 1846

I feel as happy as when Charles was born & yr. mother safe. I had written before the mail came in a long rambling letter to Sarah of my excursion to the mountains, & I have since written her a short note to express my joy that yr. little man is come into the world. May he resemble his father & mother in all their good qualities.[264]

I have been up since 4 o'cl. this morn[in]g writing for 12 hours, & I omitted to tell dear Sarah in my note to her that I [am] much pleased at the arrangement abt. the sponsors & only wish I could be present. I hope this joyful event will be balm to [her] poor parents. Such a mother to be lost to her dear children makes me very sad, for it was impossible to see & speak to her & not to love her.

Next as regards your arrangements with Peel abt. the title, I think you judged quite right. I am myself indifferent whether the foreign addenda be Lahore or Sutlege. I leave it entirely to you. I am glad you retained the old Danish pirate's name, for I seriously believe we are the younger & purer branch of Ld. Berkeley's family, now Earl Fitz-Hardinge, for he is contraband as you know.[265]

Peel's letter to me is more than I deserve. I have sent a copy to yr. mother. His friendship for me has been constant, & no gov. genl. was ever more honorably supported by his friends than I have been by him, by Ld. Ripon, the Opposition & the country. In all my papers, dispatches, and Proclamations I have been as plain in my language as possible, & when in the state tent I addressed the maha-raja & the sirdars, I was short &, I hope, intelligible, preferring the soldier's style to the attempt of acting the states-man by fine language.

The correspondence with Ld. Gough & others is curious. It will never be known & I am quite content to leave matters as they are. The govt., I believe, know & appreciate the truth.

I told you I wd. have a good case. I postponed war till the 11th hour & 3/4, &, having proved my reluctance to draw the sword, I returned it to the scabbard at the earliest possible moment. My moderation will turn out to be strength, & if I were to be vain of what has been done, it wd. be to know & feel that the Yankees & the French are envious of our success. Look to Algeria occupied for 15 years with an army of 70,000 Frenchmen; examine the character of

[264] Sarah gave birth on March 21 to Walter Henry James, later M.P. for Gateshead; in 1893 he succeeded his father as the 2nd Baron Northbourne and died in 1923.

[265] 'The old Danish pirate' refers to Harding, the son of Eadnoth, who was called 'a noble Dane' and was a wealthy merchant of Bristol at the time of William the Conqueror's invasion in 1066. His son Robert (also known as Robert Fitz-Harding) became the founder of the house of Berkeley through the friendship of King Henry II. The connection of the Hardinge family to the original Robert Fitz-Harding and, in turn, to the Berkeleys, is not fully substantiated.

the warfare: Ruzzia & Dahra fumigations in caverns, & still the people hating & loathing them.

With us the Christian character of the war has had its reward. I have only 15,000 infantry, including 3,200 British, at Lahore. Our moderation induced submission, our justice to see the disbanded Sikhs paid their arrears has made them, for the present at least, friendly. Thus, as I have often said, there is strength in moderation.

Charles is to return on the 15th June. Arthur continues for a couple of months to be with Ld. Elphinstone, who is an agreeable man.

I am, as before the war, at my red boxes, fagging away as hard as at my former period of my life.

What do the Whigs wish to do with me? What does Ld. E[*llenborough*] say? My measures have in spirit been the reverse of those in Scinde. Pray caution your mother to cultivate him. I have for 30 yrs. been on terms of friendship with him & I am too old to have quarrels.

When are you going to send back my chronometer?

I suppose I must buy Hillman's [*farm*] if it is in the market. What is the state of the case?

[*Rest in fragmentary condition*]

90. [*To Emily.*] Simla. June 23rd, 1846

My head is very steady & I am not dazzled by the praise I receive. The happiness you express is dearer to my heart than all the congratulations put together; the warmth of your feelings is the greatest of consolations. I will admit to you I am homesick, but I have well considered the effect of deserting my post just as I have received a very liberal reward; it wd. be a stain on my new escutcheon & of this I am sure, that there is more consolation for you in finding that we have not been separated without gt. cause & honorable results than if I had merely vegetated here & returned with a sum of money.

When you receive this, I shall have been more than 2 years in India. Each month, as it draws nearer to the conclusion, will be less painful, & I quite agree with you that it will be very delightful to meet at Nice, which I shall delight in as the spot which has renovated yr. health during yr. seclusion.

The climate here is mild & cool. I am more master of my time & less worked than at Calcutta, &, when I descend into the plains, the dry cold of that climate is still better. I am certain of remaining on the frontier till next Janry. Many things may happen in the interval: the Whigs may come in & may require this place, but I am for 6 or 8 months in a state of comparative ease & not subject to the hot climate of the plains. Before the end of Janry. I shall hear from the home govt. on many points & by that time the Lahore experiment will have had a tryal. Probably I shall be obliged to remain on the frontier till the beginning of 1848. If so, this will bring with it a solid consolation—the knowledge that I am in good climate.

I think of sending home Benjy early in 1848, for in 1849 he is to go to the Milty. College & he must prepare. I have just been writing to him & sent him off a packet of newspapers & letters.

Charles has dispatched 29 sketches to Walter, some to be selected for publication. Tell Walter the style of J. D. Harding's book on drawing appears to me to be the best, namely a mixture of litho*tint* & litho*graphy*. I wish the Queen & the prince who are artists to see them. The Q. may take what she likes. After her notes, I am quite devoted to her.

I am sorry Walter has given up Penn's Rocks. He is probably right, but the hope of having the two brothers as neighbours was a cherished plan, originating, it is true, in his own fancy but relinquished now very reluctantly by me, for it wd. greatly add to our happiness.

Also tell Walter that the first thing to be done with the sketches is to have them properly mounted, &, after the Queen has seen them (if H.M. condescends), then to have them framed, which prevents their being soiled & injured.

I send a mem[*orandu*]m (on note paper) & beg you will answer each question.

I sometimes fear the things are lost.

Tell Emily I have returned the necklace to Delhi. It was turquoise *enamel* with a few diamonds instead of real *turquoises*.

Dear Arty has bought each of his sisters a shawl at Cashmeer. Yours will not be ready till the end of the year.

Pray tell Lord Mahon I was delighted with his letters.

Don't forget to present poor Mrs R. Fitzroy[266] with some present & my love. Be particularly kind to Robert.

I propose you should spend £3000 a yr. whilst in England. I can very well afford it.

My plan for Charles is, after giving the 3 younger children £10,000 each, to invest the remainder, whatever it may be, & let it roll for the 4th generation of Vist. H., who will be a pauper unless we make provision for him; &, as Charles' son may be expected to be alive 50 yrs. hence (as he is not yet born), a moderate sum at compound interest will, 50 yrs. hence, be a large sum. The 2nd & 3rd vist. (don't reckon yr. chickens before they are hatched) will have £3000 a yr. each; the 4th *nothing*. If I don't do something for him, he will probably be an honble. pauper. I therefore must not lose sight of this posterity duty.[267] You & I can, I am sure, be quite *noble* enough with £5000 a

[266] Mary Henrietta, wife of Robert Fitzroy.

[267] Henry Charles Hardinge (1857–1924), the first son of the 2nd Viscount Hardinge and Lavinia, became the 3rd Viscount Hardinge in 1894. His eldest son, Henry R.

yr. to spend & S.P. to cover us. This duty may make me somewhat niggardly, but I am quite satisfied that Peel is right in limiting the pub[*lic*] grant to £5000. I had rather receive a smaller sum with the cheerful assent of the country that it is well deserved than a larger sum & unpleasant squabbling in passing it through the Commons. Pray express this very clearly to Peel & to Ripon.

Be very civil to poor Sir A. Grant. He has been a true f[*rien*]d. He has bought all my wines, sent them out, & taken a great deal of trouble. I may owe him money.

When you see Louisa N[*apier*],[268] say I regret Sir Charles was not included, making a 3rd peer. Conciliate Ld. E[*llenborough*]. It is said he is mortified that Scinde should be drawn into contrast with Lahore. Always remember he is one of my oldest friends & that he is *sensitive*. Lady Colchester has not written me a line.

I am much gratified that you have pensioned Mad[*emois*]elle A.[269] for life. This is the proper way to enjoy affluence.

About the beginning of Sep. it will be known whether Ld. Gough will retire from the command of the army or not. She [*Lady Gough*] is a clever woman & wd. wish to remain.

I wish I could withdraw with credit. I have in the wane of life been called upon for gt. exertion of mind & body. By God's mercy I was successful; it is my duty to go through. I vigilantly watch my own powers of intellect, & the instant any *decadence* makes me suspicious of myself, I shall withdraw.

Reiterate to Sir Robt. Peel that my principal good fortune has been to serve under such a master. Don't *seek* to see Croker. He has written me a very bitter letter against Peel. I go with Peel without any reservation. It is not necessary to go to war with Croker because he agrees with Stanley & other honorable men; he has a right to his own political opinion. All I object to is the violence of his enmity to the man whom I respect more than any other[270] & to whom & the Duke I have more obligations than to any other men.

If the City of London give me a gold box, you had better take charge of it & appropriate it as you like. The merchant Taylors have

---

Hardinge, died, and he was succeeded by his second son, Caryl Nicholas Charles Hardinge, as the 4th Viscount Hardinge in 1924.

[268] Ellen Louisa was married to Capt. (afterwards Lt. Gen.) Edward D. H. E. Napier (1808–70), the stepson of Adm. Sir Charles Napier (1786–1860) who, in turn, was a cousin of Charles James Napier.

[269] Not identified.

[270] This was in reaction to an angry letter dated April 24, 1846, from John Wilson Croker, the Tory politician, charging that Peel had 'ruined the character of public men, and dissolved [*the Tory party*] by dividing the great landed interest' (D.N.B., v. 130).

sent me their resolution making me an honorary member of their
Compy. Launceston has sent a very cordial address.

I have in the plains, before my fall, been riding 30 miles before
breakfast & [?was] hard as a piece of iron. There is my poor friend,
the Duke, a prisoner in an armchair with £120,000 a yr. I am now
degenerating into corpulency & shall limit myself in diet. I never
touch meat but at 8 o'cl. in the even[in]g. I walk out at 5 for 3/4 of
an hour, then work till nine; tea & marmalade, a biscuit or a potato
at one, & dinner at 8; bed at 10, except on 2 nights when I have
parties which make me an hour later.

Charles has quite got rid of the dyspepsia he had at Calcutta &
now never touches medicine. He is looking remarkably well. He is
greatly pleased at his independence & seems determined to deserve
his rank & the duties it will impose.

You had better ask Sir Charles[271] for a small book, I think printed
at Derby, on the Hardinge family & let me have the information he
possesses. Earl Fitz-Hardinge has, I believe, a very detailed history of
the family. I don't care abt. King's Newton. I shall never leave S.P.
The most prudent course is, after our death, to let Charles sell S.P. if
he chooses &, with the money he will have, buy a better estate. I have
explained all these matters to him. At my age he may, if my views are
carried out, be the *consolidator* of the family. He views the things in their
proper light &, as his characteristic is gt. prudence & forethought, he
is well adapted to be the second viscount.

[*And*] now, dearest, after all this family twaddle, I will close my
letter. Pray see the Alick Woods. His attachment is very sincere.

Who writes the articles in my praise in the Times? They are very
well done.

Let me know after you have distributed the scarfs to whom you
wish I should send others. Love to dear little Emily.

91. [*To Walter.*] Simla. June 25th, 1846

The mail went out yesterday. With me it was a race to complete in
time the various letters I had to write with my own hand. About 45
were dispatched.

I then went to a ball & did not get to bed till late, but am pretty
fresh this morning, & whilst my mind is undisturbed I wish to say a
few words on the subject of Poundsbridge.[272]

Have the foundations been laid, & what is the state of the affair?
How much subscribed, & how much deficient? I should like also to

---

[271] Sir Charles Hardinge (1780–1864), 2nd Bart of Bellisle, Fermanagh, Ireland, was
the vicar of Tunbridge and Henry Hardinge's eldest brother.

[272] A chapel then under construction near Penshurst.

see the *elevation*. I dislike a Methodist chapel so much that I connect beauty & good taste with good feeling to the Creator. Every church should be so distinct with its belfry tower denoting its holy purpose that I attach much importance to ecclesiastical architecture. I should like, therefore, to be well informed of what is intended to be done, how the clergyman is to be decently paid, before I embark in the undertaking.

I told you that Charles wd. desire that the proceeds from his sketches should be applied to the church & that I wd. give £100. If the necessity for such an additional place of worship be well established, I should be disposed to make up Charles' & my own donations to £500. There is more merit in the act *now* when, as the founder of a title in my family, I am anxious to provide for my posterity, & as a worldly duty I naturally look to that object as one of importance. But my gratitude to the Giver of all mercies ought to make me in what regards His service a free & liberal giver, & my habits when I return will be much the same as they were before. The sum I propose to give is but a tithe of that which the public men so liberally bestowed upon me.

I do not wish my intentions to be known except to yr. mother until I am ready to take my line, & I wish to know from you whether the additional church is really required now.

A sect of Sikhs in the Jullundhur have for several years been in the habit of destroying their female children when born. I have taken very strong measures to repress this horror now that the district belongs to us.

I expect to have a report from the president in c[*ounci*]l at Calcutta on my proposal that no govt. work shall be done on our Sundays. This is the case at Bombay & I wish to extend it to the whole of B. India, for there never was a wiser law in all the hearings of the question.

My heart must be of stone if, whilst there is yet day, I do not *here* attempt to do all the good I can, avoiding the risks of proselytism but opening the eyes of this benighted people by education & the practical benefits of the Christian religion.

92. [*To Sarah.*] Simla. July 4th, 1846

Fortunately Charles has returned or I think I should have deserted my post. The daily constant drudgery of official papers, now that the excite[*men*]t of war is over, is very difficult to bear, but I must have patience, be humble & grateful. My council, poor fellows, are melting in Calcutta, have had no Sikh adventures but go through the same dry labours of which I am so ungratefully tired & of which I am sure Ld. E[*llenborough*] is very envious, for he delighted in public business

&, having no attractions of domestic happiness at home, India was a fine field for his ambition.

To tell you the truth, I tore off the 1/2 sheet, for I said *something* that had better not be said, even to you who are very prudent, & I shall be so disappointed if, as I grow older, I become sharp & *acariâtre.* My grandchildren will pout & refuse to play with my scanty locks. My gallant old colleague Ld. Gough has his wife, daughter, & grandchildren about him, & he lives surrounded by his family. She, Ly. Gough, is a clever woman, & we get on very well together, but I can't say that there is one agreeable woman here to whom I could go & gossip with anything but a sense of being bored & a suspicion that the lady felt the same result. Admit, my dear Sarah, that to endure this for 2 years more is a penance. The real consolation is in the hope that I do some good, & this is so compounded of vanity & self-sufficing that I discard it. I should die if I were not worked like a post-horse, & when I return I shall be as idle as the sloth.

I am very anxious for my English letters. I devour the domestic news first & then Peel's administration. If I did not feel a strong friendship for him, I shd. be a most ungrateful man.

Love to Mrs Lambton & all yr. family circle.

93. [*To Walter.*] Simla. July 4, 1846

I have no public news worth detailing. Everything [*is*] quiet in the Punjab; our troops [*are*] healthy & happy.

During the rains everything is stationary, & the heat in the plains is excessive till the middle of Oct. but I think I shall move into newly acqd. mountains in Sep. & thence in Oct. descend into the plains & be under canvas from October till March.

I walk 2 or 3 miles in the mount[*ain*]s & ride 5 miles before dinner & am somewhat tired of the monotonous life I lead.

The return of yr. mother to England has made me *homesick* but, after the rewards conferred upon me, the *general's old bones* belong to the public service. This autumn will be most important in its results, tho' free from milty. excite[*men*]t, & I must be on the spot & await the event. By the time I embrace you all I shall be pretty well worn out—that is the end of 1848. In a few days I shall have been 2 years in India. The next 2 will pass rapidly if you all prosper at home. Here Charles is his former self before his accident. This climate agrees with both of us.

Arthur is I know not where. Bob [*is*] quite well but anxious, I think, to go home, which he won't acknowledge. He is an excellent fellow.

94. [*To Walter.*] Simla. July 20th, 1846

I send 2 more sketches, one of the durbar at Lahore, the tone & colouring of which is very good; the other a rough sketch of a Hindoo temple, which I think particularly clever. They are better than some sent by the last mail, & you can settle the selection with the gt. H[*arding*].

It wd. be a great advantage to this bold style to have them in lithotint. There is a meagreness in lithograph which only suits outlines & will not suit Charles' style. I therefore consider lithotint indispensable.

You wd. be surprized at the rapidity with which he hits off his light & shade, at once placing his figures by intuition of their appropriate places.

Send out a book of paper fixed in a port-folio, the paper prepared & warranted not to take *the small pox*, a size larger than the Lahore durbar. Let me know the state in which the sketches reach you, whether damaged or opened, etc.

My chronometer has not turned up. The best mode when the article sent is so small is to send it in my bag.

I also send a native outline of the Tage [*Taj*] which will assist the artist who has to transfer Charles' drawing of the Tage [*Taj*] to lithotint.

The sketches are sent through the Bd. of Cl.

95. [*To Walter.*] Simla. 22nd July 1846

I am delighted to read yr. acct. & Sarah's of yr. dear mother. She must spare herself & not attempt to do too much. I have recommended her, in case S.P. shd. be too cold in the winter, to go to Hastings or Dover, which is easily managed by putting her carriage in the train. In England yr. mother will require 3000 a yr., & in a note to Cox I have told him to be prepared to that amt., & that I wish him, Cox, to receive my pension of £5000 a yr. at such periods as the payment may become due. Thus there will always be ample funds for any requirement. If the bill from Calcutta arrives here in time by tomorrow's post, I shall send to Cox abt. £7000. First pay off Pott's 5000, then settle with A. Cuninghame [*sic*] how he wishes his £10,000 to be secured, to which you & Alex Wood will be parties, & if there is any deficiency I can send money home, or the pension can repay the difference, for it will commence the day we occupied Lahore, abt. the 23rd Febry. (I *think*) &, 6 months being due, you & Cox can appropriate it as you like.

Payment reqd.		*Money in Cox's hands*	8000
Pott's farm	£5000	23rd July [*?send*] home	7000
A. Cuninghame [*sic*]	£10000	Pension	2500
	£15000		£17500

Cox must discount the bills. I lose more by 10 m[*onths*]' interest than by paying the disc[*oun*]t & I secure the money; & all our Calcutta banks are in a very tottering condition.

I regret the loss of Hillman's farm, but I have no doubt Mr Woodgate did his best. Mr Waldo had no right to be annoyed that I shd. buy Pott's farm. I owned S. Park before he came to Stone Wall. He had a perfect right to outbid me for Hillman's. I leave Charles at full liberty to sell S.P. if he does not like it at my decease & his mother's.

With regard to the pension, I entirely concur with Peel. A reward for service loses its grace when it is made the instrument of party bickering &, in our jealous system of govt., if, as is most important, we wish to retain the power of rewarding poor but deserving naval & milty. men, we must take care to be so moderate that the nation shall feel their representatives have not been profuse with the public money. As to the maneuvre in the Lords, neither of the chief actors care a pin for me or for Gough. It was a trick to vex Peel & show him how powerless he is.[273] I hope he will bring in a first bill & merely in that bill grant 3000 a yr. to my 2 next heirs. I wrote originally [*I would*] have preferred a sum of money from the Com[*pan*]y & £3000 from the Crown because I should have invested the sum for my posterity, if Charles or Arthur have any. But, being deeply impressed with a sense of gratitude to Peel for the friendly & admirable manner in which he has defended my conduct & thinking him decidedly right on public grounds, both as regards future precedents & my present repute, I shall be very sorry if he gives way. My habits are not expensive. I care very little for representation in my old age &, having provided for my younger children amply, I am too much bound up in attachment & friendship with Peel not to be sensibly alive & anxious to do him full justice. And if it were not that the Parlt. wd. be up before you can receive this letter, I wd. authorize you to read a state[*men*]t to this effect in the House. Rely upon it, posterity, age, & in our time will do this great & honest man justice. I feel very indignant when I read the shameful manner in which he is attacked.

---

[273] Discussion on the annuities for Hardinge and Gough continued in Parliament from May to July (3 *Hansard*, lxxxvi and lxxxvii, *passim*). Part of the delay was caused by Peel's enemies in an effort to embarrass him. At one stage of the impasse Wellington advised Peel to resign if Parliament did not promptly pass the pensions bill (letter of 8 June 1846, in Parker, iii. 353.)

I never shall be in public life again, but of this I feel certain, such is my faith in his integrity & sagacity, that if ever I have to give a vote in the Upper H[ou]se, it will be in accordance with his views.

As to the Punjab, I believe the Sikh govt. will stand. My difficulty is the chance of what the caprices of a barbarian army may produce when the B. force retires from Lahore. Peel can't say what will be the average price of wheat pr. q[uarte]r after this measure has passed. I cannot positively say whether the S[ikh] army will submit to discipline & low pay when we retire. In the interval we have got possession of all the forts in our ceded territories. Golab S. has done the same in his. The S[ikh] army, disbanded & dispersed, cannot bring 50 pieces of artry. into the field & have no resources. We have an army of 30,000 fully equipped & highly exalted in spirit since their last victories. And if, after a patient tryal, a Hindoo govt. is an impossibility, I can then only be compelled to do what I would not have done last March— annex the country & make the Indus the boundary of this gt. empire, a brilliant termination but made practically useful & safe with existing arrangement.

I am in perfect health &, saving my stiff knee, more able to encounter fatigue than last year. How[eve]r, I hope to see the [Sikh] govt. stand & am doing everything in my power to insure that result.

I hope I take a sturdy view of my duty, divested of personal considerations. If I were 40 instead of 61, I might be tempted & I could, by passive conduct, bring abt. an ambitious opportunity. I told you after what had occurred in Scinde that England should be satisfied before a milty. G.G. entered into war. So I again say, every resource which honest cooperation can supply shall be afforded to the Sikh govt. before I attempt to annex the Punjab, but if we do it at all, do it at once on a grand scale. I think we shall avoid it, but 99 in a 100 are of a different opinion. So they were when I occupied Lahore with 10,000 B. troops. All their throats were to be cut according to Napier & Gough, & even by the last mail I have a Minute from the Duke laying down precautionary measures & after Cabool being somewhat anxious.[274] I am gratified after Cabool that one of the effects of leaving a force at Lahore will in reality be the punctual conviction of all Asia that we can do what we please, provided we do not repeat the follies of Cabool or the unmilitary proceedings of Paris & Brussels in 1830.

I have not a man on whose opinion I can rest for assistance except my foreign secry., Mr Currie. All the orders signed by him are written

---

[274] In a memo dated 19 May 1846, Wellington suggested steps to be taken to protect and safely withdraw British troops left at Lahore in case of a surprise attack upon them. Hardinge responded in a letter written on 22 July explaining with detailed figures and a sketch, the measures already in effect to safeguard the British force in the Sikh capital (Wellington Papers, 145/53–145/59.)

by me, & I accomplish many things by industry & perseverance which wd. fail in more able but less active hands. But I need not conceal from you that this eternal demand upon the mind is very wearing. I am not nervous & can sleep sound under any circumstances before or after Feroz-shah, but this system of being responsible for everything, with 100 millions of subjects & 4000 miles of seacoast & as many miles of mountain frontier, keeps my energies on the stretch & for any length of time is too much for one man. Even if my council were with me, I should derive little comfort from their aid except in revenue & judicial matters. They now send up to me all milty. & political matters, & I get through business at a quicker pace by myself. If I could with honor retire, I would. *That,* under existing circumstances, is impossible & I am sure yr. dear mother, when she feels that the necessity of awaiting the result of the Punjab is real, will be reconciled to my absence, which in no case will be extended beyond what I promised & may be more palatable to her because my career, by the aid of the Supreme Disposer of all events, has been more prosperous than I could have expected or have deserved. I reruire to be supported by the submission of my family to what is inevitable, & those who encourage other hopes do me & yr. dearest mother some harm. Marriage & children are guarantees for moral & political good conduct & ought never to be drag chains fettering our actions & enervating our minds. They soften & give a Christian tone to all our feelings & actions & make us better men in all the relations of life. It will be, I hope, a part of my merit in balancing my misdeeds hereafter that I have not, by doing my duty here, acted a selfish part at a time of life when repose is the natural indulgence of our weak nature. I am confident you will view my position in the light I have described. If the Whigs wish me to retire or treat me ill, that is another affair; but under existing circumstances I do not see my way without disappointment to say that I can leave India before the autumn of 1848—a long span on my brief career after 61.

And now, my dear Walter, I will close my letter, which has been more serious than I intended.

96. [*To Walter.*] Simla. Aug. 13th, 1846

The mail has not brought matters to the *denouement* I expected. A week, how[eve]r, after your letter left England must have brought the Whigs into office, & I hope to hear by the next mail who is to be my master in Cannon Row. It will be a gt. relief to Peel, & for his sake I shall be glad of it. I can excuse some rash & hasty words, how[eve]r personal, used in the heat of debate, but Lord G. Bentinck has shown such a malevolent vindictive spirit that I never would hold any

communication for the future with a person whose heart is that of a
fiend without one particle of generosity. It gives rise to unpleasant
reflections, considering his intimacy with Ld. Stanley, that the latter
is only withheld by prudence from taking the same course. As to
D'Israeli, he is, as O'Connell once said, a lineal descendant from the
impenitent thief crucified with our Saviour.[275]

If Peel had chosen, he could have a tale unfolded as to what passed
in 1827 between Canning & G. 4th, which wd. have shown on which
side double dealing was resorted to at that period between Peel &
Canning. I must say I should have liked to have been in the House
& entitled to speak for 20 minutes.

I can have no objection to what Mr Gleig may write in praise of
Lord Gough. There's room enough for both of us. I placed Gleig in
his present office of principal chaplain & I know him as the humourous
& ingenious author of the *Subaltern*. He has also written the history of
the Bible. He failed in his life of Warren Hastings & I can't say I
admire his novels. He wished to be bishop of Calcutta & is somewhat
a disappointed man & not at all times a very discreet man.[276]

You did quite right not to give him any letters of mine. If I am
compelled to write, *facts* according to the necessity of the case can be
adduced which wd. do the public service no good & gratify no passion
of mine. The Napiers have done themselves harm by the historian's
partial history of Scinde, & now Outram has published a book in
which violent retorts are made to disparage the Napiers.[277] The parties
are much irritated & Ld. Ripon by a milk & water line has dissatisfied
both.

Sir Chs. N[apier] writes to me that I saved India on 2 occasions.
This, from a warm-tempered man who does not like the doubtful
policy of the Scinde war to be brought into contrast with the just war
of the Punjab, satisfies me that this army is aware of the share I took
in the late campaign, for he, N., takes his impression from others, not
from me.[278]

My correspondence I leave to my children. The volumes are becoming very bulky, but my good fortune has been mercifully great &,

[275] For O'Connell's remarks about Disraeli in the Taunton by-election in 1835, see
Robert Blake, *Disraeli* (1966), 125.

[276] Hardinge was aroused by George A. Gleig's article 'The War of the Punjab'
appearing in *The Quarterly Review*, lxxviii. 175–215, which praised Gough's policies
before and during the war while implying criticism of Hardinge's.

[277] James Outram, *The Conquest of Scinde, a commentary* (Edinburgh, 1846).

[278] This praise was largely lip service and Hardinge was then unaware of Napier's
charlantry. In private letters to his brother William Napier, the general was very
critical of Hardinge's policies and regretted that the entire Sikh state, including
Kashmir, had not been conquered (W. Napier, *The Life and Opinions of General Sir
Charles James Napier* [1857], iii, 391, 400, 458–9.)

unless I am attacked, there is strength & inward satisfaction in being moderate.

What should I do about supporters? I think of taking two leopards & adding a motto. *'Posterna laude recens'* was an augmentation in 1808 when my poor brother captained the Piedmontaise[279] but I don't like it, & as I must select supporters, I think of taking a second motto—*'Fortiter et recte'*, retaining the 2 crests I now have. But I shall not place the 2 flags, the *Atalanta*[280] & the *Piedmontaise*, on my carriage. Why after a battle should I annoy the French by reminding them, as I peaceably pass through their country, that they were on such & such an occasion defeated & the national flag recording their defeat perpetrated on the pannels [*sic*] of a carriage! Any thing that creates a heart-burning had better be avoided.

Some time ago the present Lord Fitz-Hardinge had his pedigree investigated by the Heralds' Court, & I shd. like to employ the same person to settle the affairs of my supporters, arms, etc. Sir Chs. H. may be asked for all the information, pamphlets, etc. which he may have in his possession. You had better ask what is the course pursued as to the payment of the expences: Does the govt. or the person [*?entitled*] pay when the title is conferred for services to the public?

I should prefer Ld. Fitz-Hardinge's genealogies because he has already gone through the whole of the research, & will do it more accurately & cheaply for me. I should not like to enter into an indefinite expence as to pedigree. On yr. part you can say you will refer to me for instructions. There is a small tract printed at Derby 6 or 8 years ago, which gives several details which I have neglected. The Derbyshire branch was the 2nd son of the Hardinges of Berkeley Castle & settled on the property given him by his father. The 3rd son went to Ireland. There is also a story that in Dugdale's visitation to Derbyshire, he quarreled with my ancestor abt. the fees,[281] and I rather think my grandfather, the member for Eye & Secretary of the Treasury in Sir Robt. Walpole's administration,[282] had an amicable suit in the Heralds' Ct. with the Berkeley family as to our right to use the Berkeley arms. If so, these records can be referred to. The monuments in the Church of Melbourne, where our family had a chancil [*sic*], goes up to Henry 7th, but the settlement of the family in Derbyshire was in Richard the 1st or 2nd's time.

[279] Henry's elder brother, George Nicholas Hardinge, was commanding the frigate *San Fiorenzo* in Mar. 1808 when he was killed by grape shot fired from the French cruiser *Piémontaise*.

[280] The *Athalante*, a Dutch brig, was seized by G. N. Hardinge in March 1804 after a naval battle near Texel island off the Dutch coast.

[281] Sir William Dugdale, *The Visitation of Derbyshire taken in 1662, and reviewed in 1663* (1879), p. 27.

[282] Nicholas Hardinge (1699–1758) served as Clerk of the Commons for twenty years.

Sir Robt. Hardinge raised a troop of horse for Charles the 1st, lost his goods & chattels in the royal cause & was knighted by the merry King Ch. the 2nd. My brother can give you all these matters. You will find in Oxford's anecdotes that my grand-father was supposed to be the best Eton scholar & versifier in Greek & Latin of his day.

I won't bore you any further.

Your acct. of yr. dear mother is very gratifying. She is all heart & I long to be on my way home, but alas! this must not be.

There is not the slightest chance of anything like a milty. operation this autumn. At the same time these Sikh vagabonds have no patriotic virtues and only consider how they can best plunder the treasury. I am doing all I can to sustain the govt. & keep it on its legs.

Three long months will elapse before I descend into the plains. In the meantime I have as much work as ever but am quite well. I have settled some unpleasant matters which I inherited from my predecessor, one of the most able and indiscreet of men, & I hope, having the C.C. within hail, who refers everything to me, that I shall not have my time engaged in unpleasant squabblings. I think the govt. quite right in adhering to their course abt. the govt. pension.

Probably Peel will never form another govt.

I shall have had so much work in India before I get home that I shall never enlist again. Thank God! 2 years are over. I must spend the year '47 in the hills & the autumn in the plains & shall be spared the tryal of a Calcutta summer. '48 will be my valedictory year, but between this & then what may happen is too painful, & I chase away these thoughts by steadily fixing my mind on the clear line of my duty.

I am glad you seem determined to settle in the country. I suppose Brambletye is in the possession of the family—the Wrights—I thought it had great capabilities, if well planted, but rather out of the way, & I like the convenience of a rail-way. I see by a letter from Lushington[283] that a S. Eastern rail-way to Dover is to pass through Parlt. What do you say?

I like your generous sentiments in speaking of Peel's vindication & I think your description of the state of parties clear & convincing. I have more obligations to Peel than any other man & I detest those that maliciously abuse him. I suppose Carlton is unbearable Does Ld. Ellenboro' frequent it? I don't think he is cordial with Peel, & I shd. judge from Sir G. Colborn's [Cockburn] replies that he is on bad terms with his naval colleagues.[284] I am awaiting a letter from Ld. E.,

[283] Sir James Law Lushington (1779–1859) was then a member of the Court of Directors.

[284] This presumably is a reference to the differences during a Commons debate in July between Adm. Sir George Cockburn, who had been the first sea lord under Peel, and those who wanted an end to naval floggings. (3 Hansard, lxxxvii. 344–5; lxxxviii. 272–3.)

& then I will write to you distinctly on the annoyance he betrays in Indian matters.[285]

Charles is quite well, Arthur loving his time dawdling with Lord Elphinstone.

Ld. Jocelyn has shown in his correspondence with me much more practical ability than I expected. He wd. make a very good govr. of Bombay.

I hear from everybody that the little Walter is a Hercules. It makes me very happy that your family hopes are realized & your joy complete & full by Sarah's safety & return to good health after such a tryal to her strength. I long to have a game of romps with my grandchildren.

Love to dearest Sarah, to Mrs Lambton & all within your family.

97. [*To Walter.*] Simla. Augt. 31st, 1846
Private

I have received a letter from Hobhouse[286] assuring me I shall find no change in my position in India by the substitution of a Russell for a Peel ministry & inviting the most unreserved confidence.

I have recd. also a letter from the Duke, recommending me to remain till the affairs on this frontier be settled & to complete my own *glowing* work, as he is pleased for the first time to term it.

I have a letter from Ripon saying he thinks I ought to stay till next summer [*but takes*] no vigorous grasp of the subject. And I have a letter from Peel, inclining to the honorable course of not shrinking from responsibility & trusting to my own sound judgement to do what is right.

Then I have letters from yr. dear mother, giving a different version of the opinions of the 3 preceding writers who, I have no doubt, spoke gentler words of comfort to her wishes than they have to me in reminding me of my duties.

The fact is, I must in honor see my troops out of Lahore & next spring & summer pass over before I can leave my post. Ld. E[*llen-*

---

[285] Ellenborough was indignant about the post-war arrangements in the Northwest. He particularly singled out the creation of the Kashmir state and wrote to Hardinge (April 22) that 'there have been times when the treaties with Golab Singh as the minister of the Lahore government and the detaching from the Lahore dominions a very extensive territory for the purpose of placing it under the independent authority of that minister, thus rewarding a traitor, would have been measures a little too oriental in principle.' Hardinge, however, rejected this charge and bluntly asked his predecessor in a letter of 7 June if the British were 'to treat the only man who had not lifted his arm against us with indifference' (Ellenborough Papers, PRO, 30/12/21, no. 7).

[286] John Cam Hobhouse (1786–1869), Baron Broughton, succeeded Ripon. He had previously served as president of the Board of Control, 1834–41.

borough] writes very decidedly that I ought to remain. I have therefore written to Hobhouse that I will satisfy all the obligations of my public duty & not evade any of the responsibility arising out of my measures & will stay to the end of 1847. By that time everything will be in such a state that I can return in Janry. 1848 with a clear conscience. I do not like to receive £5000 a yr. &, on a principle which the Ct. disclaims, return home because there has been a change of ministry. I have no party politics to favor here. I shall go straight forward with my plans, & it shall not be said that the last public act of my life was the result of selfishness. It is doubtless not so agreeable to correspond with yr. former adversaries as your own political friends. But if I am not well treated, I shall insist upon being relieved. I am confident I have taken the right line.

Charles is anxious to see the denouement, & abt. the middle of Novr. I shall be in the Jullundhur, having gone round by Kangra & the hills. I anticipate a quiet autumn but one of some anxiety. In the interval I work like a slave, trying to leave no arrears, & the occupation, though it wears me down, makes time pass quickly.

Sir James Hogg has not written to me since the change. What line will he now take? The D. of Buckingham was 2 yrs. ago one of his gt. allies.[287]

The Whigs will dissolve either this next spring or the present autumn. If they succeed in getting a tolerable majority & can carry on the govt., which I doubt, they will be ready with a successor when the session of '47 is over. If they fail, my office is equally at the disposal of any other govt., being most anxious to retire when I can do so with honor. In the meantime I shall return here next March to be close to the frontier & hope, if my anticipations be correct, to be in England in February or March '48, taking Thebes in my way if I can muster strength for the effort.

When yr. mother finds that I shall return 1 1/2 years before the usual period of g[*overnor*]s g[*enera*]l, she will, I am confident, be satisfied that my determination has been the right one. I shall then be 63, & if my head & nerves & frame last for the next year, I shall be content to have run my race & perform my remaining duties without the constant effort which this gt. empire demands.

Arthur has passed Iskardo on his way to Ladak, touching Chinese Tartary, & will be with me the end of September. When he last wrote he was 13,000!! ft. above the sea, with a good deal of headache & difficulty of breathing—no vegetation but a few wild onions.

I admire Peel's speech, but it is open to the objection taken. His

---

[287] The 2nd Duke of Buckingham (Richard Grenville) had opposed the Corn Laws' repeal.

position in the House will be a novelty. He has shown gt. powers of reasoning, wisdom & courage, but what is to be the result? What is yr. solution of the problem?

I wish I were amongst you. This life wears me out fast, but I must never repine. Amidst the changes & chances of this mortal world, I have daily reason to praise the mercy of God.

I trust I do not tempt fortune by the effort to remain. If the Whigs wd. but remove me, the difficulty wd. be over.

Love to dear Sarah & the Ellisons if within reach, & I suppose this will reach you in Northumberland. God bless you and yrs.

98. [*To Walter.*] Simla. Sep. 18th, 1846

I have written to Mr Gleig on the subject of his article in the Quarterly & have sent the papers to Alex Wood as I was not sure of yr. movements. Alick will show you the papers if they do not bore you, & I have sent him a letter from Ld. Gough to me concurring in all my state[*ment*]s. I never answer the abuse of the daily press, but mis-statements in the Quarterly are historical, & I have desired him to correct his errors.

I have been writing a very long official dispatch to Hobhouse, I am ashamed to say, of 9 sheets of foolscap 1/2 margin. I generally try to be short, & that desire to be brief, I fear, makes me obscure, but, as in speaking I never attempt to be fine, so in writing I escape errors in writing which wd. be innumerable if I were not satisfied with being understood in a simple style.

The ministers at Lahore begin to be alarmed as the period approaches for withdrawing our troops. A man in that great city can now lie down in the hope of rising the next morning, & property is equally secure under our police. The shop-keeper now dares to complain of the khalsa soldier & can obtain justice, & such is the good discipline of our 10,000 troops that not a life has been lost in a fray, & the Sikhs, having been forced to respect us in the field, are now beginning to esteem us in quarters. We have caused their disbanded soldiers to be paid their [*?arrears*], & the intercourse has become so familiar that many prejudices agt. feringhees have been completely removed.

Still the question presses, what will become of the Sikh govt. when the B. retire? The question is one of gt. moment, & the next 3 months will be very anxious. I am alone in council & have only my chief secry. Mr Currie, in whom I have every confidence. There is not a man who can give me an idea on such a subject. In England popular subjects are ably discussed in the papers & yr. butler may, if he chooses, know as much as you of the Corn Laws question. But here nobody can see behind the curtain, & therefore I am entirely left to my own judgement of what ought to be done. My colleague, Ld. G[*ough*], is no colleague unless the council be present, & he never pretends to enter upon political matters.

By anticipation I wish you all a merry Christmas & I expect to have yr. answer to this letter abt. that day. The end of Decr. I withdraw my garrison or take a new political line of departure. I am glad I remained, for I never could have endured the shabbiness of evading any responsibility. Yr. mother will show you the letters from the Q., but never allude to them.

I leave Simla the 15th Oct. for an excursion in the hills to visit the new territory but shall be in the plains the middle of Novr. ready for any events. The Sikh army is completely dispersed; but the folly of the wisest man of the East, Golab S., is giving us some trouble in Cashmeer. He neglected to occupy the country, relying on some intrigue with a Musselmen chief, the govr. of Cashmeer appointed by the Lahore govt. This adventurer has set up for himself & will give Golab S. some trouble. In a conflict the other day Golab S.'s people were defeated & lost 100 men, & I anticipate he will have some sharp conflicts for which there was no necessity if in April last he had sent up a sufficient force to occupy the country.[288] If I were a brig[*a*]d[*ie*]r instead of a G.G., I should like to have the management of the Cashmeer campaign.

I cannot make out that Alexander ever came further than the Hyphasis, the British boundary under the Lahore treaty.

I expect the mail to arrive hourly & long for my letters.

No news of Arthur—he is amongst the Tartars. I wish we were with you in the snug Oak Room but, my dear friend, I must go through & be more cautious & painstaking than ever.

Love to dear Sarah. Kiss my grandchildren, & above all let me know how your dear mother stands the damp cold of England.

99. [*To Walter.*] Simla. Oct. 22nd, 1846. 4 o'cl. a.m., as dark *as pitch*

You will receive in a tin case a few more of Charles' sketches, some of which may be used in vignettes to the frontispiece or as affording variety by inserting 2 small sketches in one page instead of one.

I am glad the great [*J. D.*] H[*arding*] approved of what he has seen. The rapidity of the execution, I believe, is greater than that of his

---

[288] One of the more troublesome problems arising out of the peace settlements of Mar. 1846 was the refusal of Sheikh Imam-ud-Din, the Lahore-appointed governor of Kashmir, to hand over the Himalayan province to Gulab Singh. Kashmir passed under Gulab Singh's official control in Nov.

master & he never *puzzles* where to introduce his figures, which are appropriate as to attitude, costume & employments. I hope he will never aspire to minute finishing. An amateur should be rapid & effective & not waste time in arriving at the excellence of the japanned tea board, or on the other hand be indistinct by bold daubing which some mistake for genius.

I quite agree with Sarah's criticism of the gt. H., that he uses too large a quantity of yellow which we don't see in nature, & he finishes up his foregrounds so highly that the effect of the main objects in the picture are injured by the attention being directed to a rock or some flowers when it ought to dwell on the middle ground, the distance & the sky. The latter is much more important than is generally imagined & I should say very difficult to do well. Cuyp's[289] chef-d'oeuvres often depend on the aerial tints of his skies & their warmth which pervades the whole picture. The same excellence is to be found in Claude,[290] particularly in the celebrated picture of the embarkation & so on. For the last 4 months, Chas. has scarcely touched his pencil. He hopes to try the merits of the new color box you have sent him next week. If the style approaches to oils, so much the better. I admire transparency but I prefer the depth & force of the old masters to the more flimsy beauty of Copley Fielding[291] & that school of putty masters.

You will, I have no doubt, agree with the gt. man as to the best style of lithograph. His own drawings in his book on the art are conveyed in a style of mezzo-tints, very masterly, & I should hope something of this sort wd. be adopted. I would recommend the name of the place to be at the bottom of the drawing in bold letters not requiring a microscope.

As to the hall, you will do as you like. It will amuse you, &, as both Sarah & yr. mother are at the 2 ends of the h[ou]se & have a back staircase, I shd. hope (if the noise & litter of taking down the flooring & wall be done in yr. absence) that the inhabitants will sustain very little inconvenience. I propose the walls of the hall & stair-case to be hung with stags & wild animals' heads, intermingled with armour, matchlocks & milty. weapons. If Salvin[292] comes down, pick his brains as to the alteration of the windows. Mr Wells recommends large panes of plated glass &, as S. Park has no pretensions like Mr Hussey's h[ou]se to architectural consistency, combining modern carpet with ancient reminiscences, I am disposed to think single plates between each mullion wd. be advisable. I do not care much for the bow

---

[289] Aelbert Cuyp (1620–91).

[290] Claude Lorrain (1600–82).

[291] Antony Vandyke Copley Fielding (1787–1855).

[292] Anthony Salvin, a Tudor style architect, built or remodelled various prominent buildings in Kent, including Betteshanger and South Park (Newman, pp. 112n, 460).

window. I once thought of throwing one out at the end window of the drawing r[*oom*]. It wd. improve the bedroom above, but the drawing room wd. be colder with one fireplace. I am satisfied with the snugness of the old Oak Room, & if Charles prefers a better dining room he can hereafter suit his own taste. The old Chatham storekeeper built his chimneis [*sic*] so perversely that alterations are very difficult. Try if the room in which the stores of linen are kept could not have a fire-place & be converted into a bedroom for a single person. The rooms to be added had better be two stories high so as to pass through the house-maid's closet into the add[*itiona*]l rooms above stairs & through Mrs Sevant's[293] room below stairs, with a staircase *from below*.

You see by these details that I am preparing to take up my abode for the remainder of my life at dear S. Park, &, if yr. mother outlives me, my arrangements will enable her to do so with comfort as to income. I have written to Alick Wood on the subject & he will inform you of my plans. I spent a gt. deal more than usual for 3 m[*onths*] last year whilst my table was open to all the world, but next year I shall be very prudent &, with the 5000 a yr. pension, I shall be able to do very well, first for the living & next for their posterity, & a poor viscount's family, almost promoted from the ranks, need not have more than an English gentleman's competency. Nevertheless, I think it my duty as the founder of the family to do what I can for the future respectability of the old pirate's descendants, & I shall be glad to have yr. remarks.

The Cashmeer affair promises to be brought to a peaceful termin-mination.

What vile instruments I have to deal with in attempting to re-establish Eastern govts. The other day 31 chiefs of Nepaul were murdered in the council room, it is supposed by the order of the ranee or princess.[294] I send you a curious letter showing the diabolical ferocity by which chiefs in this country are excited to crime. Because the chief of a Brahmin is unjust to his vassal, the Brahmin cuts off the heads of 10 of his wives with his own hands & murders his mother & his children in order to bring down upon the unjust chief the vengeance of the deity![295]

---

[293] Perhaps a housekeeper.

[294] This resulted from the continuing struggle for power at Kathmandu involving King Rajendra, Queen Rajya, and others. The massacre took place on the night of Sept. 15 at the royal courtyard in the presence of the Queen, and victims included Fateh Jung Shah, the prime minister. Although the Queen was at least a partial accomplice, the main culprit responsible for the carnage was Jung Bahadur Rana, who in 1845 had killed Matabar Singh. Jung Bahadur Rana succeeded Fateh Jung and started the line of hereditary prime ministers who governed Nepal until 1950.

[295] Hardinge, in a letter of the same date to Hobhouse, described the gruesome event: 'A few days ago, a Brahmin, of the small district of Rewah, in Rajapootana, having a

This rascal, the Sheik in Cashmeer, lately cut two men to pieces, insulting their remains in the most disgusting manner. The Sikh horrors are too recent to require notice, but I mention these facts to show that in Nepaul, in Rajoopootana, in the Punjab & even in Cashmeer the same system of cruelty prevails. Even Dost Mahommed of Cabool, the friend of Ld. Auckland & the Miss Edens,[296] has married in three instances his daughters to Affghan chiefs whom he wished to get rid of & has not scrupled when the son-in-law was in his power, confiding in the alliance, to have him assassinated.

The maha-raja Golab Singh, whom I elevated to be an independent prince, is now abused as a cruel monster, because an equally cruel monster, the Sheik, has excited a rebellion in Cashmeer, not of the poor weavers of shawls & the agricultural population but of the Mussulmans of the hills. The insurrection is not the rising of the people against Golab S. but of the hill tribes paid by the Sheik & secretly fomented by the vizier at Lahore.

Golab S. has not committed one act of cruelty of which I have any proof & his personal character is free from every immorality but, with more ability & energy than others, he is more feared. He has behaved very ill by not taking proper precautions to occupy Cashmeer &, as he has obliged me to move 16,000 men to his support, I have taken the opportunity of insisting upon his making proper provision for the chiefs & people transferred to him. How[eve]r, I must first have the Sheik out of Cashmeer, which he has promised to vacate tomorrow, but the result I shall not hear for some days.

What a contrast between Oct. 1846 & Oct. '45. Last year the Sikh army with 70,000 reg. & 30,000 irreg. & 300 good pieces of artry. were rabid in their hatred of the feringees. Now 6000 Sikh troops are actually marching on the same route with our regts. towards Cashmeer to place a province taken from them into our hands!

I do not intend to let a B. soldier enter Cashmeer. The native Lahore & Jummo soldiery must effect this object. I speak thus openly to you because I know I shall not be quoted, but you will perceive by this state of things that I could not without discredit have left India because a Whig administration had replaced Peel's govt. All real friends of her [Emily] ought to moderate & not excite her expectations.

Pray tell Sarah, when I begged to have acknowledgements of things sent home, my meaning was confined to the certainty of their safe arrival & not to the recognition of their being acceptable. These things

---

quarrel with his raja, took out his ten wives on the road to the fort, cut off their heads with his sword, and his son murdered his mother and two or three infant children. The Brahmin then stabbed himself. And these atrocities take place in every direction' (Broughton papers, dcccliii. 207).

[296] Auckland's sisters, Emily and Fanny Eden, lived with him in Calcutta.

are packed in tin & are sometimes purloined in the packing. They are then slung on the two ends of a stick & carried by a naked man from station to station for 1200 miles to Calcutta & there embarked, thence across the desert, reshipped at Alexandria, & undergo several chances of being lost or stolen. I therefore wish to know whether they arrive safe & that is all.

With respect to Penn's Rocks, the difficulty of extension is almost fatal to the selection of that spot. As a family residence I should have preferred Brambletye, with the power of acquiring property, & before I bought my place I wd. visit it in winter. In yr. station, you & your posterity must conform to dog-days & residing in the sporting season of the year at yr. country residence. The goodness of the soil, the facility of seeing friends are important considerations, of which you are the master in selecting a family residence. Those who inherit family property have not this advantage.

It is now broad-day light & I must attend to other matters. The post for England goes out tomorrow, & I must omit nothing under Whig masters. I am sometimes surprized at what I go through. I dine with [*the*] C.C., & I shall then have been at work 16 hours with the interval of breakfast & a piece of *Parliament* at 1 o'clock.

[*P.S.*] I should be glad to know whether the Whigs wish to get rid of me *immediately*.

100. [*To Walter.*] Simla. Oct. 23rd, 1846
Private

The accts. this morn[*in*]g from Cashmeer are that the Sheik, alarmed at the advance of 10,000 B. troops in support of the Sikh & Jummoo forces, has raised the siege of the Hurree Purbut[297] & is willing to submit on the terms I have imposed. In three or four days I expect to hear that this affair is settled, & then I can make progress in the Lahore business, leaving Simla on the 26th for the Jullundhur.

I wish to have the Times instead of the M[*ornin*]g Herald.

Thank heaven I am off on Monday! I am quite sick of the work I go through, & yet I believe it keeps my body in health, that all my staff are ailing except myself by the sudden change of climate.

Love to dear Sarah, & Mrs Ellison & Mrs Lambton.

101. [*To Walter.*] Sarkote [*?Sarka Ghat.*] Novr. 3rd, 1846

It is now 4 o'cl. in the morn[*in*]g, & at 1/2 p[*as*]t 5 I march on to Mundee & thence to Kangra & other hill stations. The exercise, the

---

[297] The strong brick fort atop a hill in Srinagar, reportedly built by Akbar in 1597, where a Dogra force had been held up since early summer.

change of scene, the riding & talking instead of being glued to my chair are delightful recreations, & I am in excellent health & good spirits. I have to receive the hill rajas, receive presents & make unnecessary speeches, but still it is a great enjoy[men]t, & sometimes I meet a man whose conversation is amusing. Here the raja trains hawks, & he showed me one 24 yrs. old. The terms are mainly the same as those in Europe & were either brought from Persia here or went hence to Persia. The birds are not taken out of the nest but caught & trained & managed by opium. In 2 or 3 months a wild bird is trained to hunt for man. One killed a wild peacock this morn[in]g, another is famous for hares, others for partridges. They were kept beautifully clean & if any important feather in the wing is lost or broken they splice it with a new feather. In ingenuity & cunning they [the Indians] are quite our equals, but they have no strength of character & are very cruel.

I passed the river on inflated bullock skins. The bones, apparently, of the animal are broken & taken out at the neck, the 4 legs tied up, & the monster, thrown upon his back, is crossed by a man who paddles his way across by moving his hands & legs. The river had a small fort on the other side of which Charles has made a very good sketch.

I had a letter from Coll. [Henry] Lawrence at Golab Singh's h[ea]d q[uar]t[er]s of the 26th. The Sheik had left Cashmeer on the 23rd on his way to Coll. L. His Muhommedan confederates had dispersed & I have no doubt that he is coming in. We owe this result partly to the cowardly character of the man & partly to the rapidity with which we moved up 7000 men to the Chenab R. followed by 4000 men from Lahore, replacing them by 4000 from Feroz-poor. We then insisted that the Sikh forces should take the lead & put us, according to treaty, in possession of Cashmeer. Thus we showed a combined force of British, Lahore, & Jummoo troops amounting to nearly 30,000 men.

The Sheik was intimidated & we shall by this success, brought abt. by peaceful means, convince all parties that we will enforce the treaty, & this mode of overawing *all*, founded on the reputation of our arms & the facility with which they are moved, will save us a gt. deal of future trouble.

My next object will be to settle the question of retaining Lahore on our own terms or of giving it up the end of Decr. This keeps me on the qui vive, but a ride of 12 miles, constant occupation during the day, & sound sleep at night keep me in high force, & I am more fit for a campaign this autumn than I was last year. And I know so much more of these provinces & the Punjab that I am as confident in these affairs which now occupy me as if I were at the War Office transacting inferior business. My eyesight is improved & I scarcely ever use spectacles. In short, I am stronger than I was in England & if reqd.

I can ride 50 or 60 miles & write a dispatch afterwards. But I am frugal & temperate in my diet, & I wish Charles & Arthur may inherit the stamina I have in this upper province. At Calcutta I lost weight & was a good deal shaken.

Who is to be my successor? Are the Whigs anxious for my recall or return?

16 months will soon pass away in the stream of time & I shall be delighted to enjoy the luxury of repose, for this is the privilege of age, just as activity is the essence of youth.

In three or four days I shall hear from England & that is a day of enjoy[men]t.

Tell me if you know what conservative peers & members of Parlt. go to Drayton. I suppose Croker is still rabid. He wrote to me twice, & I was so amazed at his animadversions agt. Peel that I have not answered his letters.

What line does the Duke take? Does he incline to Stanley or is he quite neutral?

Love to dear Sarah.

102. [*To Sarah.*] Camp, 12 miles from Hoshiar-poor. Novr. 21st, 1846

We are in hourly expectation of the English mail, but my express closes in an hour & I wish to thank you for all you have done & written.

I trust in the mercy of God that the next accounts will report Lady Emily's arrival at S. Park in a convalescent state. I was greatly relieved when I heard that the cause of the illness was not the influenza, for I had been kept in a state of painful suspense for 2 days, having seen a paragraph from a London paper, which I instantly attributed to [*Dr*] McCann, & derived consolation before yr. letters arrived that he might have exaggerated the patient's state for the sake of puffing his attendance.

It appears, however, to have been very serious, & altho' I am sanguine that I shall have a favorable account, still it is very depressing to be kept in this state of anxiety. If S. Park should be too cold or damp, pray persuade Ly. E. to go at once to Hastings or Dover— both are most convenient & at the shortest notice. I know, however, that yr. affectionate vigilance will suggest the best possible arrangements. And after next summer I have recommended Lady E. to return to Nice for the winter & wait for me in the spring when we can return together.

We have ridden 12 miles to breakfast &, when the midday heat is gone, I ride to the gt. camp 12 miles further on, when we get into the plains, which extend for 1000 miles to the sea without a hill. This mountain march since the 26th Oct. has been very interesting & bracing, & I shall move out of my small tent into the spacious canopies which await me in the plain with regret. The elephants & camels are streaming in to replace the poor coolies, & my horses have arrived to take the place of the patient ponies, which have climbed over rugged paths requiring some nerve to confide in their sagacity & safety. At this very moment a fine elephant waiting for his load has gathered a bundle of long coarse grass which he has made up into a wisp & is flapping away the flies which incommode him. The Hindoo god of wisdom has an elephant's head,[298] and the anecdotes of the beast are quite marvellous, with a supple trunk in which alone there are 40,000 different muscles! with which, as it has been said of this wonderful animal, he can pick up a needle or root up an oak.

I am just in time to correct a mistake. He does not use the wisp to drive away flies but to shake off the dust before he thrusts it down his throat. I believe I was intended by nature for a patient curate in a country village, occupying his spare time in observations on birds & beasts.

God grant that yr. next letters may give me the good news I anticipate.

103. [*To Walter.*] Camp, 12 miles from Hoshiar-poor. Novr. 21st, 1846

Your accounts of your dear mother took off a great load, which had depressed me for a couple of days before I recd. yr. letters. It was particularly consoling to know that the illness had not originated from influenza, & with prudence hereafter I hope no bad effects will result from this severe fever.

We have been in hourly expectation of further letters, which has made me delay writing till the last moment, & now the bag is about to be closed. I rode in here this morning & I shall rejoin my large camp this even[in]g by a gallop on Mianee. I anticipate a good report from you, which keeps up my courage & makes me trust in God that the recovery after yr. note left England was strong & permanent.

Charles tells me the express ought to start. I have only to add that Cashmeer is quiet & the Musselman intrigue put down. But I have an acct. to settle on that head with the Lahore vizier, Lal Singh, & I shall move up towards the Beas in a few days.

Our troops have all returned to their stations. The co-operation of Sikh troops with British has been most satisfactory. The country is perfectly quiet but the mis-government at Lahore is very flagrant, &

[298] Ganesa (Ganapati).

I shall either withdraw the troops altogether or insist upon a better system of govt.

104. [*To Walter.*] Camp Hoshiarpoor. Decr. 2nd, 1846

A letter from yr. dear mother relieved me from all anxiety. She wrote confidently about herself, & all your letters are confirmatory of her own account. The explanation of the illness is also a great consolation, & I trust I shall have the happiness to hear in a few days that she is at S. Park & convalescent. She writes in most grateful terms of Sarah's affectionate care having been so instrumental to her recovery, & her whole train of thought seemed to be most cheerful & satisfactory.

The winter of 1847 had better perhaps be spent in Italy &, if she gets through this without an attack of influenza, I shall hope that the tendency to a delicate chest is no longer to be dreaded.

I anticipate that this autumn *here* will be quiet & the next summer as tranquil as its predecessor, & if, in Decr. 1847, the *pacification* is complete & I have been able to reduce the milty. expenditure, affording by safe reductions & liberal assessments in the ceded territory a relief of one million sterlg., I shall retire with a satisfied conscience & a grateful heart, every day convincing me that the Lahore policy of last March was the best for the permanent interests & security of India. The contrast between the Punjab policy & that pursued in Scinde is distasteful in some quarters otherwise friendly to me. In my position here I must not be a partisan but, if I am compelled to speak out, I can show in every instance as clear a statement as that sent to A. Wood. Since I replaced Ld. E[*llenborough*], I have acted as a friend. My forbearance has been tried, it is not yet exhausted; in his instance I will practice moderation. He recommended me to make terms with the Lahore govt. after the battle of Feroz-shahar without crossing the Sutlege, & he advised me to do so as an honorable course. I could not have done so with honor or in policy, & when, after a gt. effort, the army was at Lahore, he is the first man to carp & wail at my moderation, expressing his dissatisfaction that I did not annex the whole country. Nay more, I have a Mem[*orandu*]m of his, produced to the Cabinet & sent to me, in which an annexation is recommended, & yet *after this event* he disapproves of a course which, since Janry. 1845, I had advised & the Cabinet had concurred in considering the most politic. I won't pursue the subject.

I move my camp to the Beas R. abt. 40 miles off on the 4th to be nearer Lahore, having dispatched my chief secry. on a special mission to Lahore. The Sheik will be put on his defence for violating an important art[*icl*]e of the treaty. He, the servant of the Lahore durbar, will probably disclose in vindicating himself that he acted by orders of the vizier, & I rather think the proof will be induced. Then will follow demands, which cannot be refused, for depriving the guilty party of power, & lastly the important question whether the S[ikh] govt. will attempt to stand alone, without B. troops, or whether they will again implore us to remain, to which I can only concede on terms, not of gain, but of power. This month is full of interest &, thank God, I am quite strong & relieved in my mind from the anxiety of yr. mother's illness. You must be very cautious in appearing to know what is passing, for, altho' this scanty portion of news may be in the papers, you must remember I am not acting under the govt. of which I was a member.

Charles rode 19 m[iles] this morn[in]g, having been yesterday in a swamp shooting snipes off an elephant's back. He killed 7 1/2 couple. His activity is very great. Arthur has gone with Mr Currie to Lahore where his regt. now is stationed. From 11 till 3 it is still hot; the rest of the 24 h[ours] very agreeable.

My love to dear Sarah.

This day last year I reached Umballa & joined the com. in ch. The victories achieved have struck terror into the finest native army that ever took the field with 300 pieces of artry. The *prestige* of the Sikh army is irretrievably gone. The success which has attended our exertions during the last 8 m[onths] of peace has exceeded all expectation.

Kangra, an almost impregnable fort,[299] surrendered at the 12th hour.

The Moultan dewan refused to pay his revenue to Lahore. We interfered. The money has been paid to a rupee & he has gone back satisfied & submissive.

The ld. govr. of Cashmeer refused to relinquish the province. I sent 10,000 British[300] & 26,000 Sikhs & Jummoo forces agt. him, & he surrendered whilst the snow was falling in the passes.

These 3 events serve to fix attention on what has passed since the treaty was signed. Do they not prove that the influence of our power is felt by firm but moderate conduct? I don't like the responsibility of 10,000 troops in Lahore, which last March Gough & Napier told me wd. have their throats cut, but I know that much of the obedience is attributable to the possession of the capital. The responsibility of that measure rested more heavily upon me by the denunciations of its danger & the fear of a Cabool disaster. I bore their anticipations of mischief as the friendly councils of brave men, but I took my own

---

[299] The Kangra fort stood almost 2500 feet above sea level at the top of a mountain encircled by the Bar Ganga River nearly 150 feet below.

[300] The British troops, however, did not enter Kashmir.

course & the results are before you. What I am now going to do may be disapproved—I can't help it. It is unpleasant in great political & milty. emergencies to act with strangers, but I know Lord John is a man of honor & a fair man, & I sleep sound every night.

So God bless you.

105. [*To Sarah.*] Camp, Cham Chourassi [*Sham Churasi*]. Decr. 4th, 1846

I marched into this camp this morning, abt. 14 miles, & am proceeding to the Beas River opposite Umritser.

I have an acct. to settle with these vagabonds who got up the Cashmeer disturbance &, as it is not dignified for the G.G. to enter the Punjab, I have sent my chief secretary to Lahore to make the investigation. The vizier is in a fright & the ranee consults holy men, has her horoscope drawn by astrologers of celebrity, &, as I tell my secretary's wife, intends to unveil her weeping eyes to soften Mr Currie's heart if matters should proceed awkwardly for her friend the vizier.[301]

Till Christmas I shall keep as close at hand as possible & am making a variety of arrangements which fill up every moment of my time.

I was delighted to receive a very cheerful letter from Lady Emily full of affecte. gratitude for all your incessant attentions & soothing cares & breathing throughout her letter a contented & happy frame of mind. A thousand thanks for all you have done. I can now go through my business with energy. The last year in the hills has so improved my health that you wd. scarcely expect to see me riding twice a day &, with the exception of a slight limp in my gait, going through more active work than I could have done since you first saw me at Betteshanger.[302]

I think my sojourn here will be long enough to give the Whigs time to arrange who is to be my successor, & the certainty that it will not be distant may reconcile them to treat me with forbearance & civility. Let me know what you hear; I have no objection to hear their opinions of my demerits. The knowledge puts me on my guard. They are not bound to treat my deficiencies with indulgence, but there are those who ought to be so bound & who, from disappointed vanity, have taken a course the reverse of a friendly consideration for an absent friend.

[301] No sooner had Iman-ud-Din quit Kashmir than he claimed that his opposition to Gulab Singh had been at the urgings of the Lahore minister. Considering the charge serious, Hardinge appointed a court of inquiry presided over by Currie. Early in Dec. the court found Lal Singh guilty, stripped him of his office, and expelled him from Panjab (Minute of the Court of Inquiry, 3 Dec. 1846, B.G.L.D., pp. 27–41).

[302] Near Sandwich in Kent, it later became Sir Walter's country seat.

Peel is always to me a sincere friend. I have never had it in my power to do him any service. This I regret, for my career will close before I can prove the sincerity of my attach[men]t. I had a warm & excellent letter from him by the last mail.

I am confident he will give Ld. John a fair trial. It is quite impossible for the great country party to be led by such a Billingsgate orator as Ld. G. Bentinck.

A little boy of 6 yrs. old breakfasted with me this morning, having ridden 14 miles from our last camp. This turned my thoughts to little Walter. In little more than a yr. I hope to embrace him.

106. [*To Walter.*] Camp Sobraon. 19th [*January 1847*]

I entirely concur in & approve of all that A. Wood has done in the affair with Mr Gleig.

I have read the article. If it stands in the terms now sent, it is evident this clergyman very charitably means to raise ill-blood between me & Ld. E[*llenborough*]. My defence, or rather the correction of prejudicial errors, did not require that Mr G. should point out the insufficiency of Ld. E.'s distribution of the force in which the C.C. *then* concurred, the civil G.G. having a right to lean on the professional offr. for support in a milty. question. It shows his animus agt. me & his mortification that I did not back his application to be bishop of Calcutta.

Lord E. on his part writes letters to India *trembling* for the consequences of the force being *disseminated,* as he styles it.

I have, after reducing the Bengal army by 15,000 regular troops, a force from Meerut to Lahore of 54,000 m[en] & 120 field guns!

He, Ld. E., also talks of the treachery & power of Golab S. & the danger of our position. These things he writes & they come round to me. What does he not *talk* when Indian affairs are the subjects of his eloquence? And yet he advised me by letter to patch up a peace with Lahore without crossing the Sutlege! I would have died before I would have subscribed to such terms.[303]

He laid a Minute before the Cabinet which was not sanctioned but which was sent to me. In that Minute he does not advocate the

[303] Before he learned that the war was over, Ellenborough, in a letter dated 3 Mar. 1846, had indeed advised Hardinge: 'If there were a govt. at Lahore you might perhaps, after what has passed, make peace without dishonor, or injury to our position, on the condition of the cession of all the Lahore dominions on the left bank.' However, Ellenborough had added that 'there is no govt. at Lahore and can be none and I fear the die must be considered to have been cast by them & that you have no alternative but must take the whole country—that is, if *you can*' (Ellenborough Papers, PRO, 30/12/21/7).

annexation of the country. He was so unintelligible that neither Currie nor I could interpret his policy.

The battle of Sobraon brought us to Lahore with 3,400 B. inf. & 11,000 n[ative] inf. &, with other arms, abt. 24,000 men. Gough & Napier both concurred that *annexation* was impossible. It was not my policy but, in the opinion of any reflecting officers, it was impossible. Now Ld. E. descants in a different tone.

I wish I had had him for 5 minutes by my side on the night of Feroz-shahar. Or that I had him here in this camp for one hour of milty. explanation!

107. [*To Walter.*] Camp Pattiala. Febry. 5th, 1847

I have been here for the last 3 days, the maha-raja of this district[304] being the most wealthy & important of our Sikh-protected chiefs; he was also loyal & an exception to the great mass of the chiefs & population who, if we had been beaten at Feroz-shahar, wd. have turned agt. us & cut all our throats. The whole system in these states is very unsatisfactory, & during this summer we must endeavour to place our defective administration on a better footing.

Everything is as peaceable at Lahore as at Calcutta. The policy is approved by the press & by the principal men of experience in the civil & milty. service, but the army, sighing for promotion, are met by the always ungrateful duty of reduction, & rail-ways & canals have superseded siege trains & pontoons, & all our engineers will shortly be occupied in the avocations of peace. This is a disappointment, & my policy is contrasted with Lord E[*llenborough*]'s as adverse to the army's interests. And so it is, so it would have been if Lord E. had ever got to Lahore, for in a Minute of his laid before the Cabinet & sent to me, he does *not* advocate annexation. The value of a native Hindoo state interposed between us & the Kyber is the true policy, for we have not the means out of Sikh revenue to administer so large a country on the English expensive system of civil servants highly paid & a large regular army with European officers.

I await patiently the verdict of the Parliament & the country, &, having conferred on the army many advantages during the last 2 years, I bear their disappointment very philosophically & pursue my own course of conscientiously doing what I believe to be right.

I shall be at Simla at the end of March & for the remainder of the year get through as much work as I can, watching the progress of events in the Punjab.

I lose my secretary, Sir F. Currie, which I regret very much. Sir

[304] Narinder Singh ruled Patiala from 1845 to 1862.

George Pollock returns to England & Currie takes his seat at the council board.[305]

I recommend you converse in the House with Lord Jocelyn. He lives with Palmerston & the Whigs & hears all that is passing, & Hobhouse probably will not be coy if you approach him. He writes in a very encouraging strain, but I have no great confidence in my master, for last year he was an advocate for annexation. Peel, I anticipate, will entirely approve of the recent policy.

I hope this time next year to be on my way home.

Charles has not done much lately in the way of art, & the cold has been so great as to render our tents disagreeable & our fingers stiff. Arthur is *volage* & I cannot fix him to any steady work. Bob [*is*] very steady & useful & affecly. attached to me. We shall all return together. It is quite refreshing to count my future service here by *months*, for I never have a respite from labor & care. Yet I think I am more active than when I left England, & now that the business has become more familiar I get through it with more confidence & ease. Still, my dear Walter, the holding of such a highly responsible office under Whig rulers is irksome & I long for my return. The next 11 months will, I think, enable me to retire with honor.

As to the hall, I await the architect's plan with curiosity. I now & then purchase some arms & the heads of stags for its decoration, & [*at*] the end of March I expect you will make the acquaintance of a very fine ibex's head.

Don't forget the dimensions of the dining room curtains.

If money is required, recollect that the discounting of the bills before they become due is no loss.

I hope you will be able to suit your taste & Sarah's by a country place in which you can display your taste & employ your leisure. You appear to me to be indifferent about Parliament & Hull is, I think, out of the question, but you will never regret the experience you have derived from 10 yrs.' practice in St Stephens. At my age, I feel happy that I have no elections before me, & I shall subside into a quiet old gentleman, occasionally going down to the House of Lords.

I have been writing since 4 o'cl. in bed & am cramped & cold in my fingers, & my two black servants are waiting to rub me down with the horsehair gloves.

108. [*To Sarah.*] Camp Pattialla. Febry. 6, 1847

I have been here 4 days, settling with the maha-raja the abolition of all transit duties through his territories. He has voluntarily relin-

[305] Henry M. Elliot (1808–53), a member of the East India Company's civil service, succeeded Currie.

quished his rights. All the other chiefs will follow his example &, for the future, trade on this frontier will be perfectly free. He is a very young man & during the war was loyal to us, whilst his neighbours in these states would, with few exceptions, in case of defeat have destroyed us. He has been giving us durbars & fireworks in Eastern splendour, & I have been giving him 17 guns instead of 13 when he enters or leaves my camp, the no. of guns fired being as distinct & certainly a more audible recognition of rank than the difference with us between a lord & a duke. I have also increased his trays of shawls to the no. of 42, to which great importance is attributed, & I shall praise him for his enlightened liberality in the Calcutta Gazette. I have also given him some villages which belonged to the disaffected worth £4000 a yr. And then in another case I have confiscated estates on this side [*of*] the river worth £30,000 a yr. belonging to one chief, who retains about the same income on the other side. Pattialla has about £220,000 a year & is loaded with pearls & jewells [*sic*].

I make short speeches in durbar which are translated by the secretary to the attending chiefs, & the scene is sometimes very interesting & generally very picturesque. Little boys attend to represent their family, & one little urchin, whose father has been dispossessed & the infant established in his place, cried with fear, having never been out of the women's apartments. But I brought up to him my secretary's son who is 6 yrs. old & rides 10 & 12 miles a day. The little raja was 7, & it comforted him immediately. I have ordered the child, who is now my ward, to be put on horseback every day.

In this progress the chiefs flock in to pay their duty to the paramount power so that I have a court drawing room once a week & large dinner parties, as I pass near stations occupied by our troops, of 50 & 60 covers.

How happy I shall be to exchange all this pageantry for the society & repose of dear S. Park. In an office of anxious care & unceasing solicitude, I begin to feel the want of relaxation. I never know what it is to be free from urgent demands on my time, &, if I did not snatch moments of writing to my friends from 4 till 6 o'cl., I should be compelled to be silent. But the life I lead is full of exertion mentally & bodily. At six I shall be up & ride 13 miles to breakfast. All my staff are gone on to Umballa to play against the garrison a match of cricket except Charles, this being the departure of our mail for England. But everything is so quiet, I have very little to report.

I expect the govt. will about this day receive in England the ratification of the late Lahore treaty,[306] & I shall not hear from my

---

[306] A more comprehensive Anglo-Sikh treaty, signed in Hardinge's presence on Dec. 26, 1846, at Bhairowal, removed Rani Jindan from her role as regent. Though the treaty established a council of regency consisting of eight Sikh notables who were to

masters till the middle of March. I know that the measure is quite right, & increased years & hard work have not made me *fussy*.

Seven months in the hills will be passed quickly in spite of all the forebodings of the Indian press which, paid by the army, hates peace, with the exception of 5 or 6 of the most influential papers. In this country, as in Europe, success is the criterion of the merit, & the best plans may & do frequently fail from causes amongst barbarian powers which no foresight can anticipate. From week to week the most prudent man in so extensive an empire cannot conjecture what may happen. Mutinies & conspiracies are always reported to be hatching & every detail from every quarter passes through my hands. I am rejoiced to have had this ordeal &, when I embrace you all at S. Park, my dear wife will be repaid for all her painful sacrifices if, as I expect, I can go through successfully to the end. I really am stronger than when I left you.

God bless you.

109. [*To Walter.*] Camp Shamlee. Febry. 20th, 1847

We are in a state of perfect quiet, & I expect that we shall remain so. Of course the inveterate habit of centuries of violence & rapine cannot at once be changed, but we shall have no insurrections.

For the last 8 yrs. since the Affghan war, we have incurred in consequence of that war at least a debt of 13 millions, or in round numbers in interest borrowed 1 mil. a yr. In 1849 or 1850 I expect the annual deficit will be abolished by reductions & improved revenue, &, as we are about to be engaged in very expensive canals & railways, I propose to raise the money for these by annual loans, raised for these special & distinct uses & not for general purposes. An annual deficit for the army & state expenses ruins our credit. A loan for a canal to be repaid out of profits carries with it as a govt. measure none of the distrust of an overgrown army which the state cannot pay.

I am very confident of an abundant harvest in these sandy plains; the rains have been attended with a most healthy vegetation &, instead of a famine, three days' heavy showers will give the people nearly a double harvest. The revenue will also profit by it & I shall not have to encounter during my last year of govt. the miseries of a starving population.

---

serve at the G.G.'s pleasure, the real power was concentrated in the hands of the British resident who was not only to steer the regency council but also to have unlimited control over the Sikh government for eight years, at which time Dalip Singh's minority would end. In addition, Lahore was to pay for the permanent stationing of a British force in Panjab (B.G.L.D., pp. 41–54.)

I hope to leave Simla for Calcutta in Novr. & embark in Janry., but I do not wish the dates to be known, for I shall not write to the govt. on the subject for some months—that is, until I see the working of the Punjab arrangement, until I hear from the ministers their verdict on my conduct, & until I ascertain the probable fate of the Whig govt., my own opinion being that they will be able to struggle through their difficulties. I shall probably write to Sir John Hobhouse definitively & decidedly in May next, have his answer the end of July, & another answer relating to the arrival of my successor before the end of October, & I shall then move towards Calcutta the beginning of Novr. Your mother will, I hope, clearly understand that between April & the end of October the heart of the season renders it very unadvisable that I should move at any intermediate period.

Further, I do not think it politic that my anxiety to return to England should be bruited forth to the ministers. I am in a high office from which they cannot eject me unless they have good cause to disapprove of my conduct. My usual period of service does not expire till July 1849; I shall anticipate that period by about 20 months. I prefer, of course, that they should feel I accommodate them rather than that they should appear as according to my wishes. It is not of much importance but it is the most prudent course to take, & I should be glad to find that my family adopt it. In the House & at the club you can state to those with whom you converse such as Jocelyn, Mahon, George Byng[307] & those connected with Indian affairs that I do not intend to evade any difficulty or avoid any responsibility, that I adhere to the line I took when the Whig ministry came into office, but that I am ready at any moment to attend to their wishes, bearing in mind the difficulty of moving from Simla before the end of October on acct. of the rains & great heat. In short, I am ready to vacate at their convenience rather than for my own release from office. The accommodation is to be theirs, not mine. If they say, 'Then let the G.G. remain' (a very unlikely wish for hungry Whigs), I have the satisfaction of having my conduct approved by both the govt. parties in the state, & family arrangements can always extricate me from such an improbability. Nothing but the disturbed state of the Punjab will induce me to stay, & this contingency will not occur.

Your mother had better not make any arrangements to meet me in Italy. I shall be anxious when I move from Calcutta in Janry. 1848 to make my way direct to England, & that season would be most unpropitious for her travelling through France. I shall proceed through Egypt & from Marseilles in all probability to London.

---

[307] George Stevens Byng, the 1st Viscount Enfield, was the secretary of the Board of Control from July 1846 to Nov. 1847.

I have gone through a pretty sharp ordeal for a sexagenarian, fettered in the field & left to my own resources in council, & if I can leave India after a probation of 3 1/2 years, liberated from all danger of external enemies, the army loyal, the country prosperous, & public credit improved by equalizing the expenditure & the revenue, to which in a large colonial empire I attach the greatest importance, I shall retire to my roses at S. Park a worn out but unhated public servant, who nearly after half a century of service has a right to repose.

My health is good but the labour & anxiety is incessant, & I really want rest & relaxation. And as I *more* than keep my promise to your dear mother, I consider the line I have indicated, of retiring after a service of 3 1/2 years, just to myself & fair to the Whigs, whilst to the Ct. of Directors I have, by remaining after the Whigs came into office, confirmed a principle to them of some value: that this great office is not so strictly political as to be of necessity held by a party man.

I want to know how far the remittances of money to England will pay for Pott's farm, £7000; Fanny's portion, £10,000; a loan to Cunynghame, £2000; & the additional allowance for yr. mother's expences such as [*the*] London house, carriage, etc., before I send any more money to England.

I hope to hear that Alick Wood & Woodgate have purchased £15,000 in the 4 pr. ct. Calcutta loan. My family arrangements when this has been done are nearly completed, & Charles will probably in Janry. next have his own nest egg of £10,000 saved out of his income &, with common prudence, the family affairs will go on very well.

You had better inform Peel of my intentions. I shall receive the govt. decision in April, & if I could I shd. be disposed to come away then—but the weather is adverse for traversing 1000 miles down to Calcutta, & it wd. be an earlier retirement than that which I have named to Hobhouse, namely the end of 1847. I feel very confident that I shall have no serious difficulties in the interval. I shall have reduced the army a year before my successor arrives. Every milty. arrangement will have been *permanently* made, the deficit will be lowered 1 mil. & not exceed 1/2 a million for 1848, & I am not aware of any awkward legacy left behind, such as a B. native army in a mutinous state & the Punjab in one of anarchy with a powerful army of 100,000 men & 350 pieces of fine artry. I went to India forswearing war & I have kept my promise. I might have been a more popular man in Indian history by planting the B. standard beyond the Indus & adding a kingdom to our overgrown empire, but to me in my old age (I hope without dotage) the triumphs of British moderation & justice can never be less a subject of inward congratulation than those even of our milty. prowess. I shall as a Christian soldier feel a conscious

satisfaction that I have done as much as possible by peaceful negotiation & as little as could be avoided by force. I told you if I drew
the sword I would be sure of having ample justification. I drew it at
the latest & returned it at the earliest period to the scabbard, &, if
our milty. reputation & national character for good faith have not
been injured in my keeping, I feel confident that the policy, under
very difficult circumstances, has been the best for the interests &
security of B. India. This is only for yr. own eye. The verdict upon
my measures belongs to others, not to me.

110. [*To Sarah.*] Camp near the Ganges. March 5th, 1847

First I hope the canny bairns are both well & thriving & comforting
their mother for all her anxiety. And next, as the spring is advancing,
that you will enjoy its genial influence & court the sun's rays, which
here is the greatest of tyrants & is already beginning to be too hot.

I proceed to the Ganges tomorrow to inspect a plan for a canal
already commenced but interrupted by the war, by which that mighty
river is to be brought through a sandy district of 800 miles in extent,
irrigating 2000 square miles of land & producing food for a million
of people & mitigating, if not altogether preventing, the famine produced by drought. It will cost a million, &, the add[*itio*]ns to our army
having of late years cost a million a year, peace has been obtained,
milty. reductions to the extent of 30,000 men are making, & I shall
get rid of a deficit in our revenue of 1 mill. a yr. The famine would
as a matter of finance cause us to lose a mill. by the impossibility of
paying rents & the necessity of feeding the people, & I am now as
eager about aqueducts as bombs & shells & villainous saltpetre a year
ago.[308]

I am to see the valley tomorrow across which the Ganges waters
are to be brought on piers to the level of the country. This will alone
require 5 yrs. to construct, & the whole undertaking will be some
redemption of our character, for hitherto we have done very little for
the people, & our constant companions wherever we establish ourselves [*are*] a barrack & a gaol.

I have for the last 20 months had doctors visiting canals to report
on the malaria & disease which they engender. The report is now

---

[308] Encouraged also by new official reports that the Ganges Canal, with proper
safeguards, would not cause malaria, Hardinge ordered its construction resumed,
telling Hobhouse that the canal would be a work 'of peace and prosperity' (21 Feb.
1847, Broughton Papers, dcccliii). Hardinge sanctioned an annual disbursement of
£240,000 to finance the project which was completed in 1856 and ultimately irrigated
large areas of the Gangetic plain.

before me & I am becoming very learned in enlarged spleens & so on, but, on a comparison of blessings & of evils, the balance is immensely in favor of securing food for the people.

When I have settled this point, I intend to have 3 or 4 days' holidays in tiger hunting, then make my way through the hills to Simla & be quiet till October when I hope to leave everything on this frontier perfectly quiet & wend my way to Calcutta &, early in Janry., embark for Egypt.

The mail the end of this month will bring us the verdict of my masters in England as to recent events at Lahore. I anticipate approbation & have every reason to be quite satisfied with Hobhouse & the Whigs.

Tell me, who is to be my successor?

Do the Whigs abuse me for holding a lucrative office?

Give me good accts. of my wife & of all dear to you. The heat affects the paper. My love to your dear mother & sister. How happy I shall be to see you all.

111. [*To Walter.*] Camp Deera [*Dehra*]. March 15th, 1847

I rode in here this morn[*in*]g—a most beautiful spot under the hills of Missouri [*Mussorie*]. I halt tomorrow & then proceed by the mountain road to Simla.

After visiting the great aqua-duct [*sic*] at Solani & the stupendous work at Hurdwar of turning the River Ganges into the canal for 800 miles, 75 feet wide at top & 10 ft. deep, running at the rate of 3 m[*iles*] an hour, I proceeded to some wild forest scenery intersected with wet nullahs out of which grass & reeds grew upwards of 20 ft. high.

I resolved to have a week's holidays with the boys, having had scarcely a day's cessation from work since I came to India. We took with us 40 elephants, & the field operations were entrusted to a Mr Harvey,[309] a civil offr. of some tiger celebrity in these parts.

The first day we formed excellent lines, with our 40 monsters moving through the reeds as easily as we walk over a stubble field at home, &, after a good deal of fatigue to one not accustomed to the motion of an elephant, we were passing through some high grass close to the trees under which an hour before we had taken our luncheon when my elephant was suddenly attacked by a tiger, which Mr Harvey fired at, causing the animal to turn again into the grass. We saw him trot away within 100 yards & fired but missed.

Bob Wood & two other gentlemen on the other side of the morass

---

[309] George Frederick Harvey (1809–84), a member of the Northwestern Province civil service, later became the Commissioner of Agra.

were cut off from us. We gave chase but soon lost the animal in the long grass. By an instinctive preference for the representative of royalty, I was urging my elephant driver into the verge of the swamp when the tiger, after 2 loud roars, sprung 7 or 8 ft. high at the head of the elephant. A step on one side threw the tiger on the elephant's side where he hung by his teeth & claws for a second, & in falling to the ground I shot him in the body, but evidently with little effect, for in rising he sprang *en croupe* on the nearest elephant, trying to get into the howder [*sic*]. He held his position for 30 or 40 yards, biting at the native behind who hit him with a wooden mace used in driving the elephant. The gentleman in the howder [*sic*] would not fire. The terrified animal rolled & plunged to get rid of the tiger, & our friend Mr Davison[310] could with difficulty keep his seat.

I got up close enough to give the tiger a shot without injury to the elephant, & Charles, coming up on the flank, gave the tiger 3 shots, the last of which brought him to the ground where the noble beast still attempted with his last gasp of life to make a desperate struggle. We soon put him out of his pain.

Bob Wood & his friends at abt. 100 yds. saw our adventure but were cut off by the morass of access to us. Davison could not fire, & the 4th gun, Mr Harvey, seeing that the tiger could not escape but that there was some risk in firing into the elephant as well as the tiger, did not interfere.

We had thus the satisfaction of killing a very fine fighting tiger who charged me twice. My elephant was only slightly hurt, & we returned to our tents with our gallant victim in the highest spirits.

I had him skinned instantly except the head, which I sent off to my doctor, who, as agreed upon, took out the skull & jaws &, having saturated them with arsenic & soap, drew the skin over again, filling the cavityies [*sic*] with cotton, & the next day, when I saw him, he looked quite beautiful. He is greatly admired, being 9 ft. 5 [*inches*] from nose to the end of the tail & perfectly well marked.

I propose to send him to Mr Ledbetter.[311] With glass eyes & a red leather tongue he will be a perfect specimen for the hall—a reminiscence of my last days of activity in India & perhaps in after years some recollection to Charles of his having been associated with his father not only in his labours but in his sports.

The next day being Sunday, we halted. On the 5 following days we killed 2 more tigers, inferior to the first in size & courage & rather mobbed them to death by nos. than in more equal combat. The animal is so fierce & active that he takes many shots before he falls, & whilst it lasts the excitement is the finest in the world.

[310] Not identified.
[311] A taxidermist.

The sport is also very agreeable in seeing the wildest parts of the islands of the Ganges but above all in watching the wonderful sagacity of the elephant in the various positions of difficulty in which he is placed. If a bough hangs over the howder [sic] as big as a man's thigh, he snaps it off to let the howder [sic] pass. He pushes down small trees with the greatest ease & walks through the thickest jungle of reeds 20 & 25 ft. high clearing his way with his trunk, which touches every spot of ground to ascertain its soundness before the foot is trusted to make a step in advance.

I rode one upwards of 80 yrs. old. They are very sensitive if a fly settles on their hide & quite furious from terror if a bees' nest is disturbed. This happened partially on one day & reminded me of poor [Alex] Grant's mishap at Drayton. He was seeking a partridge he had shot & trod in a wasp's nest when we saw him at a distance cutting various capers & suddenly plunge his head into the grass, bringing the skirts of his shooting jacket over his head & exhibiting his sitting feature high in the air on which with instinctive rage the wasps settled, as is the hiving custom of these insects, when he roared with pain, for his garments were very thin, till the gamekeeper came up to the rescue. We all behaved most barbarously except Lady Peel who, when he came to her, bandaged with a turban, exclaimed, 'I hope you have not been shot?' & impassionated his sufferings. What a curious love we have to see & dwell on the ridiculous in others! I have been laughing aloud at the recollection of poor Grant's tormenting antics.

I bore the toil of being 8 or 9 hours at a time cooped up in the howder [sic] very well. The sun was hot but I am quite well, though some-what stiff & bruised.

I have just seen a *fat* captain who is settled here, he reminding me that last year he was my escort with 50 men towards Sobraon & that the rate I went at for 15 miles placed 18 horses in hospital. I tried to defend myself against this charge & recollected that in his exertions he burst his pantaloons & was obliged to ride for decency in his cloak. He admitted to the retort & that I waited 2 or 3 minutes for the adjustment of his toilette.

In this out of the way place I have picked up about 25 persons to dine here. Tomorrow I shall have as many more, & at Nah[a]n I dismiss all my heavy baggage & shall not see a soul till I reach Simla.

By the way, if Salvin builds over the south wing, the iron girder will have to sustain not only the chimney, etc., of the bed-rooms above but also the additional rooms.

I suppose the new dining room chimney may be so constructed as to act as a buttress, otherwise the interior walls may bulge in when loaded with a 3rd story.

112. [*To Walter*.] Camp Nah[*a*]n. March 21st, 1847

Confidential

I have had during the last month a sharp correspondence with Ld. Gough who very indiscreetly & busily endeavoured to cast suspicions on a field offr. of our staff & through him indirectly on me. I have made him unsay the most important parts of his accusatory state[*men*]ts agt. Coll. B[*enson*], & I have not answered his fulsome assertions of personal friendship for me & my great qualities.

The whole proceeding has impressed me with the deepest conviction of his being a very shabby fellow. Even now he adheres to state[*men*]ts which he knows to be false as regards offs. of this army because in the Quarterly his fabrications have been inserted in letters from himself or someone abt. him, & he dares not *again* encounter Mr Gleig's displeasure for exaggerated information.

The correspondence is curious & has turned out very much to his annoyance.

It is not quite over. The perusal [*of*] some of these days will very much interest you.

Don't say a word to yr. mother on this subject.

113. [*To Walter*.] Simla. April 15th, 1847

I have a beautiful imitation of the screen in the Taj in teak wood. I send the dimensions. How can it be applied [*at South Park*]? The carving is equally well finished on both sides so that its perfection of carving would be diminished by being fixed against a wall. The perforations constitute much of its beauty, & it is a classical reminiscence.

I have also a five-sided window in carved wood from Lahore, very prettily worked. I think this would look well by being fixed on the wall at the landing place of the new staircase looking into the hall, as is the case at Hatfield. It will harmonize very well with old Oak [*Room*] armour & stags' heads.

The tiger is in excellent preservation—the head entire with the skull & teeth, etc. I propose to fix him against the wall. That is, the tail up to the ceiling, the skin stretched like a bat agt. the wall & the beautiful monster's head so fixed as to be springing on the spectator. This vagary of mine will show his size & skin, & the head, which is fine with Mr Ledbetter's art, will be nearly as ferociously beautiful as when alive.

I have got some old Sikh armour for the hall which I prize, for the art seems to have been known in the Punjaub before Alexander's time. The chain & steel armour of Porus, inlaid with gold, was greatly

admired by Alexander & the Macedonians, according to Arrian.[312]
These reminiscences of India will in afterlife be a source of satisfaction
to Charles & will ornament the walls of an old veteran very appropriately.

I have only 6 months to get through at Simla & I hope to clear off
every unsettled question & to leave this gt. empire in profound peace
the end of Decr. with no external enemy that can give my successor
a day's uneasiness & no deficit for 1849.

I am reducing 35,000 men, & next spring the new gov. genl. may
reduce 10,000 more, but it is right that he should exercise his own
judgement in this matter, & he shall not complain that I have left
him too weak in milty. means.

114. [*To Walter.*] Simla. April 20th, 1847
Private

I have had a mass of detailed business on my hands connected with
army reductions & canal augmentations—that is, what I save in
discharging useless soldiers I apply to purposes of more lasting &
peaceable utility. In two years I have no doubt we shall have a surplus.
The 5 pr. ct. loan will close very shortly, the old 4 pr. cent having
failed 2 years ago before the war; & our next estimate from April
1848/49 will make the revenue equal to the expenditure.

I am overworked & look forward with delight to New Year's Day,
hoping to be on b[oar]d ship the first week in Janry.

Hobhouse says in his last letter that he has consented to print
extracts from my dispatches in consequence of Ld. Jocelyn's wishes &
others of my friends. I knew nothing of it. I have taken no part in the
matter &, if you know anything abt. [it], be so good as to let me know.

I concluded the late treaty *before* I could receive the Whig approval
of the measure. Bad or good, it is my own act. Sir James Hogg in his
letter to me approves, & strongly.

Hobhouse's approval is to me cold, & I evidently perceive that he
& probably Palmerston wd. have preferred annexation. Ld. John &
the Cabinet *entirely approve*. How[eve]r, I have taken the opportunity
of the entire approbation of the Cabinet to beg to be relieved the end
of Decr. & requested Hobhouse to inform H.M. of my resolution, in
strict accordance with my letters written when I was urged to remain
on the Whigs coming into office. I shall write to H.M. myself today.
Everything is perfectly quiet on this frontier, & I am going on as
usual.

Ld. G[ough] is my most obedient serv[an]t. He has fallen greatly in my estimation. The correspondence is curious & I have not spared him, but he has dined with me &, for the sake of the public service, I am courteous & cold.

We have got 2 or 3 ladies who can sing & play, & after dinner the dining room is cleared & we adjourn for an hour. I really begin to believe I have a taste for music. Pray encourage Emily to cultivate her music & singing.

How I long to be with you. Eleven months must still elapse till the end of Febry.

115. [*To Walter.*] Simla. May 2nd, 1847

I send you some parcels of seeds gathered in the mountains of Nepaul. I would advise you to divide them into lots & distribute some of each to those who take the greatest interest in shrubs.

The mountain palm tree wd. be a curiosity & I do not understand why it should not thrive in England.

Now that I have declined to continue in India, I anticipate a more cordial time in the official dispatches. The private letters are full of assurances of support but they mean very little, & I shall be delighted to be released from a position in which I believe Sir John [*Hobhouse*] & Ld. Palmerston do not approve of the *moderation* policy pursued in the Punjab but are still dreaming of Russian aggression!

Lord John [*Russell*] was very cordial & like a gentleman. I rather think the Cabinet are divided on the subject of the Punjab—some for & others agt. annexation.

How[*eve*]r this may be, I have already reduced 24,000 men. The revenue is flourishing & in April from 1848/49 there will be a surplus after 9 years of deficiencies following that greatest of follies, the Affghan war, which cost 12 mill. sterlg. The Punjab war will cost the state abt. £600,000 & the permanent revenue from the ceded territory £500,000 a yr., being more than all the territory ceded after the Burmese & Nepaulese wars.

I do not know what selections Hobhouse may have made from the correspondence since March 1846,[313] but this is the fact—that every dispatch is written in my handwriting, & most of the letters signed by the secretaries or Mem[*orand*]a [*are*] also written by me, & that I am solely responsible for everything, & that, if there is censure, it deservedly belongs to me.

I do not wish Hobhouse to be told that I doubt his sincerity because

---

[313] Eleven dispatches and enclosures from Hardinge to the Secret Committee, dating from 3 Sept. 1846, to 2 Jan. 1847, and dealing with Panjab affairs, were presented to Parliament and published in Mar.

he wd. have preferred a policy of aggrandize[*men*]t, as it wd. only sour him & the Palmerston clique. I have no doubt after a squabble or two we shall part in Decr. very good friends. But in writing to you I conceal nothing.

The mail is expected on the 4th. My best love to dear Sarah.

116. [*To Walter.*] Simla. June 9, 1847

I send you a drawing of the teakwood screen, but I really know not how it can be applied at S.P. I hear it is beautiful, being a fac-simile of one in marble at the Taj. It is a mixture of Italian & Saracenic, both sides equally well carved.

You say in one of yr. letters that there is a feeling that Sir John Littler has not been rewarded. This is no fault of mine, for I have issued [*a*] strong G[*eneral*] O[*rder*] in his praise, & he is now [*a*] provisional member of [*the*] council. He is at this time staying with me here & I have recommended him for the G.C.B. The hitch is at the Horse Guards.

As to reductions in the army, this ungrateful [*task*] must be done, & I have reduced 30,000 men in Bengal & 15,000 in Madras & Bombay but with such contentment that I send you an extract from the Bombay Times.[314] Lord E[*llenborough*]'s popularity consisted in rhapsodies of marching the n[*ative*] army to Constantinople through Egypt. My line has been to speak merely the truth, to do them substantial services in just cases but not to march to the Indus & perpetuate our debt *merely* to give them promotion by a large milty. augmentation. This is the real state of the case, & popularity obtained by flattery is so fleeting that it is of no value; &, as to abuse, I know, as regards the army, it is undeserved & it never comes across my mind, for a 20 yr. seat in the Hse. of Coms. makes a public man very tough in his hide & allows to unjust censures.

You may hear of plots & treasons at Lahore and disturbances elsewhere. The papers must find news & constantly exaggerate what they hear. My own expectation is that everything will be quiet. I shall have remained in India 22 months next Decr. *after* the Lahore treaty &, having evaded no Punjab responsibility, I may surely return without the imputation of having left all the difficulties of my policy to my successor. On the contrary, I shall leave him without an enemy, the army purified of extra nos., & the exchequer with a surplus instead of a deficit for 9 yrs. In short, my dear Walter, I have no misgivings, without indulging in vain delusions, for I am seldom satisfied with my

---

[314] Not found. Hardinge seems to be referring to the editorial of 20 Jan. as reprinted in *The Bombay Times*' bimonthly summary of intelligence, Feb. 1, 1847, p. 13.

own efforts, always imagining that I might have done my work better, but this emulation at 62 keeps me awake, & I think my public papers during the last year the best of my life, altho' I always seek to be as plain as possible.

Love to dearest Sarah.

Robt. Wood is much better & is quite safe if he will but be prudent by not acting as if he were quite well.[315]

117. [*To Walter.*] Simla. July 6th, 1847

I was very glad to see that you hit off a just point in debate in the education question & that Peel, Graham & the ministers agreed with you that the R. Catholics ought not to be excluded.[316] It is, as I know *here,* a most difficult question everywhere, but we must, to make civilization a blessing, educate the people & if possible in Christian principles (*not here*), for it has this merit over every other, that it is practical morality of the purest kind, supporting a man in this world by giving him peace of conscience &, in the next, hope of eternal happiness. It fulfills more conditions in alleviation of suffering humanity than any other system & its perfection is a proof of its divine origin.

I am expecting the mail any hour, but the rain has been very heavy for the last 24 h[*ours*] & I dare not risk the chance of delaying our express.

The Punjab is wonderfully tranquil. My resident, Lt. Coll. Lawrence, is a very fine fellow but has been too long in India. He is suffering from ill-health. I expect him at Simla in a few days.

I can answer for peace during the next 6 years. Can Ld. Palmerston say as much for Europe?

I am expediting the milty. works at Aden as fast as possible. It is an important promontory at the entrance of the Red Sea & the last stage for our steamers to Suez & Egypt & the first from Egypt to China. In case of war, Algeria & the Lac Français, as they call the Mediterranean, will be the scene of action; Gibraltar, Malta & the Ionian islands will play their part, & on this side our little port of Aden will be an important link in the wonderful chain of our communications with the Celestial Empire. I have rendered Aden as compact as

---

[315] He had a serious bilious attack accompanied by high fever.
[316] On 22 April, during a lengthy Commons debate dealing with education, Walter 'unfeignedly regretted' the attempt to deprive Catholics of the right to an equal education. Alluding to the reforms of recent decades, he declared: 'During the present century, they had removed the Roman Catholic disabilities; yet it was impossible to deny that the proposed scheme, as far as the Roman Catholics were concerned, did, by excluding them, create a new Roman Catholic disability' (3 *Hansard*, xci. 1177–8).

possible. The Bombay govt. & their engineers had projected works for 4000 troops, 2000 of which were to be gunners, thus *permanently* draining the Bombay presidency of troops & entailing a very heavy expense. I have reduced the troops to 1200 in peace & 1700 in war, lowered the works & batteries by more than £50,000, but the gt. saving without any real loss of efficiency is in the men & the wear & tear on their health.

I have just sent home a Mem[*orandu*]m of 16 sheets on this subject in reply to a report of 362 par[*agraphs*].[317] I fear we cannot finish the works under 3 years, & we shall have a breeze after Louis Philippe's death. I should like an expedition from Gibraltar to Egypt as the *finale*, shaking hands at Cairo with my Indian friends from Aden.

The Palmerston *night-mare* of an attack on India by Russia & Persia is still persisted in. I hope Ld. John will show him a letter I wrote to Lord John on that subject. We have paid dearly for the solution of that problem, but the Affghan expedition settled that point.

I am anxiously waiting an announce[*men*]t of Lord Ellenborough's marriage with Miss Monk. You will be amused with our correspondence.

I also expect an answer from Hobhouse as to my solicitation to retire. It was gratifying to receive cordial invitations to remain from Ld. John &, what is not in the ordinary course, from *all the Cabinet*, but nothing shall induce me to depart from my line. I shall have remained 2 years since the war & have evaded no difficulty or responsibility arising out of my policy, & I shall leave India at peace & with a surplus, having reduced 50,000 men & yet keeping an army of 50,000 men on this frontier, which costs no more than if it were dispersed over Hindostan.

I keep up appearances with G[*ough*], who is most submissive. You will one day at S. Park read *the* correspondence. The attempt to lower me has signally failed & with disgrace. It was founded on a lie & persisted in by a garbling & suppression of his own witness's evidence, & the offs. whom he attacked to get at me have recd. from me with his consent a full vindication. The fact is that he boasted to his lady & wrote to his son of conversations with offs. which never took place. She, believing them to be correct, managed the correspondence &, when every offr. denied his accuracy, he garbled the evidence of his nephew[318] to sustain a lie, not considering the infirmity of his memory & the weakness of his understanding. How[*eve*]r, the affair is now

---

[317] Hardinge, in a letter to Hobhouse on 7 July 1847, called his Aden Memorandum 'long winded' but expressed relief that the matter had now been resolved (Broughton Papers, dcccliv, 60).

[318] Col. (afterwards Gen.) John Bloomfield Gough (1804–91) was then on his uncle's staff.

past. I refused (as he wished) to burn the letters, & I leave them & various other documents to Charles, & I shall probably, when I get home, write an acct. of the three years in India for my children.

As soon as the mail goes out, I shall add a codicil to my will, which I have not looked at since I left London but which will provide amply for yr. mother in case she should survive me &, in other respects as concerns the children, confirm all my former intentions for their benefit. In the changes & chances of this mortal life this is a proper precaution, & I am quite satisfied with the arrange[men]ts secured for the living & the precautions taken for posterity.

I now get up at 5 instead of 4 & take more sleep, but I am eagerly attempting to clear off all undecided subjects before I wind up my concerns & am in perfect health.

I am raising all the precautionary measures taken for the occupation of Lahore & shall place another European regt. there. I know I shall be held responsible after my departure, & my successor shall find practical proofs of my care to place this frontier in a state of perfect security. The advanced position at Lahore gives us the Punjab without the expense. In fact, we receive £220,000, which merely covers our expenses & which wd. be equally incurred if the troops were on this side [of] the Sutlege, & it has enabled us to reduce 50,000 men. The finances are improving. Canals & roads are making & yet we shall make our revenue equal our expenditure for the first time this 9 years from May 1848.

[*P.S.*]
Bob is quite right & getting on rapidly.

118. [*To Sarah.*] Simla. July 6th, 1847

Pray tell Walter that Charles will by the next mail send £1000 for Salvin's alterations & probably £3000 more in the following 4 months, by which time I hope we shall be near Calcutta & the end of December on our way to Egypt.

In less than 6 months I hope to be on ship-board, leaving this vast empire at peace, with its finances equal to its wants, but they are the most inconsistent & incomprehensible of God's creatures.

Exclusive of suttee & infanticide, the Rajpoot brahmins of high pretensions to sanctity & antiquity of race commit the most atrocious crimes ostentatiously on the plea, when justice is refused, of casting the reproach of their crimes on the head of the chief refusing the satisfaction they demand. A few days ago I read a report that, during the last 6 months in a district of Raja-pootana, a brahmin having had 2 bullocks stolen, went to the chief &, as the chief could not discover the thief, the brahmin, to show the depth of his annoyance, cut off his own mother's head & cast it at the raja's feet.

In another case the remission of a fine was requested & refused near Ajmeer. The man goes with his friends to the chief, one friend stabs himself to death, & the *fined* man brings forward two aged men with the avowed purpose of immolating them if the money fine be not remitted. The raja succumbs, the rascal walks off triumphant with his dead friend's body.

Another man, having had his crops plundered, went to the chief where the depredator was supposed to be &, having no proof & obtaining no redress, he cuts off his mother's head, & another relation cut off his aunt's head, & threw them at the chief's feet. In this last case, the raja imprisoned both the murderers to pass 7 yrs. in irons, & this sensible remedy gives gt. dissatisfaction!

At Odeipoor several years ago, the raja had a very beautiful daughter, & 2 chiefs disputed her hand in marriage. A sanguinary war wd. have resulted [*from*] the offended feelings of the chief refused. The beautiful princess in full durbar pathetically begs to be put to death to save her country from war, & the father, advised by his council, consents. This is a much finer subject for a poem than Helen's elopement with Paris, but the fact is true.

And yet the extraordinary fact is felt every day & every hour that these ferocious men submit themselves to *us*, &, if each black man took up his handful of sand & by a united effort cast it upon the white-faced intruders, we should be buried alive!

Our courage, our justice & good faith so surprize their faculties, & their habit of submitting to what they deem to be destiny is so strong, that we have seldom any attempt to throw off the yoke.

The boys are well & Robert Wood quite convalescent.

119. [*To Emily.*] Simla. July 6th, 1847

I have written to Walter & Sarah & the Woods & have postponed writing to you as our English mail is hourly expected. Charles is [*in*] the adjoining room exchanging a drawing with a fellow artist, a daughter of *Nimrod*'s who is married, very appropriately, to a cavry. offr. The lady, who is very pretty, has just returned from Scinde, has for 2 yrs. been living in a tent at 128°! & is alive & healthy! She has a very good drawing of Sir Chs. Napier, & in some respects [*is*] a very clever artist, particularly in horses, her father Mr Apperley having written the best book on horses ever published, under the title of Nimrod.[319]

---

[319] Probably 'Nimrod' [C. J. Apperley], *The Horse and the Hound: their various uses and treatment* (Edinburgh, 1842).

Charles improves daily. Each successive sketch excels its predecessor.

I gave Arthur a public rowing before the staff at breakfast for sitting all last night whispering to a pretty girl, a sister of Lady Currie's, & making himself remarkable by his attentions. I quizzed him severely, explaining that the young lady came out to be married &, unless he *proposed*, it was selfish to engage her attentions so exclusively. He bore it very well, for we all hit him a slap, & I hope it will arrest a silly habit. I am so occupied I cannot attempt to educate him, & his idleness is excessive. I shall be glad to have him in England under such a man as Sir F. Smith before he goes to the Milty. College, & I must get him through that useful institution to which I owe so much before I die.

I am quite at ease about Robert Wood. He is working steadily & usefully as of old & is an instance of how much may be done by perseverance & care.

As for me, I am nearly worn out. Prepare the dust-hole. I now take another hour in bed & don't rise till 5 & am the better for the add[*itiona*]l repose.

I reckon Salvin's expenses at £2000, £1000 for the church, &, with some wine accts., £1000 bills to pay in London, & nearly £1000 to bring me & my staff home, or £5000. Adding what may be deficient to make up Fanny's portion, I shall be very close-run, but I hope you will receive yr. beggar as if he came full-handed with Golconda's mines.[320] Charles & Arthur, like provident sepoys when they return to their villages, take their shawls in their hands to lay at yr. feet. The tiger which I bring with me must be my substitute. He is a noble monster & greatly to be admired. But I forgot that I have some worked curtains for yr. bed-room & boudoir, which are warm & pretty. The natives keep their shawls in a press, with a screw to tighten the pressure similar to a butler's press for napkins, etc. The insects can neither get in nor breed insects, & it is so simple that it is worth yr. notice.

I am anxiously awaiting the verification of the report in our papers that Lord E[*llenborough*] is about to marry the Bishop of Gloucester's daughter. What an extraordinary man he is. The presence of a lady will improve Southam,[321] but I do not think we shall be pressed to be witnesses of his connubial happiness. When I hear the fact announced, I shall write to congratulate him.

Our affairs at Lahore go on admirably. The country has never been so quiet &, if the resident's health resists the climate & his hard work, peace will not be disturbed during the prince's minority of 6 years.

---

[320] The capital of the medieval Bahamani kingdom fabled for its gold.
[321] Ellenborough's estate in Gloucestershire.

Everything in other quarters is equally prosperous—50,000 men discharged with gratuities without a murmur, the finances improving, & our expenditure for the next years reduced by *one* million & a quarter, covering all deficiencies & realizing a surplus for the first time in 9 years. I am in great hopes to leave the country in a still more prosperous state &, altho' I am bored out of my life by the details I go through, I am conscious of the value of this attention to business, & I believe those about me appreciate its results.

I am quite well, very temperate & regular in exercise, & never wake from 1/2 p[*as*]t 10 till 5. I have not time to be ill. Let me know the size of the new dining r[*oom*].

From the description you gave in your note to Charles of yr. conversation with Graham, it seems as if he were inclined to be my successor. I did not see his name the last summer & autumn as a visitor at Drayton. Is he as intimate as ever with Peel? Or did he expect a peerage?[322] I hear he & Ld. Stanley merely speak as they pass by & have had no communication since Stanley's retirement. I esteem it a great consolation for my banishment here that I have had none of these political quarrels on my hands, & when I return I will do all the good I can but, being only fit for the retired list, I will never take political office again, & [*in*] my opinion Peel never will unless some gt. emergency shall force him in by the united wishes of all parties. I suppose he will protect Lord John as long as he acts on conservative principles, & this is a safer line than to trust to D'Israeli & co.

The neglect of the Queen must be accidental. Hobhouse wrote me the other day that I had in H.M. a sincere friend at court. The fault is in those around her.

I shall not receive a positive answer from Hobhouse to my request to retire till the mail expected here a fortnight hence, but I shall receive an answer to my solicitation to resign on hearing of his approbation of the treaty unaccompanied by any offer for my continuance in office.

I will wait till tomorrow before I close my letter.

[*No closing*]

120. [*To Walter.*] Simla. 20th July 1847

I send you a mem[*orandu*]m on the S.P. alterations. We are all for the enlarged hall &, as Constable[323] will probably attend to the South

---

[322] Hardinge would have preferred Graham as his successor. 'I hope for the sake of India,' Hardinge wrote to Hogg, 'Graham will be selected. He has great experience, sound judgment and [*is*] indefatigable in business' (23 June 1847, Hogg Correspondence, 342/6).

[323] Apparently a builder working with Salvin.

Wing first, I hope we shall be in time to include the bedroom above Mrs Milner's[324] room as part of the hall.

I suppose the alterations will be finished the end of Sep. &, as the walls are old, the plastering may proceed the end of that month.

What should you say to bookcases 6 or 7 ft. high, white & gold, the white highly glazed & the gold liberally bestowed? The style of work is like Japan, being white instead of black, but I don't see any way to the distribution on the walls, leaving room for watercolor drawings, which must hang low. This kind of work is well made here in India, if I had correct plans.

I have a brass door imitated from the silver door of the temple at Umritsir—height 6 ft. 7 [inches]; breadth, or rather width, 4 ft. 7 [inches]; opening from the centre. What shall I do with it?

I propose to write to Hobhouse that I expect to see my successor at Calcutta by New Year's Day or to meet him, if more convenient, at Cairo, say the 1st Febry. Both arrangements assume that I leave Calcutta the 1st of Janry. This is in accordance with the earliest day fixed by me. I have a letter from Hobhouse expressing his regret at my determination & enclosing me a note from the Queen, of which I send yr. mother a copy & which is very gratifying. A reluctant acceptance of office, followed by public approbation & terminated by a voluntary retreat, gratifies my ambition in retiring from public life, but I have 5 months still before me & it appears an age. Hobhouse assures me nothing is settled as to my successor & that I shall know as soon as it is. The Marquis of Tweed-dale retires also in Janry. from Madras, & Napier from Scinde probably at an earlier period.

I find time to write to you by getting up an hour earlier, but the work is really too much for any man, &, exclusive of family attachments, I shall be rejoiced to be relieved. The chairman & Court of D. press me to stay for one year more. Nothing shall induce me to consent to remain & nothing can keep me except an insurrection or extensive army mutiny, neither of which will occur.

On the 23rd July I landed in India, & in 3 days I shall have served 3 years, but which period in events embraces six. I hope you are all satisfied that I acted right last year in consenting to remain till the end of 1847. I have evaded no responsibility, & I have reduced 50,000 men. The army recognize the propriety of all these measures to extricate the country from debt, altho' the more ardent heroes in the lower grades give vent to their disappointment by defamation in their press, which I entirely disregard. I know that I have attended to their real interests &, having *dared* to take a line of moderation & peace, I am not to be frightened from my duty by popularity-hunting considerations.

[324] Not identified.

I shall be quite ready for a game of romps with my grand-children, &, if you succeed in becoming the owner of Betteshanger, which I think a delightful country, I shall rejoice in the facility with which the two houses can communicate, for I suppose it is about 12 miles from Dover.

121. [*To Emily.*] Simla. July 23rd, 1847

This day 3 years ago I landed in India! I ought to be grateful to the Almighty for preserving you & our children through all the chances & changes of this mortal life! For myself, a sexagenarian, I have had my trials. I begin to feel the incessant anxiety of ever-lasting business &, although my bodily health is good, I certainly want repose of mind. My nerves are good, but the eagerness to get through what I have in hand is as youthful as ever, &, as I have now only 5 months to serve in India, I am alive to the necessity of great exertion to clear off arrears, and I shall not be at ease till the end of Oct. when I am on the march to Oude to read a lecture to the king & thence to Calcutta, embarking the end of the year.

I have written to Hobhouse begging that he will leave me at full liberty to embark the 1st Janry. whether my successor arrives or not. He in his last letter assures me nothing has been decided & that I shall know as soon as it is settled.

I send you a copy of a letter from the Queen,[325] which is very cordial & handsome. I have just answered it. I never have recd. your acknowledgement of those I sent you last year & one this year. Pray let me know the date of the last you have received.

Your warmth of attachment & Charles' (yr. brother's)[326] habit of exaggeration make you both imagine that higher honors are in store for me when I return. Rely upon it, there is no such intention. I have done nothing since March 1846 to merit such a distinction, & Hobhouse & Palmerston, disliking the policy of 1846 & disgusted with the ambush of their milty. disasters & heavy debt from which India has since been extricated, will never desire to up-hold me. Most sincerely I declare that, as the object of all public honours is not to reward individuals but to record & perpetuate some important service & principle which, in my instance, has already been done & very liberally, I cannot see how they would be justified in taking the course assumed to be probable by yr. brother. Furthermore, my d[*eares*]t friend, it is most desirable that you should not be blinded by yr. partiality to suppose such a thing likely. People say these things to

---

[325] Not found.
[326] Charles William Stewart, the 3rd Marquess of Londonderry.

you as a *feeler*, to ascertain your sentiments & report them, but I know your tact is too sensitive & discriminating to be deceived by such strategems, & as to being com[*mander*] in chief, I never wish to be in any harness but yours for the rest of my life. I am so surfeited by over-work that I loathe the very thought of losing my liberty regained.

You will judge how all my feelings are turned towards home by the letter I have written to Walter about S. Park. I send it to you, not knowing where he may be, & after you have read the papers, if he is at Tunbridge Wells, he will relieve you from the worry of giving orders about the alterations of the hall. If he is not within reach, you must, if time presses, request Mr Woodgate to settle the affair with Mr Salvin & Constable. You will observe I am decidedly for enlarging the hall, & Charles is still more anxious on that point.

I revised my will made in London, dated May 1844, & when we meet the beginning of March, I will explain the state of our family affairs, which is as satisfactory as I would desire. When I took leave of you, a 4 years' banishment, a doubtful adventure, & a bad climate were before me. In less than 4 years, in 3 1/2 years I leave India with the consolation that your life has not been sacrificed, which it wd. have been could you have followed me, & that I return in good health & in good repute after a short but sharp tryal. This, d[*eares*]t, is an anticipation of 6 months, but I trust in the mercy of God that these hopes will be realized.

Napier will return, I think in 3 or 4 months. Lady Napier has been dangerously ill & his health very much shaken. He is a very fine fellow & as a lion is more to be admired than [*Sir Harry*] Smith—very different men & both of great merit.

I dislike public dinners & I never know what to say when I have to return thanks, & I don't think age & labour have brightened my imagination altho' they may have sobered my judgement. By that time the town will be tired of yellow Indians & the thrice-told stories of Indian wars.

I am interrupted by a secretary with boxes. The mail does not go out for 4 or 5 days; for the present, adieu.

24th

I have got through a good deal of business & am in a forward state for the mail. During the last month we have had a report that Ld. E[*llenborough*] was to be married to a Miss Monck. As you are silent, I don't believe there has been any foundation for it. I hear he has declared himself a follower of Stanley's. However, the election returns will shuffle the political cards to enable some one party in the state to have the means of govt., for nothing can be so bad as an equally divided state of parties. I shall adhere to the most able & most honest statesman, Peel, & take no marked line & probably seldom attend the House.

By the next mail I shall have a letter from Hobhouse in reply to my observations on letters of his to me, with which I found fault. He is most cordial in his private letters & querulous in his public, which I don't approve. Now that he has got my resignation he will be more civil, & Charles may propose to one of his daughters. I should not be surprized if *he* is out of office after the elections are over.[327] He is a clever man, without being a man of business &, I suspect, is governed by Lords Palmerston & Auckland, both of whom have no objection to pick holes in my papers & escutcheon. The result of their inter-meddling was the greatest disaster & disgrace which our arms ever suffered, shaking this empire to its very foundation, lowering the prestige of British invincibility, elevating the hopes of our enemies, & loading the finances of the state with 30 millions of debt for the folly of such a political *night-mare* as a Russian invasion of India.

I have reduced 50,000 men, & we are out of debt next year as far as realizing a surplus revenue, & this has not been the case before for 9 years. I have written to H.M. & told her these facts,[328] sending a copy of my letter to the minister. I let Hobhouse know everything I do & have no secrets serving under a Whig govt., but rely upon it, although they wd. have preferred my remaining here for another year, my measures so opposite to theirs are not palatable.

Let me know how Salvin proposes to manage the ceiling of the hall & when the whole, including the enlargement of the hall, will be finished. What would he do with the terrace? Walter proposes flower beds on each side [*of*] the terrace. Would Salvin enlarge the garden towards the south, so as to have a *pendant* to the lower terrace? Would he reform the fountain or abolish it? Would he put plate glass into the windows?

I think Burke ought to fence off the ivy by keeping up the rails or boarding it up, for all the bricks will have to be carried up on the side where the ivy grows. What [*do*] Mrs Allnutt & Woodgate say to these alterations? Burke had better provide 300 doz. roses to bud in the spring [*of*] 1848. How happy I shall be to saunter idly from the terrace to the tangle accompanied by you, admiring the growth of the shrub or regretting some absent favorite nipped by an unkindly frost whilst I was broiling under an Indian sun.

[327] Hobhouse was defeated in the 1847 election at Nottingham but re-elected from Harwich in 1848. His tenure as president of the Board of Control continued uninterrupted until 1852.

[328] Actually he wrote to the Queen only on 27 July expressing 'most sanguine expectations that peace has been securely established beyond the Northwest frontier as well as throughout India' (V.A.P.).

I must beg you to be at peace with the royal tiger. He is a noble monster, & Charles will be unhappy if you reject him from the Indian memorabilia to be hung up in the hall. I make a point also of introducing the Lahore window through yr. passage into the hall because I am sure you will like it. Walter has the exact dimensions of the window, & the workmen can at once prepare the aperture, altho' I do not think the window can reach S.P. till March.

Can Mr Salvin's ingenuity find a place for 2 highly ornamented Sikh guns? They should not be exposed to the weather.

As to the Taj screen, your ingenuity must find a place for it. I sent the plan a month ago to Walter. I hope you are not much disturbed by the workmen.

27 July

My despatches for the mail are very heavy in every dept. & really very satisfactory, & I have got through them in good time & feel the repose of a coal bearer in throwing down his last load. But what will it be when I step on board the steamer? I think of taking a favorite horse home with me if he is quite sound, & if not, he will be taken care of for life in India. Charles has got a kennel of dogs of all kinds, &, with 12 pheasants for the Queen, our ship will be a Noah's ark.

I am quite joy-ful in having made all my arrangements to leave Calcutta in any case the 1st Janry. Lord Tweed-dale also returns at the same time. The 2 other govts. of Madras & Bombay are subordinate to the govr. genl. &, as he, Ld. T., is proud & huffy, I don't think he is very cordial, [I] having been obliged to object so some of his arrangements. Conceive my charge extending over an empire whose frontier by sea & by land is 12,000 miles in circumference! & in every possible subject the other govts. refer to me; & the result of my 3 yrs.' experience is that common sense solves the most difficult subjects in the best manner. At the same time a huge portion of the business is milty., & in that branch the Ordnance & War Office trainings have been of great value.

I am going to write to Lord Ripon in reply to his note from S.P. If you see Lady Peel, tell her of the Queen's cordial note. As to Ld. E., I have not heard from him lately. You will like to read Peel's letters to me since Decr. 1845. They are warm-hearted expressions of friendship of which I am most proud. Croker, I hear, clings to Ld. Ashburton & will probably never be received again at Drayton. Who constitute the Duke's society at Stratfield-Saye & Walmer?

Pray, d[eares]t, be careful of yourself this autumn & winter & look to the warming of the house now that the workmen are in it, improving upon my suggestions in the Mem[orandu]m I have drawn out for Walter. I don't care to have hot air in the rooms but the passages, staircase, anteroom, & hall are indispensable, & the stove should be very large & simple. The old stove must be worn out.

I hope the Cunynghames are staying with you. Have you been well supplied with vegetables & fruit?

122. [*To Emily.*] Simla. Augt. 12th, 1847

Your letter of the 22nd June from S.P. was most acceptable. You seem to be in excellent health, & every month is hailed by both of us as a nearer land march by which the wanderers may more surely find their way to their native home.

The government of this mighty empire is the great & closing event of my life. After 3 years of arduous labor, a voluntary retirement is rendered respectable by pressing invitations to remain at my post, but I shall relinquish power, my dt. friend, not only without any lingering regret in retiring to a private station but with the feeling that I am more happy in resigning an empire to return to you than if I had other honors awaiting me by the success of an administration of peace after the anxieties of war. Every offer that I refuse is a grateful & devoted duty to you &, my health being good, you are known to be the attraction which draws me willingly to home, & if there is any sacrifice of ambition it will never cost me a sigh. I only claim the approval of my own judgement in having fairly awaited the result of my own measures. Having accomplished this honorable end & evaded no responsibility, I feel I can return to you without meriting the accusation that I have received huge rewards & selfishly deserted my post. I hope you will feel that I did right. Twice I have had to take decided measures of policy without instructions & in the midst of great difficulties. If I had escaped from these responsibilities by moving from Lahore to England, I should not have been happy that such a step was right. Now I return with a clear conscience & shall leave not a sigh behind. There may be a little excitement as the end approaches to leave nothing undone, but upon the whole these cares are overwhelmed & lost in the delight of seeing you & my children once more. This hope gains strength every month, & we bandy our congratulations to & fro like eager school boys for the breaking up, for the boys are most anxious to return.

Arthur has taken a passion for chess & plays very well. It sharpens his powers of combination & I encourage it. There are not above 2 or 3 men who can beat him at Simla. Charles as usual is very steady in all his ways, prudent & moderate in all his desires & very popular.

Robt. Wood is very well, considering the damp state of the weather. We are enveloped in dense fogs & pouring rains, & a good many people are suffering, so that it is scarcely to be expected that Bob should be quite well in this weather, which will last for another month. But he is quite safe & in good spirits.

Well, d[eares]t, you are in the midst of brick & mortar & I suppose the annoyance will be over the end of Sepr. I should like to know the size of the new dining room & the enlarged hall. When the whole is completed, I am certain I shall like it very much. I have ordered some curtains for the 3 windows of the new dining r[oom] of a coarse shawl wool, very warm & comfortable, but a French or English woolen carpet will be more to the purpose than any of the flimsy substitutes of the East.

I fear, d[eares]t, we shall not be able to afford so large & expensive a town house as Wm. Gladstone's or poor Sir George Murray's. The ground rent & taxes are always very heavy & my income, with allowances to Charles & Arthur, will not suffice for a town & country h[ou]se unless the former be very moderate. However, there is ample time for these arrangements.

Charles & Arthur must be put up at S.P. as they formerly were. We shall have pulled down 5 rooms & gained 4 in the new attics. Unless you can change the store room into a bed r[oom] upstairs, we shall have rather less room than we had before as far as putting up our friends is in question, & this makes me anxious to have the rooms on the kitchen floor well aired by the stove in order to accommodate men servants without going upstairs. Still, there will be a great improvement in the comfort & appearance of the house, &, under Charles' future circumstances, it is in size just what it ought to be. The old pantry will suit me admirably but on no account must you give up yr. dressing r[oom]. I have 3 curtains for you, with E.H. embroidered on them, for yr. rooms are to the north west & require to be warm in winter. As to curtains, I shall provide you from India. The carpets will be our heaviest expense, & for economy & comfort I believe the thickest will be the best even for bed rooms, not nailed to the ground but capable of being taken up & dusted. As to the disposition of the furniture in the drawing r[oom], I wd. advise you to consult Salvin & also for the dining room. What wd. he do with the terrace, fountain, lower terrace & tangle?

I am much concerned to hear yr. account of poor Mr Wells. He is a perfect sample of an English gentleman, spending his fortune in good acts & in good taste. No ostentation & no parsimony, a cheerful giver of his goods, discriminating those who most disuse his bounty, protecting the arts, & seeking agreeable society amongst clever men. I believe he is 78, & at that age who can expect to be free from infirmity?

I see the Duke opportunely gives his powerful support to the govt. Lord Grey did not speak on the Portugal question. I suppose he &

Ld. Palmerston don't go on very harmoniously together.[329] Grant is quite at a loss to predict which way the elections will go. My opinion is the Whigs must gain from the indifference & apathy of our divided party. I complained in one of my letters to Hobhouse that in his official dispatches there was a disposition to pick holes in my arrangements, & I answered one of his dispatches officially &, I believe, triumphantly. His answer is very humble in the official letter, & in his private he admits I am right & begs me to do exactly as I like, for that he will support *all my acts*. This is for yr. private information. For the remainder of my term I expect perfect cordiality, now that my office is at their disposal. As to Lord Ellenborough, I do not expect his approval of my measures. Is it true that he is going to be married to Miss Monk?

The mother of the little Lahore prince is giving us some trouble in tutoring the boy to displays of resistance to the durbar. She is very profligate, & under her care his education will be very bad. I would send her away, but, as in Queen Caroline's case, these naughty women some-how or other manage to enlist public sympathy in their favor when any strong expedient is resorted to. I should be glad to bring her to this side before I go. The boy might then be properly educated. He is a very nice little fellow & it is a pity he shd. be in such hands.[330]

I should be glad to have an acct. of my grandchildren. What is the difference in looks & character between the boy & the girl? For I take as much interest in dear Walter's children as if they were Charles'.

I have written to Adolphus Vane[331] either to come to Calcutta in Decr. or to meet me at Lucknow early in Novr. I have written to yr. brother recommending him not to leave him at Bombay. My time is now so short I can do nothing more. As neither Castlereagh[332] or Seaham[333] have children, they should steady his character under some better master than old Cotton[334] & marry him in a few years. A

[329] Grey was secretary at war and the colonies under Russell.

[330] In June Rani Jindan, divested of political power since the Bhairowal Treaty, was suspected of plotting Henry Lawrence's murder, but the charge was never substantiated. 'The rani as usual is said to be at the bottom of it all,' wrote Charles to Walter on 9 June, 'but much is attributed to her in which in reality she has no share' (Charles Hardinge Letters, i). Later in Aug., Jindan was accused of humiliating Tej Singh, the regency council president. The moralistic Hardinge, who had long considered the Rani to be a noxious influence on Dalip Singh, personally approved of her removal to Sheikhupura, some 25 miles from Lahore. She later found asylum in Nepal. Eventually the Rani joined Dalip Singh in England where she died in 1863.

[331] Adolphus Vane (1825–64) was the third son of the 3rd Marquess of Londonderry.

[332] Adolphus's half-brother Frederick was then styled Viscount Castlereagh; in 1854 he became the 4th Marquess of Londonderry.

[333] Adolphus's elder brother George was then styled Viscount Seaham; he was later the 5th Marquess of Londonderry.

[334] Not identified.

sensible woman would do him more good than a bon-vivant like Sir Willoughby.[335]

Arthur talks resolutely of going through the senior dept. of the Milty. College. If he has application he can do anything. His health seems perfect, & without being handsome his countenance is expressive & prepossessing, & he is 2 inches taller than I am & well made, quick at repartee, a great talker to the ladies, & popular with the men, & not spoiled by the *toadying* of being the G.G.'s son. He is very obedient, for I don't treat my sons as if they were children, altho' I insist upon being the master whenever the occasion seems to require it &, my authority being seldom exerted, our relations are most intimate. I have preserved the little volume of Milton, & when I request a few hundred lines, he acquiesces with a good grace.

What can I bring home for Grant? He has taken all the trouble of ordering & paying for my wine. Pray consider & give your more fertile suggestions.

I am sorry to hear that the Duke of Buckingham's affairs are in so bad a state.[336] With many weaknesses he has some excellent points in his character.

I don't think the Parlt. about to be chosen will be long lived, & I should hope parties will 'ere long become more settled & property regain in the senate the ascendancy it ought to have, if that be possible under the Reform Bill.

I hope to pass through Paris on my way home, but this will be at the severest season of the year, the end of Febry., & I should infinitely prefer meeting you in dear England, for you ought not to expose yourself at the meeting of the London season. We must hire a furnished house for 6 months from Febry. to the end of July, or for 3 months or even for 1 month, so as to have a *pied-à-terre* on arrival, & we can settle our choice after due consultation together in April or May & not be fettered for 6 months with a residence we don't like. For comfort the house in Carlton Terrace built by Arbuthnot[337] wd. suit us in every respect (except in expense), & I believe a fat wealthy brewer of pale ale now occupies it & has no intention of leaving it. You would be vis-a-vis the Ripons.

All you say & do abt. the Goderich affair is most judicious. I never wish a daughter of mine to marry for wealth & titles, nor to fall into the other extreme of marrying a handsome adventurer without the means of supporting her in her own sphere in life. If Emily were to

---

[335] Possibly Sir Nesbit Josiah Willoughby (1777–1849) who had a colourful though checkered career in the English navy.

[336] Buckingham's assets were sequestered in Aug. 1847, following his bankruptcy.

[337] Sir Hugh Arbuthnot, a military veteran, sat in Parliament for nearly forty years.

like the lord, the affair wd. be different; but from what you say, he is inclined to prefer the more brilliant cousin.[338]

14 Augt.

I am on the point of closing the mail—very tired, & I hope to be renovated in 48 h[*ours*] by yr. letters, which may be expected on the 16th or 17th. The weather [*is*] very damp & misty but Robert [*is*] pretty well.

I have written a long letter to Hobhouse & I presume we shall separate in Decr. on good terms. His explanatory letter more than satisfies me.

What line does the Duke of N[*?ewcastle*] take?

I must say I am quite gratified in not being obliged to undergo the drudgery of the canvassing of a borough. Even dear Launceston was a bore, altho' they always treated me honorably. Repose is the essence of age, & I long to be at rest, but I will go through to the end, & I am up before 5 every morning. Only 4 months & 1/2 more & I am on the blue waters!

If you meet with *fat* Lady Littler, be very civil to her. She is the wife of Sir John. George H[*ardinge*] is now here—a great good-looking youth & gentlemanlike, but I don't think there is anything in him. I could never bear to have a son of mine in *this* service.

Charles has received some of the lithographic prints from his sketches & is highly pleased with them, but in my opinion they fall far short of the coloured originals. The great H[*arding*], however, has done them as much justice as the style of print would admit of, & probably better than any other man.

And now, dst. wife, good bye.

123. [*To Emily.*] Saharan-poor. Oct. 31st, 1847

On the 26th I left Simla, having had a farewell dinner at Lord Gough's, on which occasion he eulogized my milty. as well as pol[*itica*]l services but broke down in his speech, which I suppose we shall have in the papers, written out by Lady Gough. If it resembles what he said, it will surprize you by its excess of praise, future honors, higher rank, & so forth. I had to answer him, & I took the opportunity of praising my old comrades by name & of avoiding to vindicate my policy, which each year convinces me will require no vindication.

I then descended into the plains, dining with the genl. offs. as I

[338] George Frederick Samuel Robinson, styled Viscount Goderich from 1833 to 1859, the second but the oldest surviving son of the 1st Earl of Ripon. The 'more brilliant cousin' very well could be Henrietta Anne Theodosia, a granddaughter of Ripon's brother whom Goderich married in 1851. Goderich was later, as marquess of Ripon, Viceroy of India, 1880–4. Emily Caroline Hardinge never married and died in 1876.

passed through, travelling by night & receiving visitors by day. Here I am quite in repose & free from interruption in the house of the son of Sir John Harvey who was inspector genl. of police when we were in Ireland & who was my comdr. in ch. on the tiger expedition—a very amiable & excellent man. He lost a favorite daughter 3 m[onths] ago &, having been 20 yrs. in India, has determined to go home with his wife & boy on furlough.

We dine at 4, & I have this morning walked over the botanical garden & the shed. I get into my little carriage at 6 & travel all night on my way to Meerut. The carriage is the same that I had during the campaign & drawn by men, & I contrive, notwithstanding the shaking of my old bones, to get some sleep. From Meerut I proceed to Cawnpoor & shall dispatch the mail from thence to England. It is still very hot in the middle of the day, but I am in excellent health & still better spirits. Arthur is in advance, & I am accompanied by Charles & Bob & am more free than I expected from the interruptions of business, altho' I am waylaid on my route by those who really wish to shake me by the hand or have some favor to ask. This is the first grand movement homewards, & we are like holiday school boys. No one can say that I leave a difficulty behind me which has not been provided against, & this gt. empire is in a perfect state of tranquillity, & I pledge myself that it will remain so.

I am each day, as the hour of my labour approaches, more grateful to God for His mercies. I had 11 aides-de-camp in action—5 were killed, 5 wounded, & the 11th, our dear Arthur, spared. To bring back the whole party unhurt is an interposition of Providence as marked as the successes which have attended my efforts, & I should be the most unfeeling of men if I did not reflect upon & appreciate the manifestation of such mercies in my person. As I am drawn across these sandy plains by human beings, I contrast their state. I pass in review my life in India, the decisions I have had to make, the alternatives I might have adopted, the probable results, & my reveries always terminate by fervent aspirations to heaven that I may be worthy to receive the favors which have been vouchsafed unto me, in the number of which your health & happiness stand foremost. So pray take care of yourself & be cautious of large crowded parties & any exposure which may affect yr. health.

Major Mayne has come down from the hills to see me before I leave India. He was as a boy frequently at S. Park in Mrs Allnutt's time, & we have talked over many of our old neighbours. These subjects & the complete repose of this quiet house, the conviction that the public security will last, that I have evaded & leave to my successor no heavy responsibilities, that I am on my way at last to rejoin you—all these thoughts pass across my mind, enter deep into my heart, & make me resign an empire with so light a conscience that it is a portion of my happiness to impart these thoughts to the faithful friend of all my cares & joys.

God bless you.

Meerut. Novr. 2nd

We got in here at 11 & had a night in bed at the house of the genl. off.'s com[mand]er, Sir John Grey,[339] a relation of Lord Grey's & formerly a very good offr. but the worse for wear after a residence of 6 yrs. in India. This day I am to see another very fine Sikh regt. raised by me the beginning of last year, abt. 200 of whom fought agt. us. They are very fine men & greatly superior in size, strength, & resolution to our sepoys. I presented the colors to one of these regts. on my passage through Umballa & have 4 more in the hills. Some of the heads of depts. will be with me in the course of the day, but I hope to be quiet till the evening when, after a quiet dinner with the general, I shall be again en route for Cawn-poor where my camp is formed, the last milty. pageantry in which I shall indulge in India. The weather is still hot from 11 to 4, but delightfully cool during the night.

It is not improbable the mail may come in today, in which case I shall have time to answer you before my old bones resume their shaking practices in the carriage. Here we shall have horses instead of men, a change most congenial to my feelings. Steamers & rail-ways will rapidly advance the civilization of this interesting country & enable us to fulfill our mission &, by the blessings of a permanent peace, the happiness of the people & the power of the govern[men]t must both increase. What a contrast to Novr. 1845 when I was moving up to the frontier!

The state ceremonies at Lucknow will keep me till the 23rd Novr. when I shall move on Allahabad, embarking on board the yacht the 27th & reaching Calcutta abt. the 12th or 15th Decr.

The steamer for Ld. Dalhousie will bring him to Calcutta without fail the end of the month, & I feel confident of being on board the first week in Janry.

The probability is I shall bring Adolphus Vane home with me.

It is near our breakfast hour, & I don't give up the hope of receiving letters from you, d[eares]t, this day.

Bungalow abt. 90 miles from Cawnpoor
Novr. 4th

We performed 86 m[iles] during the night & at daylight I found cooks of the king of Oude had come in during the night to prepare a

[339] Sir John Grey (1780?–1856), who had served in India under Wellesley, returned to India in 1840. He later became C. in C. of Bombay from 1850 to 1852 and was promoted to lieutenant general in 1851.

breakfast for me here, &, amongst other meats, a cold ham which, for
a Mussulman prince, shows a very great advance in getting rid of his
prejudices. In like manner a Hindoo raja of Bhurtpoor with whom I
dined in 1845 gave several dishes of roast beef, the cow being the
sacred animal!

I sleep pretty well in the carriage but, as the stages are short, I am
roused every hour, & this is my 7th night of being on the road.
Tomorrow I have 90 miles to Cawnpoor. Then our state ceremonies
begin, the last of my Eastern pomp & pageantry, succeeded by a quiet
fortnight on the Ganges preparatory to the closing & more bustling
scenes at Calcutta.

No mail [is] in! It is *not* reasonable that I should become more
impatient as the term of separation shortens, but so it is. I shall
endeavour to restrain it.

I hear Lord Dalhousie talks of sending Ldy. D. to Simla & of taking
his chance of rejoining her hereafter. If our rail-way were completed,
it would be very feasible. He is a young man & has the world before
him. I am nearly worn out, & these precautionary measures of his only
heighten my satisfaction & make me rejoice that my emancipation is
so near at hand.

Arthur was to write to you from Meerut & enclose the newspaper
of our farewell dinner at Simla. The press here is nearly unanimous
in its praise of my administration, altho' it is of no great importance.
I really hope the warm-hearted people of England will have expended
all their laudations on Sir Harry Smith, or that Napier may still
precede me. After dinner speeches of thanks are very troublesome &
embarrassing, & if my looks did not betray me, I should, like Pollock,
be disposed to stay at home with you; it is to be my lot to be put on
my tryal through excess of kindness.

A turn in the other direction is not unlikely. The Times & the govt.
papers are very cool, whilst Hobhouse is warm & publicly not over-
sincere. Our Sutlege war will not cost the state half a million & the
Affghan policy upwards of 20 mill. with all its misfortunes. For 9 yrs.
we have each yr. been borrowing from 1 to 2 mill. & I leave a
surplus, having by milty. reductions & other beneficial arrangements
improved our finances by an annual sum exceeding 1 1/2 mill. We
are at peace everywhere, our milty. reputation higher than before,
with canals & rail-ways in rapid progress throughout the country. I
have been absent from my colleagues for upwards of 2 years, & I
know they claim no share in these matters. I write to nobody, to prove
to my Whig masters that I am faithful to them, & this you can explain
to Peel & all those of our friends—Ripon, Herries, etc.—to avoid all
misapprehensions. Also that I am of no politics, for I think it wd. be
wrong after an absence of 4 yrs., the last 30 [?20] months under the

Whigs, to take any marked line. My desire & intention is to be quiet, for I really require relaxation, & my own position & the state of my own party justify this course, & whilst I admit it is of no great importance, yet it is as well that I should be very clear on this point.

I join my camp tomorrow morn[in]g &, having a night's shaking before me, I have ordered some tea for dinner after the king of Oude's sumptuous breakfast.

[*November 6*]

[*P.S.*] I came into camp yesterday morn[in]g [*November 5*], having mounted my horse 2 miles from the troops drawn up to receive the G.G., had a large breakfast at 9, a dinner in the even[in]g &, after a night's sound sleep in my bed, am up at 5 to dispatch my express for England. Everything everywhere is so quiet, I have nothing to report. This ought to satisfy my Whig masters, for it is not accidental but permanent & resulting from the policy pursued.

I have had 8 days' travelling & am very fresh, which I attribute to the elasticity of my spirits. On Monday & Tuesday I have large dinners to [*sic*] every offr. & his wife at this station. The king of Oude crosses the frontier on Tuesday & breakfasts with me in public. I do the same on Wednesday in his camp & then march on to Lucknow &, after various ceremonies which will occupy me until the 23rd, I take my departure & move as rapidly as I can to my steamer on the Ganges, which will sail on the 28th, & I shall reach Calcutta the 15 or 18th.

Adolphus Vane is here but laid up with a severe earache at the house of a Colonel Campbell. I shall see him today & I have no doubt from what Charles reports of his, Vane's, feeling, he will jump at the notion of returning to England with me. He has no love of travel, no research or love of learning or of sport & I apprehend neither the talent or energy of either of his parents.

Arthur is expected tomorrow night. I send a copy of the talk between me & the C.C.[340] on the evening preceding our departure. The Woods may like to see what I said of Bob, which he amply deserves.

The next month will soon pass, & in less than 2 I shall be on my homeward journey. I ask of the best informed around me whether I leave any difficulties behind me. The answer is *none*, & I therefore shall rejoin you with a light heart, conscious that by so doing I have violated no public duty.

[340] Untraced.

124. [*To Sarah.*] Cawnpoor. Novr. 6, 1847

I was very much grieved to hear of yr. dis-appointment, but at these moments I close my eyes & fancy I can see before me your two little darlings, giving to one or the other of their little faces more or less of the features of their dear parents. But these waking dreams will soon be turned into joyful realities & I shall scan each little face with the deepest interest, recollecting what Walter was at 5 years old with a sensibility which has never left him.

I have been travelling for 7 nights following &, after a sound sleep in my tent last night, am quite refreshed. In short, I never was in better health & everything everywhere within this great empire is perfectly quiet.

Two years ago I stayed a day at this station with Sir Robert Dick who was then, poor fellow, all anxiety to follow me. He fell at Sobraon,[341] & I take back with me those I brought out in health, credit & delight. At every step I take in my homeward journey I find cause to be grateful to Providence for the great mercies I have received.

The rain is falling heavily & the mail must go off this even[*in*]g, but I will write to you from Lucknow after I have read a lecture to the poor king in *private*.[342]

Love to Walter.

125. [*To Walter.*] Soona-mookee yacht, 7 days from Calcutta. Decr. 3rd, 1847

We are swimming down this fine stream with the current at the rate of 70 miles a day, & this easy mode of voyaging suits a man who longs for repose, for his work is immoderately heavy & from which I shall be relieved in less than a month.

Every part of the country is quiet—the harvest most abundant & the crops for the spring most promising, the river crowded with boats, & trade increasing; but in Calcutta the merchants are in a state of

[341] Maj. Gen. Sir Robert Dick (1785–1846), an officer in the Madras Army since 1837, was one of the last English casualties at Sobraon.

[342] Hardinge had been dissatisfied ever since his arrival in India with the corruption and lawlessness in Oudh, and conditions worsened under Wajid Ali Shah (1822–87) who took over as nawab in Feb. 1847. On Nov. 22 at the British residency in Lucknow, Hardinge asked Wajid Ali to put his house in order or ultimately face the alternative of a British takeover of Oudh's internal administration. Apart from telling Hardinge that he considered 'his counsels as if they had been addressed by a father to a son,' the nawab said little 'and made no promises with reference to his future intentions' (Board's Collections 112885, enc. 17, letter 33, MS. in IOL).

gloom[343] & alarm until the next mail shall decide their fate—which is due in abt. a week.

I wrote some important papers in this yacht in Oct. 1845. We were then tugging up agt. the stream; now I am floating down with every prospect of resigning the govt. of this gt. empire satisfactorily. The reduction of the army is accomplished, that odious task is out of Lord Dalhousie's way, & the revenue is benefited by a million sterlg. of reductions & by another mill. in various other ways comparing 1848 with 1845, & I am confident that the peace is lasting & cannot be disturbed.

I have written a long despatch on Oude & I hope to reconcile the good faith which is due to an allied prince with the mercy & justice which we are bound to dispense towards an oppressed people. I rejoice that my last political despatch is one in which I can strongly advocate the right of humanity.

I calculate I shall have to remain abt. 20 days in Calcutta before I embark, which is more than I wish, altho' I have had the good fortune to continue on the best of terms with all my colleagues, & I shall be glad to renew my intercourse before we part forever. I am doing all I can to ease Ld. Dalhousie of milty. decisions which wd. be irksome to a new G.G., & at my time of life I care very little for professional popularity, provided the right measure be done in the right way.

I have had Napier to manage for 3 1/2 years, & I believe I am the only man with whom he is on good terms in high office. I have done this by the most frank & friendly communications, defending him on all occasions when I could, & his Whig friends are delighted that they have got rid of him. With gt. merit, he is wild and *entêté*, & with his temper soured by the Indian press he is at 65 a little crazy, still full of fire, & all his eccentricities are of an honorable character; it is impossible not to like & not to admire him, but Dalhousie will rejoice to find him out of his way. He has left Scinde in good-humour with this government & Hobhouse, his wrath being, how[eve]r, still unappeased agt. Outram & to a certain extent Ld. Ripon.

Ld. Tweed-dale goes home dissatisfied with the Court, which he thinks ought to have given him more support. He is not very partial to me, I believe, for I have had to pull him up on milty. points of

---

[343] The collapse of the London-based financial institutions such as Cockerell, Larpent and Co; Lyall, Matheson, and Co; and Church, Lake, and Co was announced by their branches at Calcutta in Nov. Many Englishmen in India, including Hardinge, had invested with one or more of these institutions. There was speculation that yet others might fail. These developments caused 'great gloom and despondency' at Calcutta (*The Friend of India*, 25 Nov. 1847, p. 738), and shook investors throughout British India.

difference, &, when Ellenborough was recalled, he expected to have been appointed G.G. His missionary zeal has also been unfortunate & he goes home in Febry. out of humour.

Mr Clerk has just got into harness at Bombay[344] & appears to me to be an amiable & able man, but Hobhouse writes in a dissatisfied tone & somewhat inconveniently makes me his confidant.[345]

When I contrast my good-fortune in resigning this govt. by a voluntary retirement with the acknowledged approbation of both my masters, the Bd. of Control & the Court, I cannot but feel grateful to Providence for such unmerited favor. In this very cabin 2 years ago I had a difficult problem to solve & had many anxious moments. I moralize on the events which have occurred & am thankful.

The army & the civil service, the community at large & the vagabond press of India have become unanimous in favor of the policy, not on acct. of its merit but its successful results, for in this country where every man has his fortune to make, opinions on public matters are formed on personal calculations of interest. The army has been disappointed of promotion & has been reduced 60,000 men by a moderate policy, lucrative civil promotion has been marred by the non-annexation of the Punjab, & private hopes have suffered whilst the public exchequer has been replenished by 2 mill. a year, & we possess the Punjab in effect as securely & more cheaply than if our reluctant troops were in the Kyber Pass. The annexation wd. have cost nearly one mill. a yr. These results have of late been so well argued, particularly in the Bombay Times,[346] that I, who expected to be unpopular with those whose hopes I had disappointed, am spoken of with favor. But the essential point is that I am conscientiously satisfied I have done right, & I venture, as you will outlive me, to predict that a quarter of a century from the signature of this Lahore treaty, peace will have prevailed in India. We may have a mutiny or expeditions to China & Egypt, but peace is secured, & with it & railways, the country will rapidly advance in prosperity & civilization. I

---

[344] Sir George Russell Clerk (1800–89) took over the governorship of Bombay from George Arthur. Clerk had served in India from 1817 to 1842 in various positions including political agent on the Sikh frontier and lieutenant governor of the Northwestern Province.

[345] Hobhouse was annoyed by Clerk's lukewarm attitude toward army cuts, and wrote to Hardinge: 'I somewhat distrust that gentleman and have no hesitation in telling you, as indeed I tell you everything, that if that appointment was to be made over again, I do not think he could be governor of Bombay' (6 Sept. 1847, Broughton Papers, dcccliv. 53–4).

[346] *The Bombay Times* continued its strong support of army reductions. In an editorial on 6 Nov. 1847 (p. 876), it advocated further curtailments, in fact suggesting that Hardinge should be 'doing away with drums and fifes, and substituting in their places buglers armed with muskets' to save almost four more lakhs of rupees.

promised to govern the country on the policy of peace & all my measures have been consistent in producing that result. As a genl. offr., I have curbed & reduced the army to an amount *twice* as large as the home govt. expected at the same time that I have increased the pensions of deserving classes, augmented the sepoy's privileges, & conferred boons on the Europeans when in equity they were entitled to them. These acts of severe economy & of just liberality have been freely canvassed, & when I have retired from the scene, the army will acknowledge that I have, with some show of severity, done it good service & been its friend. I therefore have never complained of the press, conscious that I was acting justly, & at the moment of my retirement the acknowledgement is becoming very general. I state these points frankly, but, as the press is patronized by the E.I.C. army & lives by its favor, it is a fair argument to advance that the approbation of the press implies that of its patrons, & to neither have I ever pandered or ever will. As is usual on the departure of a G.G., my administration will be discussed in India, & I have the boldness to make these remarks to you in anticipation of the verdicts which may be given. I admit it is not of much importance what such a venal press may say, but I have been led into this strain by a former letter of yours in which you urged me no longer to defer retirement, as the army would dislike any reductions & Sir John Littler's friends were dissatisfied. You were justified in drawing such an inference from what was then passing, but by remaining at my post to complete the superintendence of my policy & the milty. reductions, I think I have over-come the difficulties I should have had to encounter if I had prematurely retired a year ago. But again, my dear Walter, all these explanations are of little importance if I have acted right, & if my acts have been adverse to the personal interests of those who constitute public opinion in India, & if, on my retirement, my acts be approved by these interested parties, then I have a right to infer that it is the triumph of truth over self-interest & that my acts have been right.

Viewing the question of annexation vs. non-annexation purely in financial considerations, the direct & absolute possession of the country up to the Kyber Pass wd. not be a politic or expedient measure, even if it could *now* be done after a more intimate acquaintance during the 2 last years, since we have made ourselves popular with the people & rendered the country more quiet than it has been in the memory of man. If we had attempted it at the moment of victory (exclusive of the want of means) when the country was disorganized, the people impoverished, & national sympathies, in a truly national struggle, arrayed in all their intensity agt. us, we could not have ventured on any reduction of our force, & for several years to come the insecurity of the tenure might have entailed upon us the same necessity. During this period of settling ourselves in a conquered country in the only vulnerable point of our frontier, instead of saving 2 mill. a yr. as is now the case, we must not only have spent this sum but probably a mill. in add[*itio*]n. We must indefinitely have postponed the gt. object of making any colony pay its own expenditure, &, after spending in the Whig war policy since 1838 27 mill. & borrowing from 1 to 2 mill. a yr. for the last 9 yrs., we must have increased this debt, the march of improvement in our own immense provinces must have been retarded & the permanent occupation of the Punjab wd. have saddled us with a permanent deficit instead of a surplus which is now secured.

The last 2 years have created wonderful revolution in the sentiments of the Sikh people towards their foreign conquerors, & this revolution has been brought abt. by moderation. Two years ago our rule wd. have been that of victorious masters. Now the people respect & admire us & wd., I really believe, rejoice in being governed by us. Two years ago we heard of the fertility of the country. Now, having examined the country with our own eyes, we have arrived at more just & sober calculations of its value.

With Sikh estab[*lishmen*]ts, milty. & civil, Coll. Lawrence hopes to have a surplus of £50,000 a yr. out of a revenue of 1 mill. Suppose we were to take the 1 mill. a yr. & substitute European agency & establish[*men*]ts & our B. system of land assessments & were to distribute justice & employ European regts. on the frontier. We must be prepared at all points, not only at Lahore but in the remotest corner beyond the Indus & in constant collision with turbulent hostile tribes of Musselmen in the passes & mountains. Each regt. of additional Eur[*o*]p[*ean*] inf. costs £60,000 a yr.; the surplus now is only £50,000 a yr. We must have built forts & erected public establish[*men*]ts, b[*arrac*]ks, etc. As the Punjab is *twice* the area of the Bombay presidency, a more difficult country & a more warlike race, it may safely be inferred that, if Bombay now costs 4 mill. a yr. for its management, that we would not occupy the Punjab on the B[*ritis*]h system with 1 mill. a yr.

The Sikh army is only 32,000, & this force defends our frontier. If they get a slap in the face from Affghan tribes, it is a Sikh & not a British defeat. This army, by improved regularity of pay & increased pensions, is now on the frontier, defending it cheaply & cheerfully for us, &, as we uphold them who are for the greater part Hindoos agt. Musselmen, they, who know what we have done for them & attribute their improve[*men*]t to our intervention, are already greatly attached & may be relied upon.

We have 2000 miles of internal navigation by large rivers, but I don't attach much importance to them as they are very difficult, & the Punjab population is in a cul de sac, with the Kyber Passes &

Himalayas bounding them on 3 sides so that, in reality, the notion of opening out the resources of central Asia by the Indus, Scinde & the Punjab is a delusion, which only exists in Lord Palmerston's speeches. I have some curious information on this point showing what the Punjab yielded 250 yrs. ago in the Emperor Ackbar's time, in Aurangzabe's time, & at the present day.

But I should weary you by these details, & I write au grand galop. Suffice it to say that our victories over the most warlike Hindoo army of the East have made every n[ative] state abandon all hope of being able to contend agt. us in the field, a notion which the Affghan disasters had encouraged & the enormous milty. power of the Sikhs had rendered not improbable, & which hope was justified by the severe struggles on the Sutlege. We have convinced Asia that territorial aggrandizement is not our object & that, altho' we have conquered & now employ & trust the last independent army & kingdom of India as attached to our interests, we are, in point of milty. strength, by a different disposition of a reduced army, in a more imposing attitude than before, having 50,000 men & 120 field guns on the frontier, an exchequer with 2 mill. a yr. *more* in it than in 1845, & with universal confidence in our stability. I release you from this hasty rhapsody.

[*P.S.*] We are determined to go up the Adriatic, land at Venice & proceed by the great Tyrol or by Basle, whichever is the most rapid. This is on Waghorn's[347] recommendation. It is more speedy than by Marseilles & Paris or by Southampton, tossing abt. in the Bay of Biscay in the stormy winds of March, with a line, *Poste restante,* Venice.

[347] Lt. Thomas Waghorn (1800–50) of the Royal Navy was a strong advocate of public steam transportation between England and India via the Red Sea and established a shipping firm, Waghorn & Co., in 1840.

INDEX

Pompey's Pillar, 19
Portugal, 230
Porus, 153, 215
Pott's Farm, 47, 100, 164, 209
Poundsbridge, 179
Precursor, 69, 95
Punala, 41 n. 88
Pyramids, 21, 24, 25

Quarterly Review, The, 186 n. 276, 191, 214

Railways, 58, 63–4 n. 130, 106 n. 185, 204, 207
Rajendra, King of Nepal, 194 n. 294
Rajputana, 194 n. 295, 220
Rajya, Queen of Nepal, 85 n. 168, 194 n. 294
Raleigh, Capt. Frederick, 80
Raleigh, Sir Walter, 80
Ramsay, James *see* Dalhousie
Rana, Jung Bahadur, 85 n. 168, 194 n. 294
Razzias, 27, 176
Redleaf, 79 n. 157, 170
Richmond, Col., 37 n. 85, 51 n. 111
Ripon, Frederick John Robinson, Earl of, 74, 81, 122, 127, 178, 179, 228, 236; and Goa, 91; and Hardinge's policies, 43, 47, 48, 81, 103, 111, 128, 131; and Hardinge's selection as gg, 4, 6; opinion of, 71, 75; and Panjab, 37, 72–3, 108, 163, 165, 169, 172, 175; and Sind, 37, 95, 239
Roslyn *see* St Clair
Royal College of Surgeons, London, 63 n. 129
Russell, Lord John, 148, 189, 203, 223; and Ellenborough's recall, 57 n. 119, 85–6 n. 169; and Hardinge, 11, 12, 172, 202, 216, 219
Russia, 14, 219

St Clair, Sir James (*later* 2nd Earl of Roslyn), 258
St Germans, Edward Granville Eliot, 3rd Earl of, 74 n. 144
St James Park, 165
Salah Al-Din Ayyub (Saladin), 23 n. 67
Salamanca, 5
Sale, Florentia, Lady, 43–4, 46
—, Maj. Gen. Sir Robert Henry, 43, 46
Saltoun, Alexander George Fraser, 16th Baron, 87–8
—, Catherine, Lady, 87

Salvin, Anthony, 193, 213, 226, 227
Samangarh, 41 n. 88
San Fiorenzo, 187
Sandhawalia, Attar Singh, 31
Sarkote, 197
Sawantwari, 54 n. 114, 81 n. 160
Seaham, George Henry Robert Charles, Viscount (*later* 5th Marquess of Londonderry), 231
Shah, Amjad Ali, Nawab of Oudh, 29 n. 71
—, Fateh Jung, 194 n. 294
—, Rajendra Bikram, King of Nepal, 41 n. 89
—, Surendra Bikram (*later* King of Nepal), 41 n. 89
—, Wajid Ali, Nawab of Oudh, 235, 237–9
—, Jahan, Emperor, 118 n. 195, 122
Shakespeare, William, 39, 109, 159 n. 237
Sheikhupura, 231 n. 330
Shepherd, Capt. John, 6, 74
Sheppard, Mr, 82 n. 164
Shikarpur, 41
Sikh Army, after Bhairowal Treaty, 243; expedition against Jammu by, 37, 51, 54, 56, 59, 61, 64; fighting ability of, 136, 151, 157; holds Gulab Singh prisoner, 73, 75, 76–8, 81; lawlessness of, 29–30, 36, 43, 50, 56, 59, 75, 76–8, 107, 111, 114, 121–2, 125; postwar condition of, 154, 163, 184, 201; role of panchayats in, 56, 77, 94, 107; in Sikh War, 132–49
Sikh Kingdom, anarchy in, 29–32, 37, 40–1, 45, 49–50, 51–2, 56, 64, 76–8, 81, 85, 107, 111, 121–2, 130–1; after Bhairowal Treaty, 204, 218, 222, 231, 242–3; penalties of defeat, 152–8; postwar conditions in, 158–61, 163, 181, 184–5, 188, 191, 199–200; and Sikh War, 9–10, 132–51
Sikh War *see* Sikh Kingdom
Simla, 10, 60, 68, 93, 104, 108, 120, 147, 154, 155, 157, 160, 192, 196, 204, 208, 213, 215, 233; scenery of, 161, 169, 170
Sind, annexation of, 3, 120, 128, 174, 176, 186, 200; and Hardinge, 29, 37, 53, 85, 95, 119
Singh, Baldeo, Raja of Bharatpur, 123 n. 201
—, Balwant, Raja of Bharatpur, and Hardinge's visit, 123–6